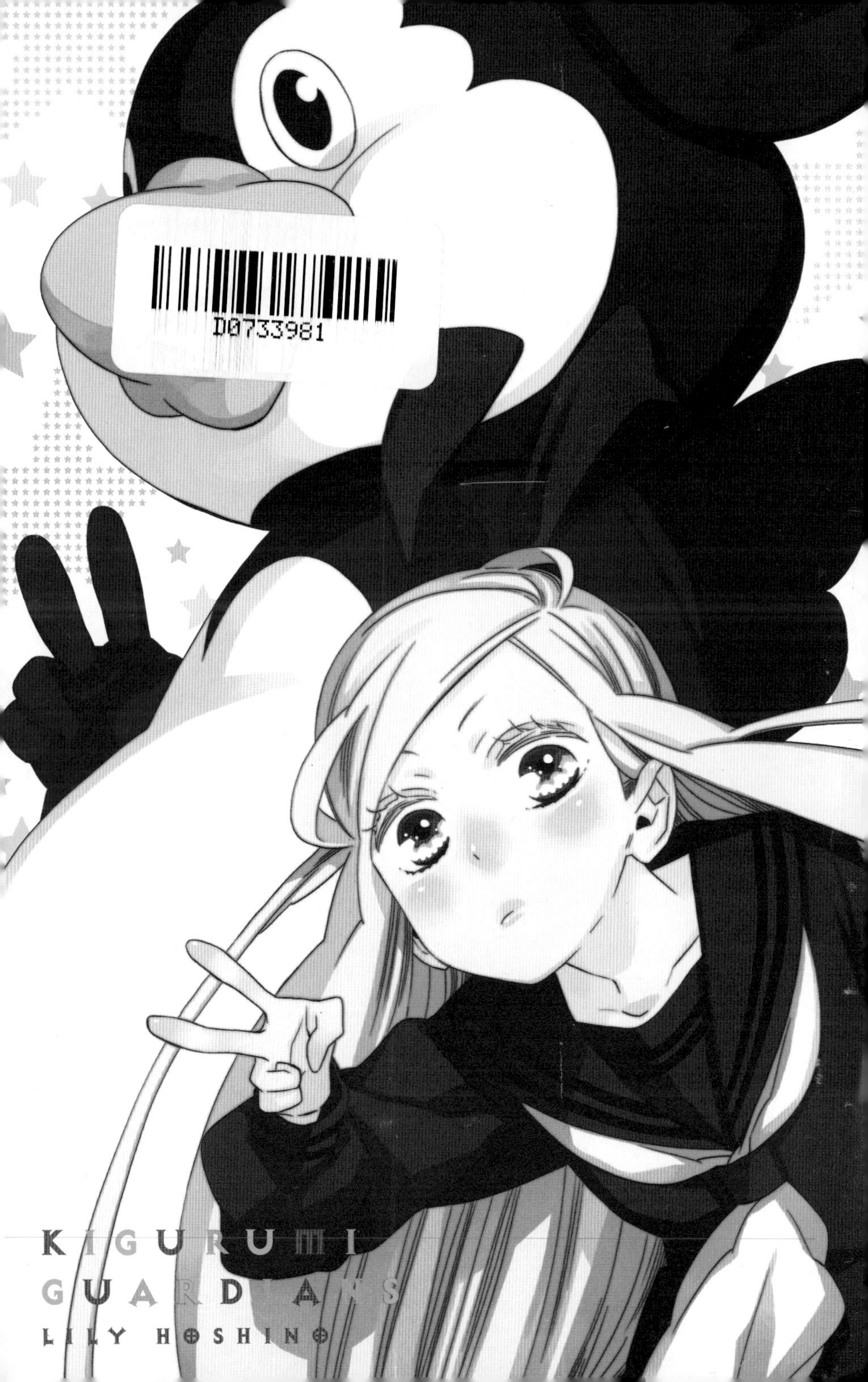

KIGURUMI GUARDIANS

LILY HOSHINO

GINGER

KIGURUMI GUARDIANS

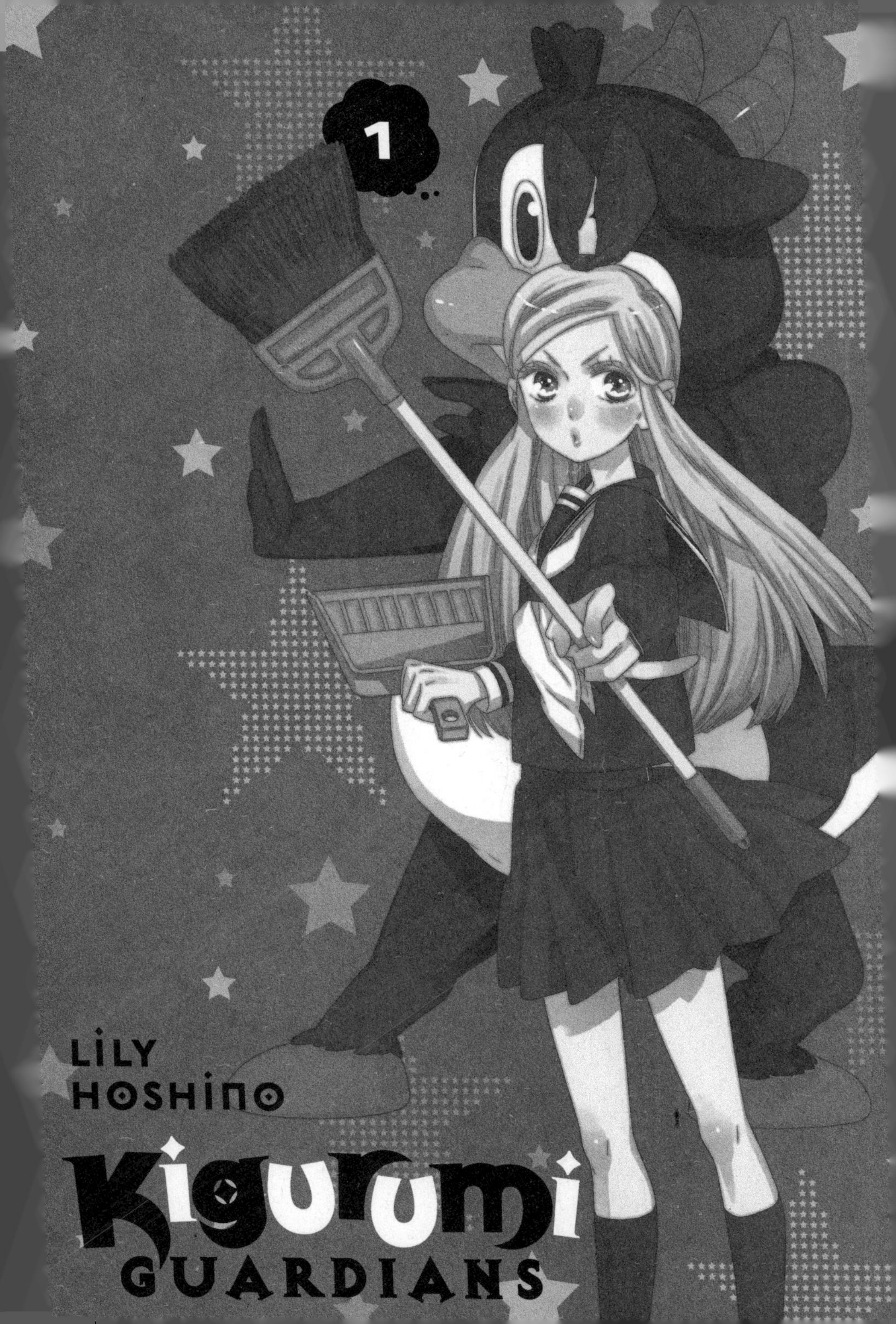
1
LILY
HOSHINO
Kigurumi
GUARDIANS

CONTENTS

CHAPTER 1: THE CHOSEN ONES 007

CHAPTER 2: ISN'T IT ROMANTIC? 035

CHAPTER 3: THE FAIREST
OF ALL THE SECOND-YEARS 061

CHAPTER 4: THE FIRST SHELL 087

CHAPTER 5: THANKS 113

GUARDIANS

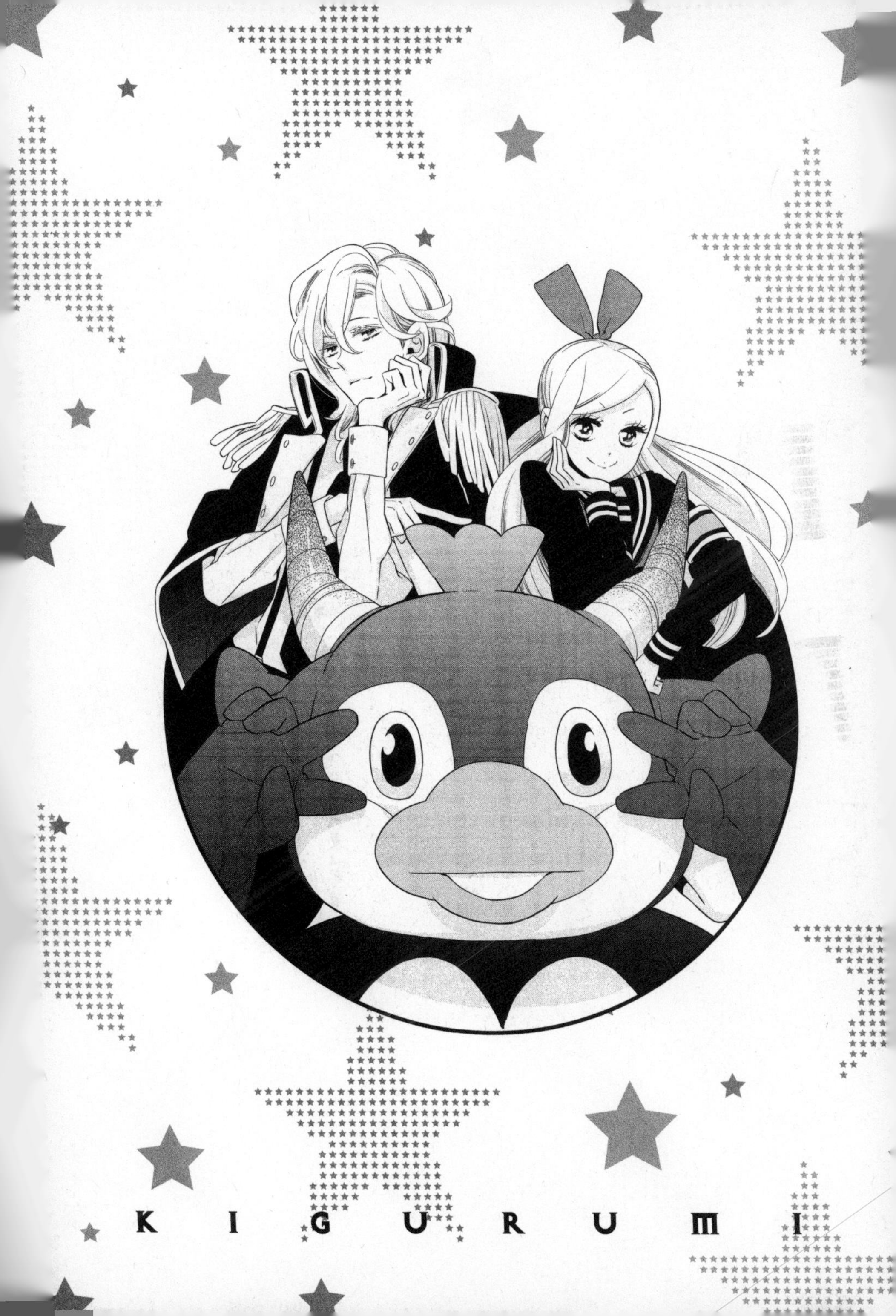
K I G U R U M I

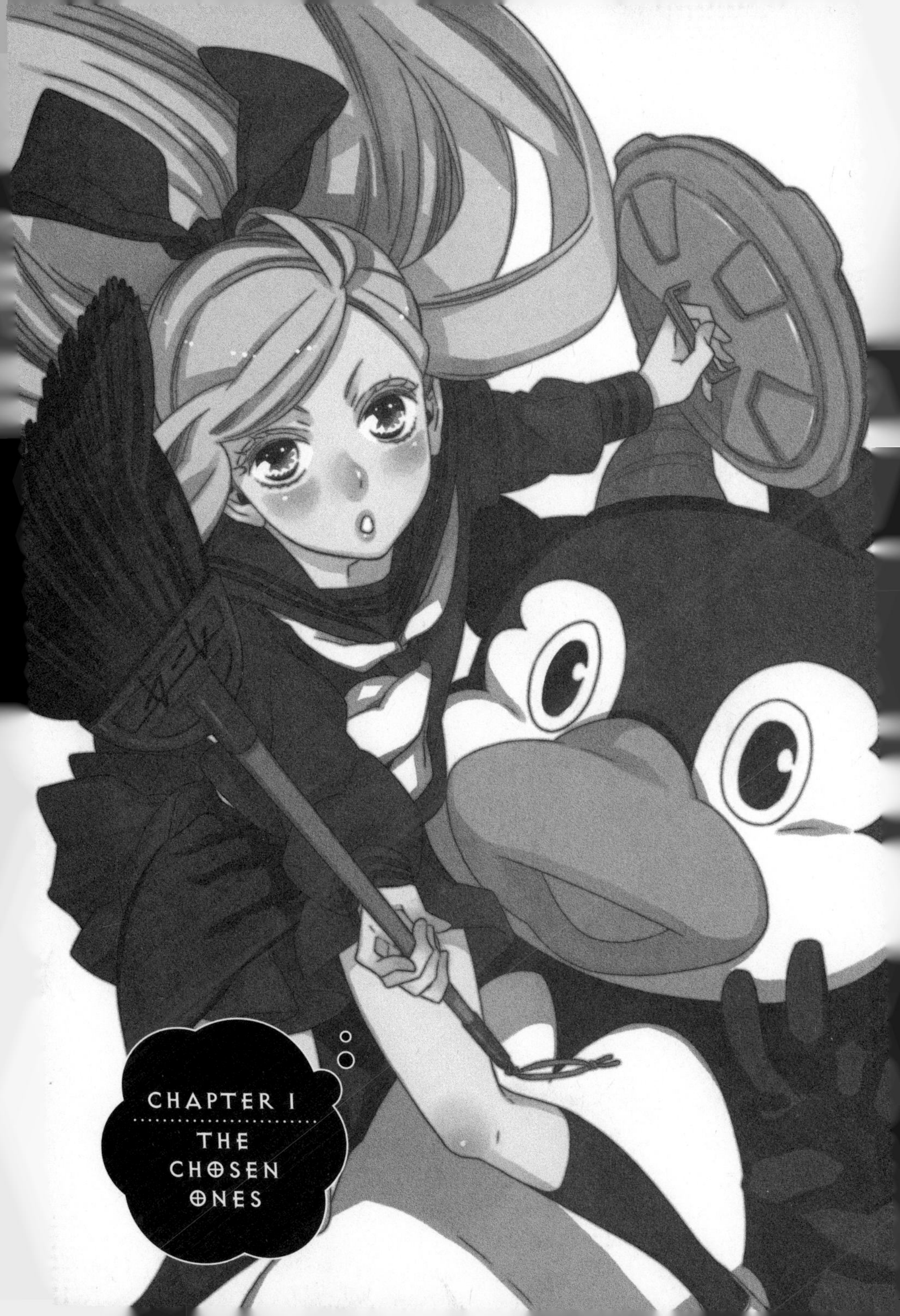
CHAPTER 1
THE CHOSEN ONES

Kigurumi
GUARDIANS

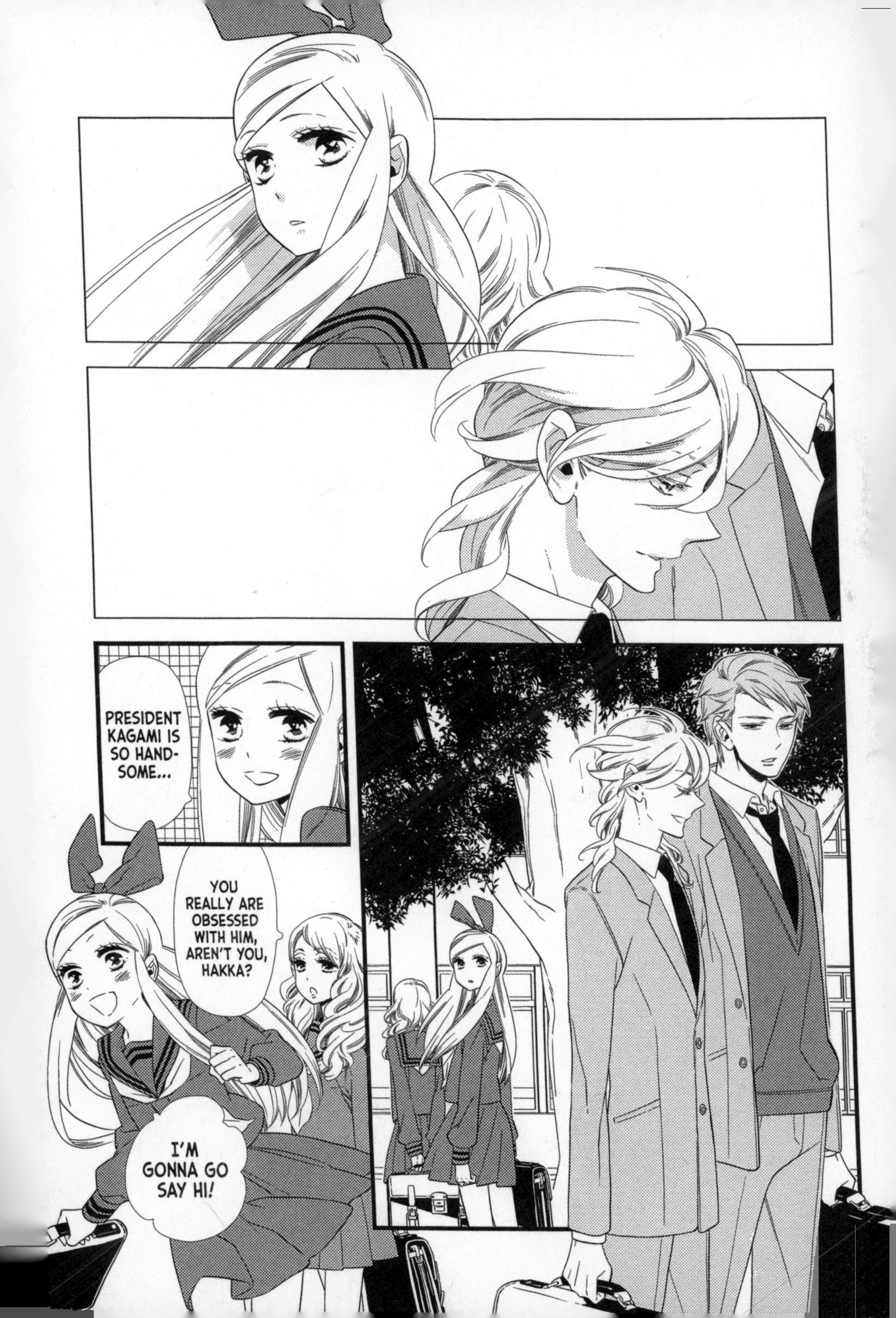
PRESIDENT KAGAMI IS SO HAND-SOME...
YOU REALLY ARE OBSESSED WITH HIM, AREN'T YOU, HAKKA?
I'M GONNA GO SAY HI!

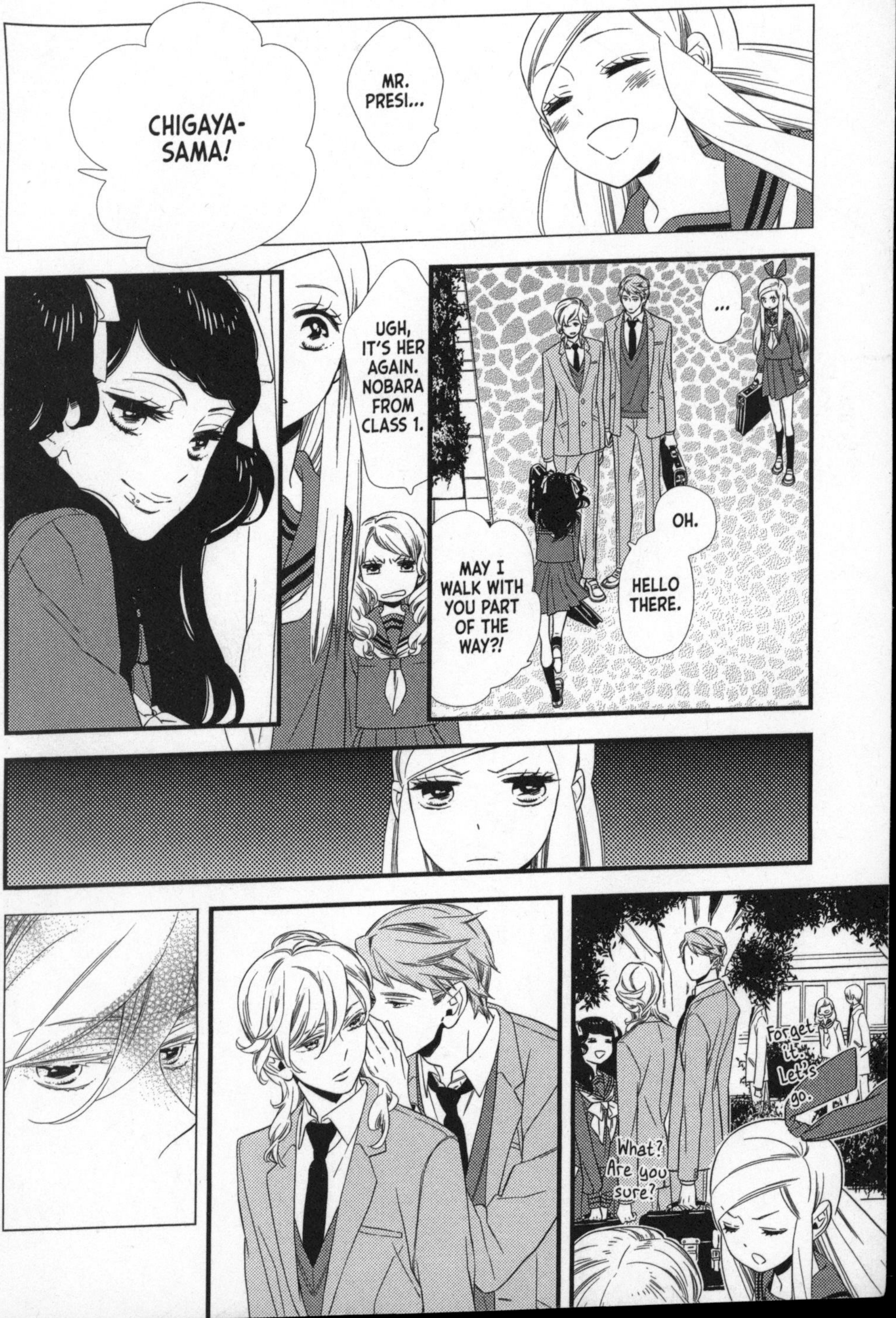
MR. PRESI...
CHIGAYA-SAMA!
...
OH.
HELLO THERE.
MAY I WALK WITH YOU PART OF THE WAY?!
UGH, IT'S HER AGAIN. NOBARA FROM CLASS 1.
Forget it. Let's go.
What? Are you sure?

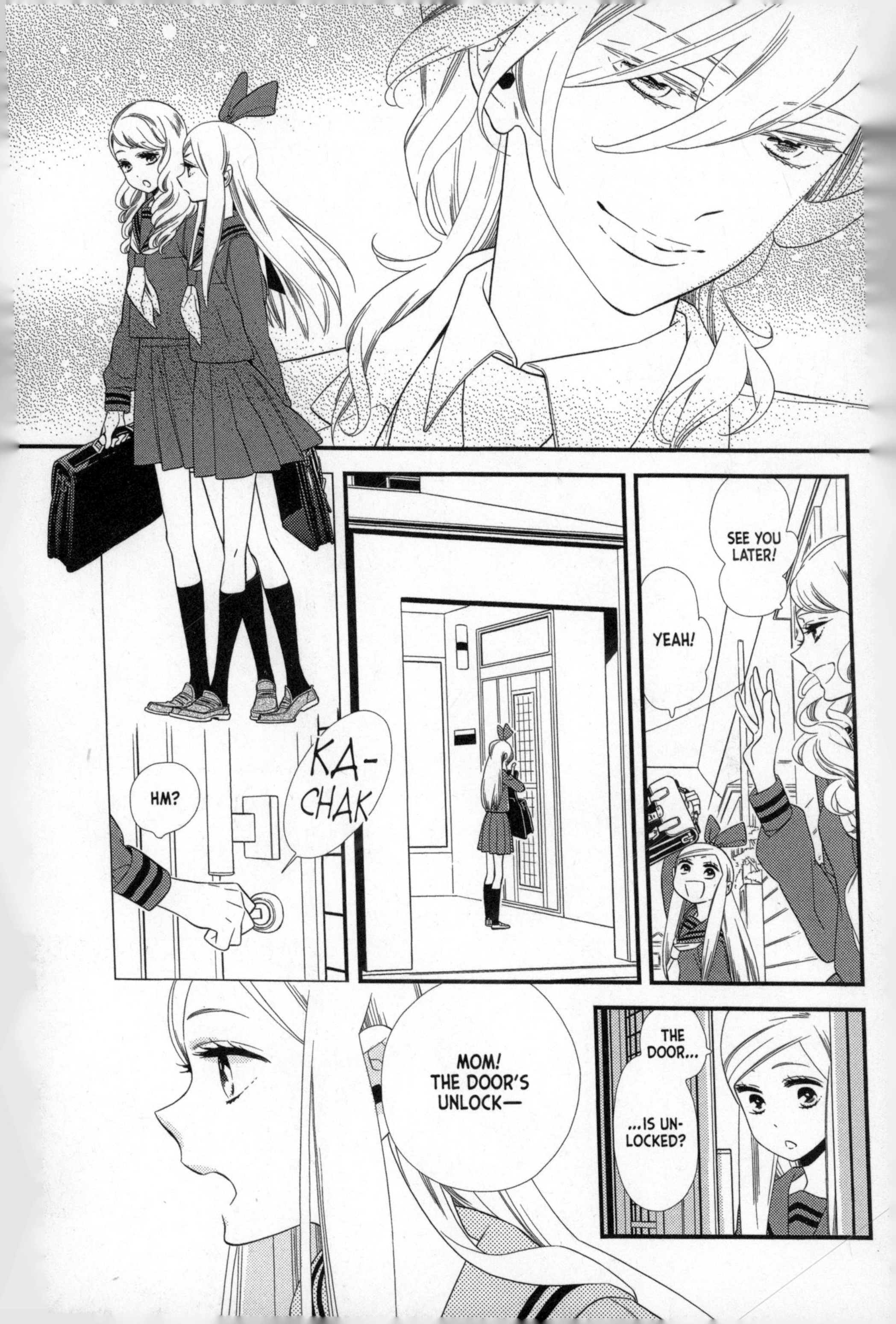
SEE YOU LATER!
YEAH!
HM?
KA-CHAK
THE DOOR...
...IS UN-LOCKED?
MOM! THE DOOR'S UNLOCK—

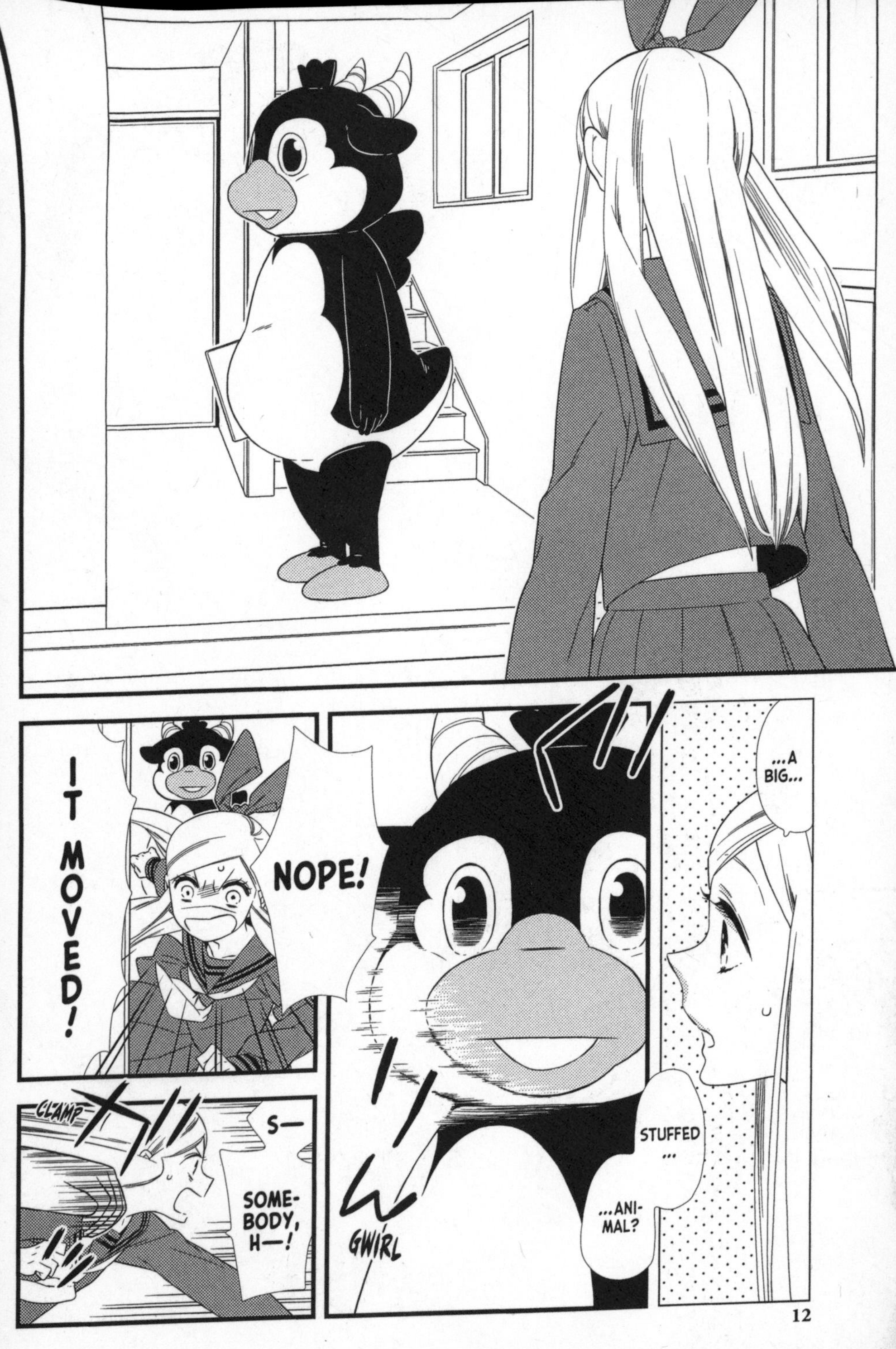
...A BIG...
STUFFED ...
...ANI-MAL?
GWIRL
NOPE!
IT MOVED!
S—
SOME-BODY, H—!
CLAMP

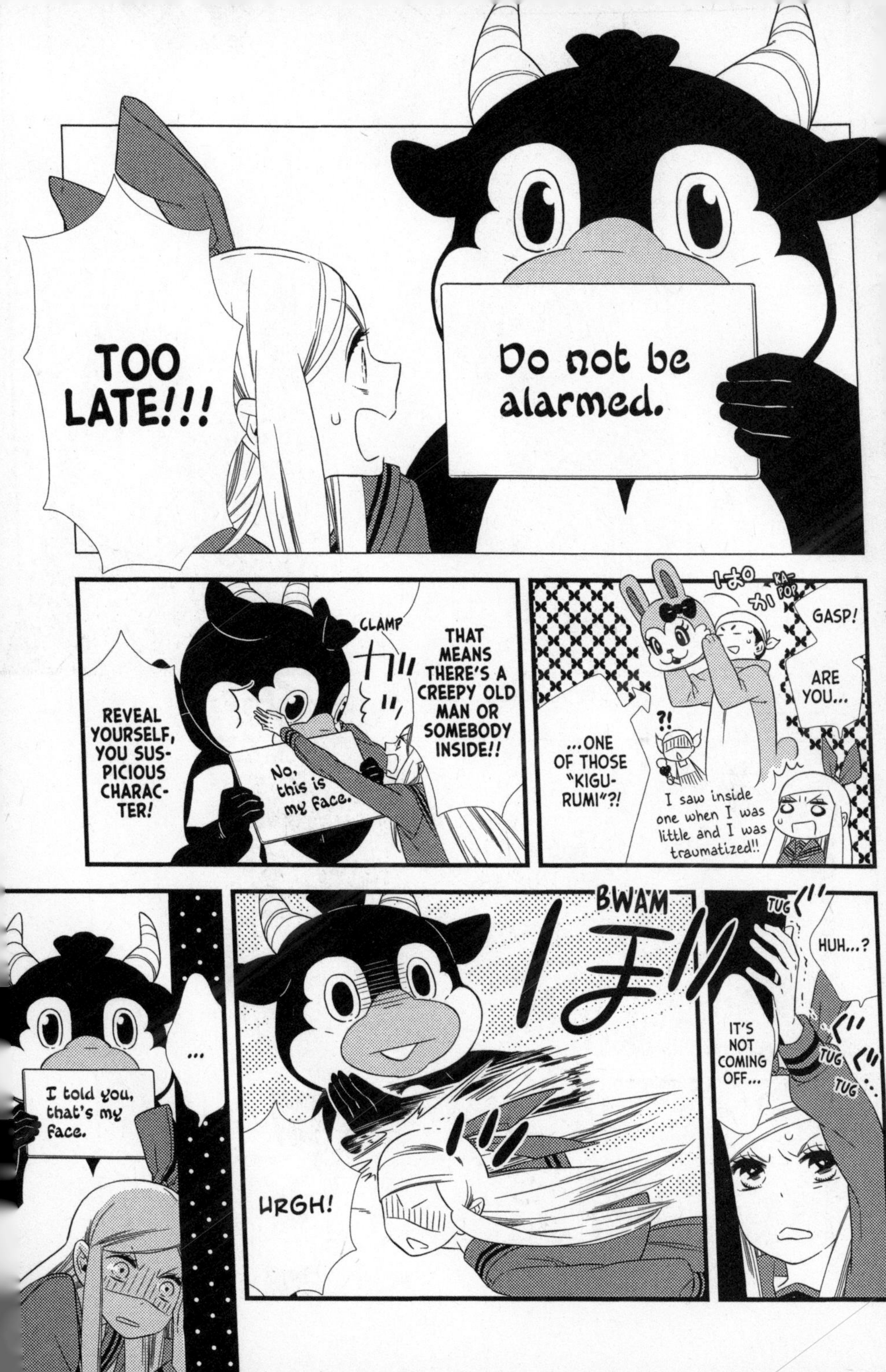
Do not be alarmed.
TOO LATE!!!
KA-POP
GASP!
ARE YOU...
...ONE OF THOSE "KIGU-RUMI"?!
?!
I saw inside one when I was little and I was traumatized!!
CLAMP
THAT MEANS THERE'S A CREEPY OLD MAN OR SOMEBODY INSIDE!!
No, this is my face.
REVEAL YOURSELF, YOU SUSPICIOUS CHARACTER!
TUG
HUH...?
IT'S NOT COMING OFF...
TUG
TUG
BWAM
URGH!
...
I told you, that's my face.

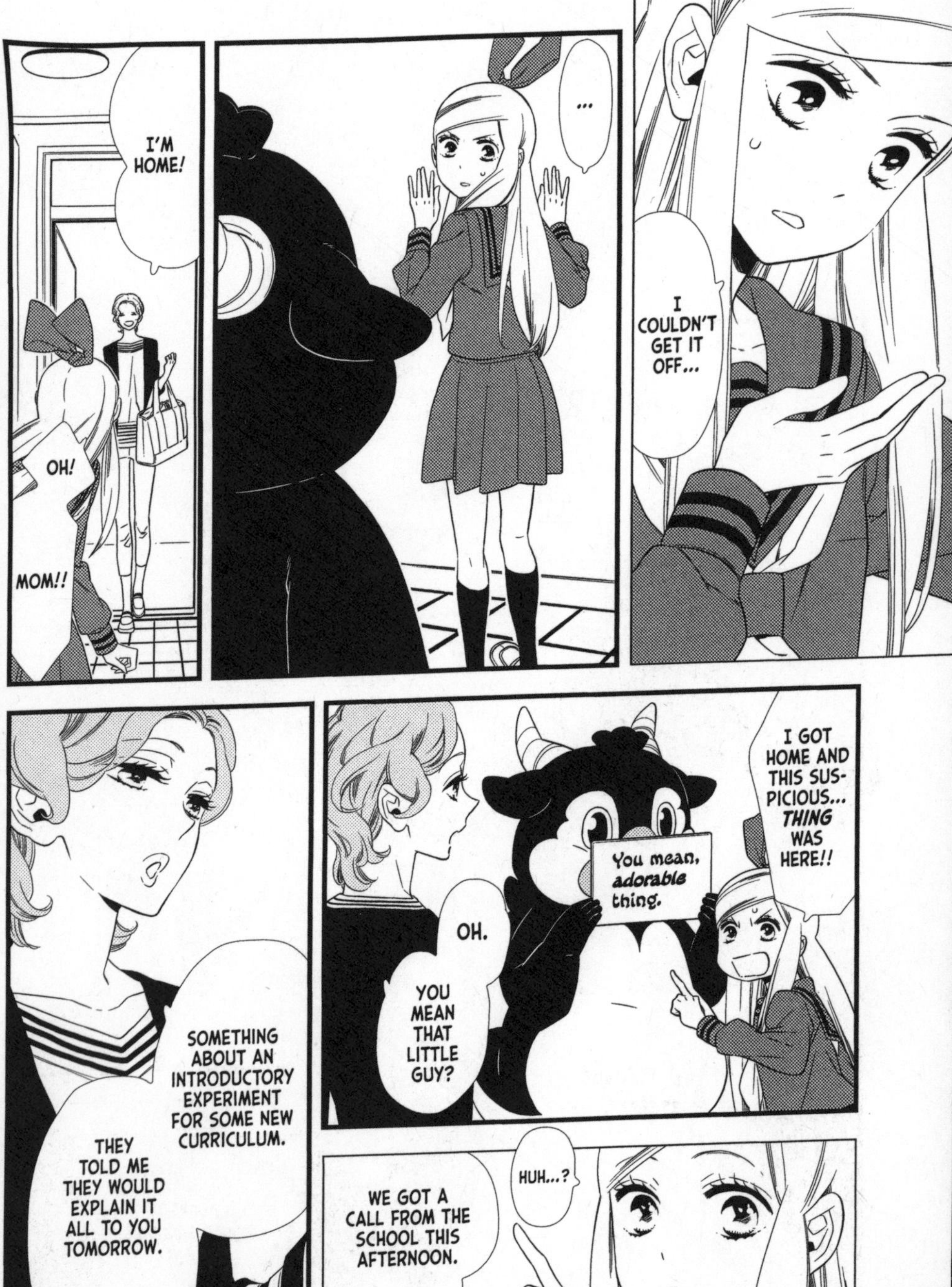
I COULDN'T GET IT OFF...
...
I'M HOME!
OH!
MOM!!
I GOT HOME AND THIS SUSPICIOUS... *THING* WAS HERE!!
You mean, **adorable** thing.
OH.
YOU MEAN THAT LITTLE GUY?
HUH...?
WE GOT A CALL FROM THE SCHOOL THIS AFTERNOON.
SOMETHING ABOUT AN INTRODUCTORY EXPERIMENT FOR SOME NEW CURRICULUM.
THEY TOLD ME THEY WOULD EXPLAIN IT ALL TO YOU TOMORROW.

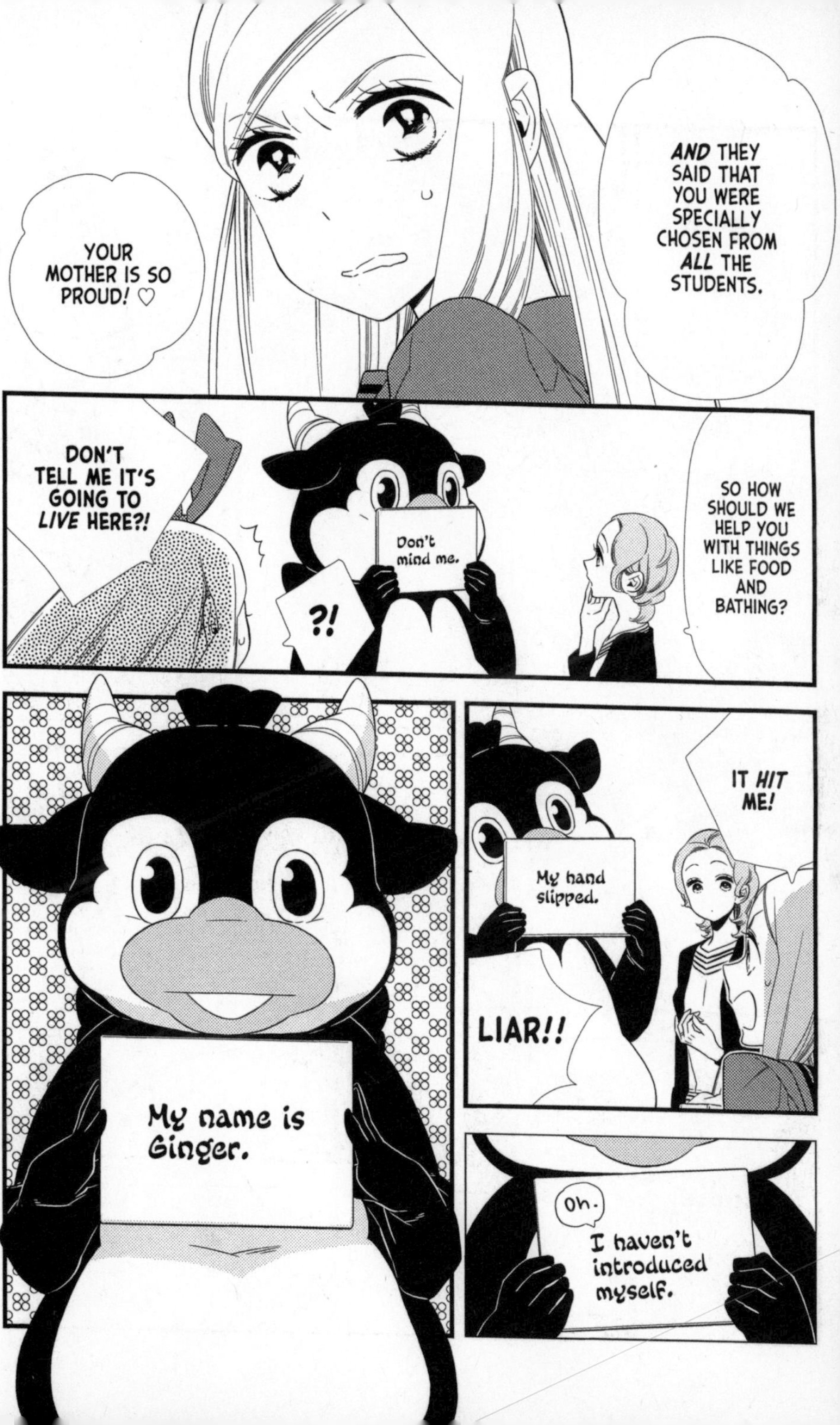
AND THEY SAID THAT YOU WERE SPECIALLY CHOSEN FROM ALL THE STUDENTS.
YOUR MOTHER IS SO PROUD! ♡
SO HOW SHOULD WE HELP YOU WITH THINGS LIKE FOOD AND BATHING?
Don't mind me.
?!
DON'T TELL ME IT'S GOING TO LIVE HERE?!
IT HIT ME!
My hand slipped.
LIAR!!
Oh.
I haven't introduced myself.
My name is Ginger.

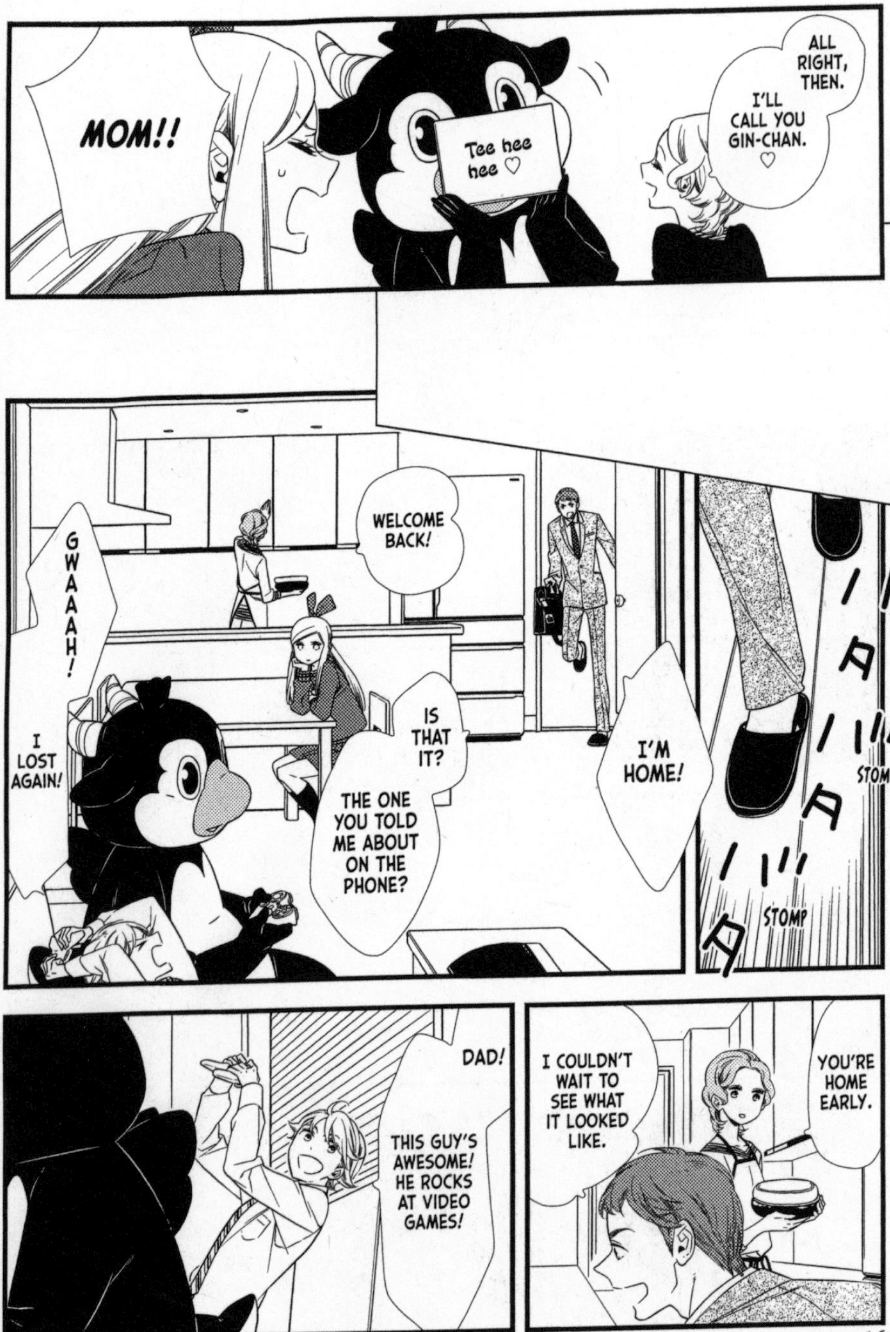
ALL RIGHT, THEN.
I'LL CALL YOU GIN-CHAN. ♡
Tee hee hee ♡
MOM!!
STOMP
STOMP
STOMP
I'M HOME!
WELCOME BACK!
IS THAT IT?
THE ONE YOU TOLD ME ABOUT ON THE PHONE?
GWAAAAH!
I LOST AGAIN!
YOU'RE HOME EARLY.
I COULDN'T WAIT TO SEE WHAT IT LOOKED LIKE.
DAD!
THIS GUY'S AWESOME! HE ROCKS AT VIDEO GAMES!

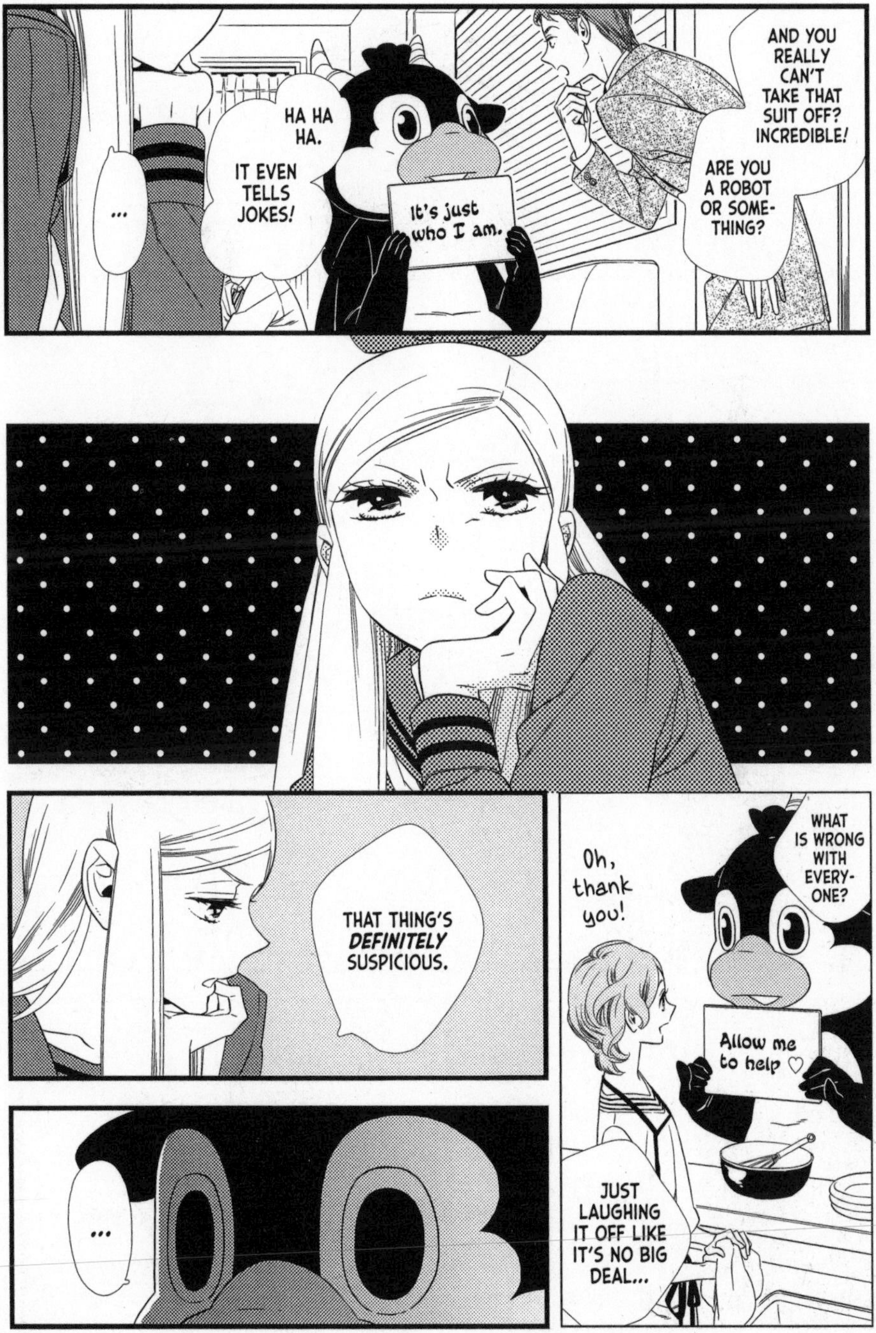
AND YOU REALLY CAN'T TAKE THAT SUIT OFF? INCREDIBLE!
ARE YOU A ROBOT OR SOME-THING?
It's just who I am.
HA HA HA.
IT EVEN TELLS JOKES!
...
WHAT IS WRONG WITH EVERY-ONE?
Oh, thank you!
Allow me to help ♡
JUST LAUGHING IT OFF LIKE IT'S NO BIG DEAL...
THAT THING'S *DEFINITELY* SUSPICIOUS.
...

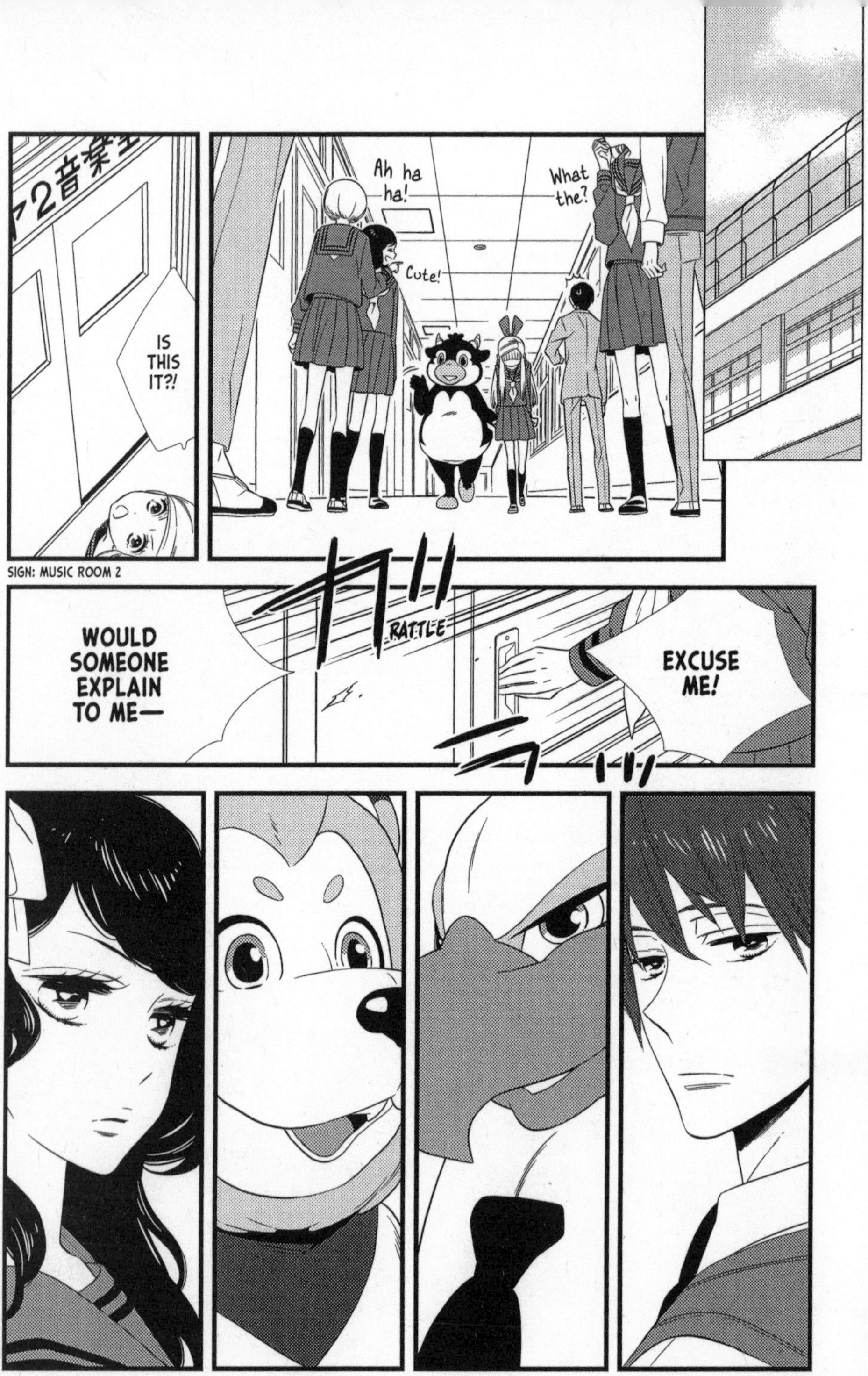
What the?
Ah ha ha!
Cute!
IS THIS IT?!
SIGN: MUSIC ROOM 2
EXCUSE ME!
RATTLE
WOULD SOMEONE EXPLAIN TO ME—

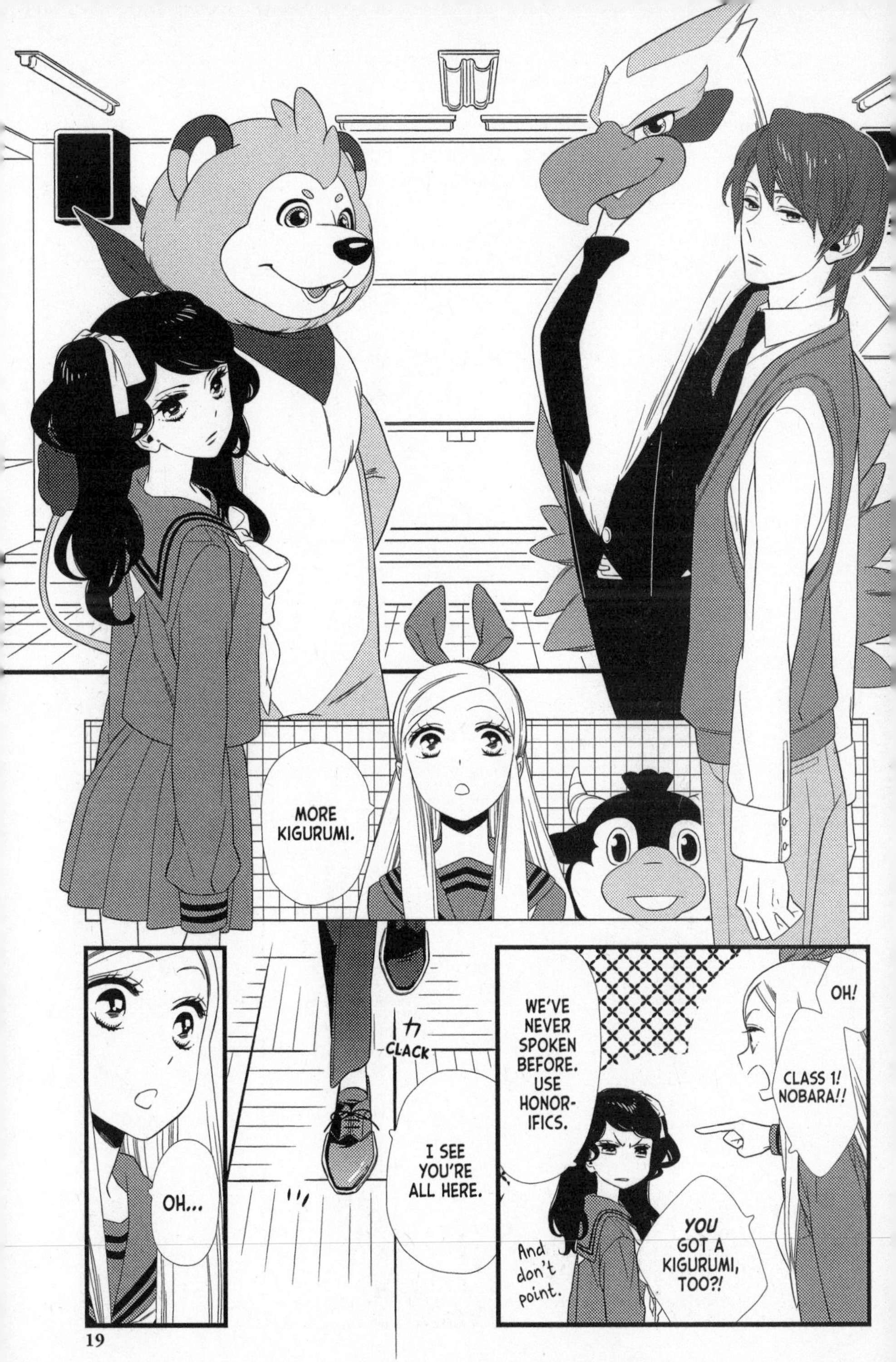
MORE KIGURUMI.
OH!
CLASS 1! NOBARA!!
YOU GOT A KIGURUMI, TOO?!
WE'VE NEVER SPOKEN BEFORE. USE HONORIFICS.
And don't point.
カ CLACK
I SEE YOU'RE ALL HERE.
OH...

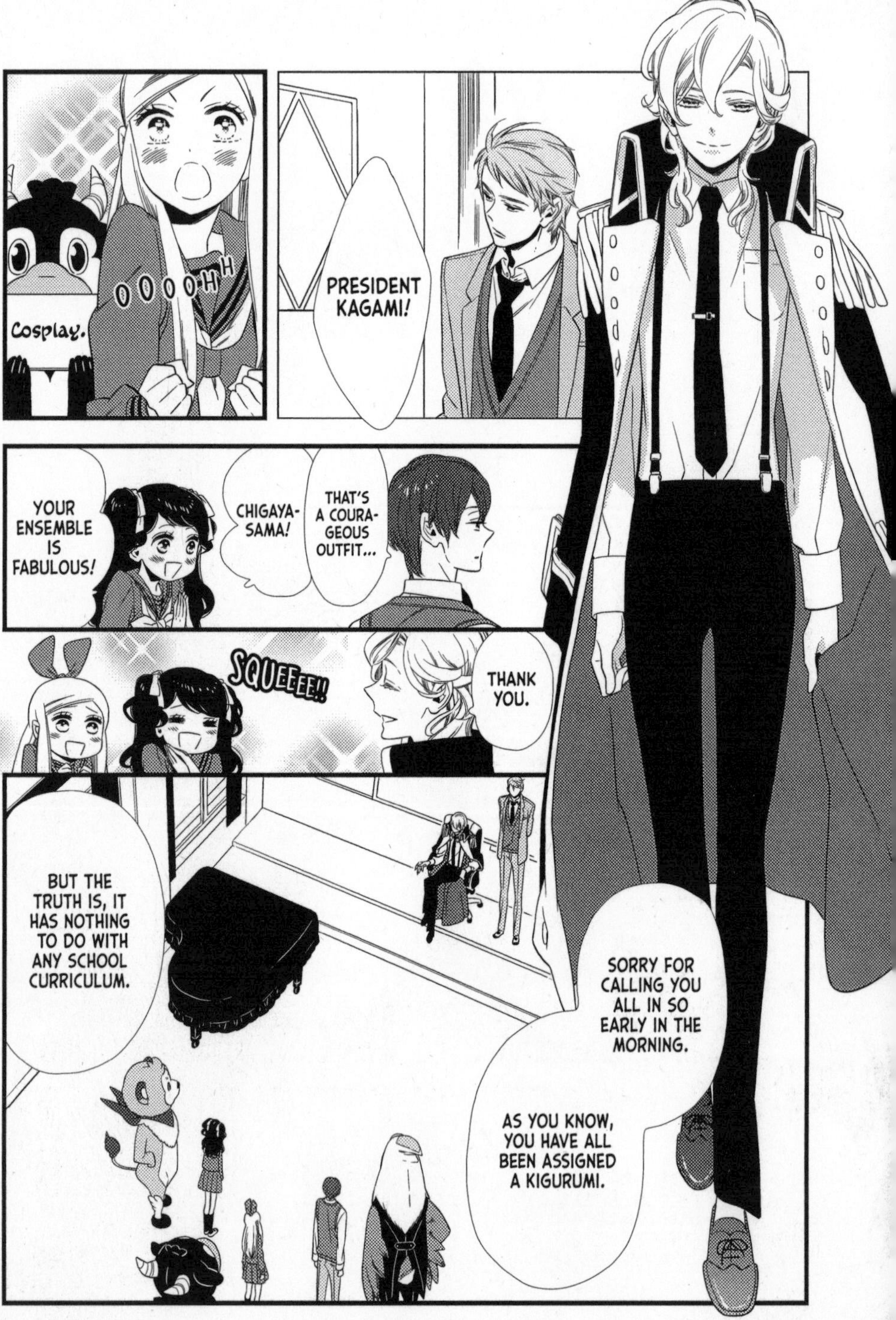
PRESIDENT KAGAMI!
OOOOHH
Cosplay.
THAT'S A COURAGEOUS OUTFIT...
CHIGAYA-SAMA!
YOUR ENSEMBLE IS FABULOUS!
THANK YOU.
SQUEEEEE!!
SORRY FOR CALLING YOU ALL IN SO EARLY IN THE MORNING.
AS YOU KNOW, YOU HAVE ALL BEEN ASSIGNED A KIGURUMI.
BUT THE TRUTH IS, IT HAS NOTHING TO DO WITH ANY SCHOOL CURRICULUM.

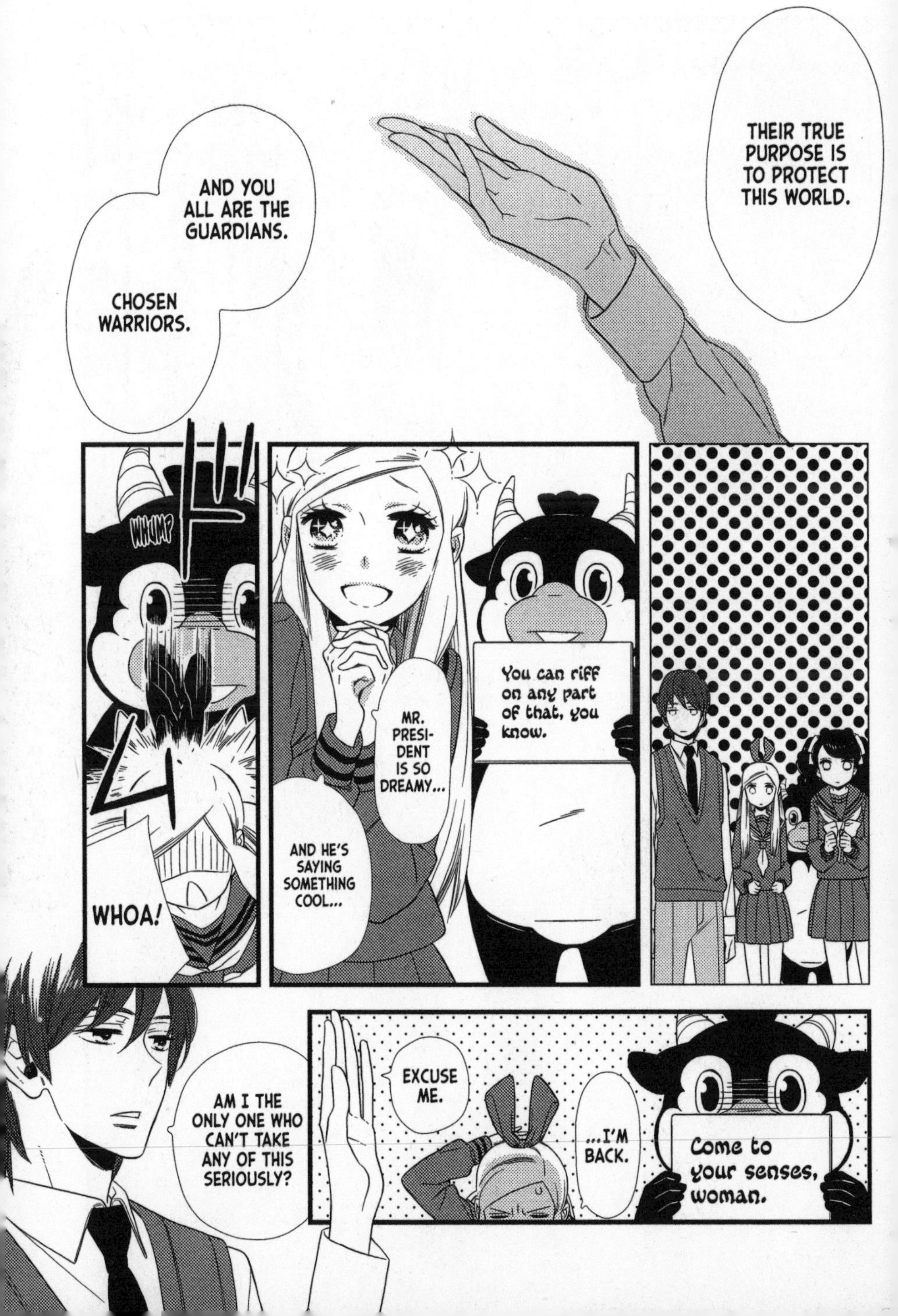
THEIR TRUE PURPOSE IS TO PROTECT THIS WORLD.
AND YOU ALL ARE THE GUARDIANS.
CHOSEN WARRIORS.
You can riff on any part of that, you know.
MR. PRESIDENT IS SO DREAMY...
AND HE'S SAYING SOMETHING COOL...
WHUMP
WHOA!
Come to your senses, woman.
...I'M BACK.
EXCUSE ME.
AM I THE ONLY ONE WHO CAN'T TAKE ANY OF THIS SERIOUSLY?

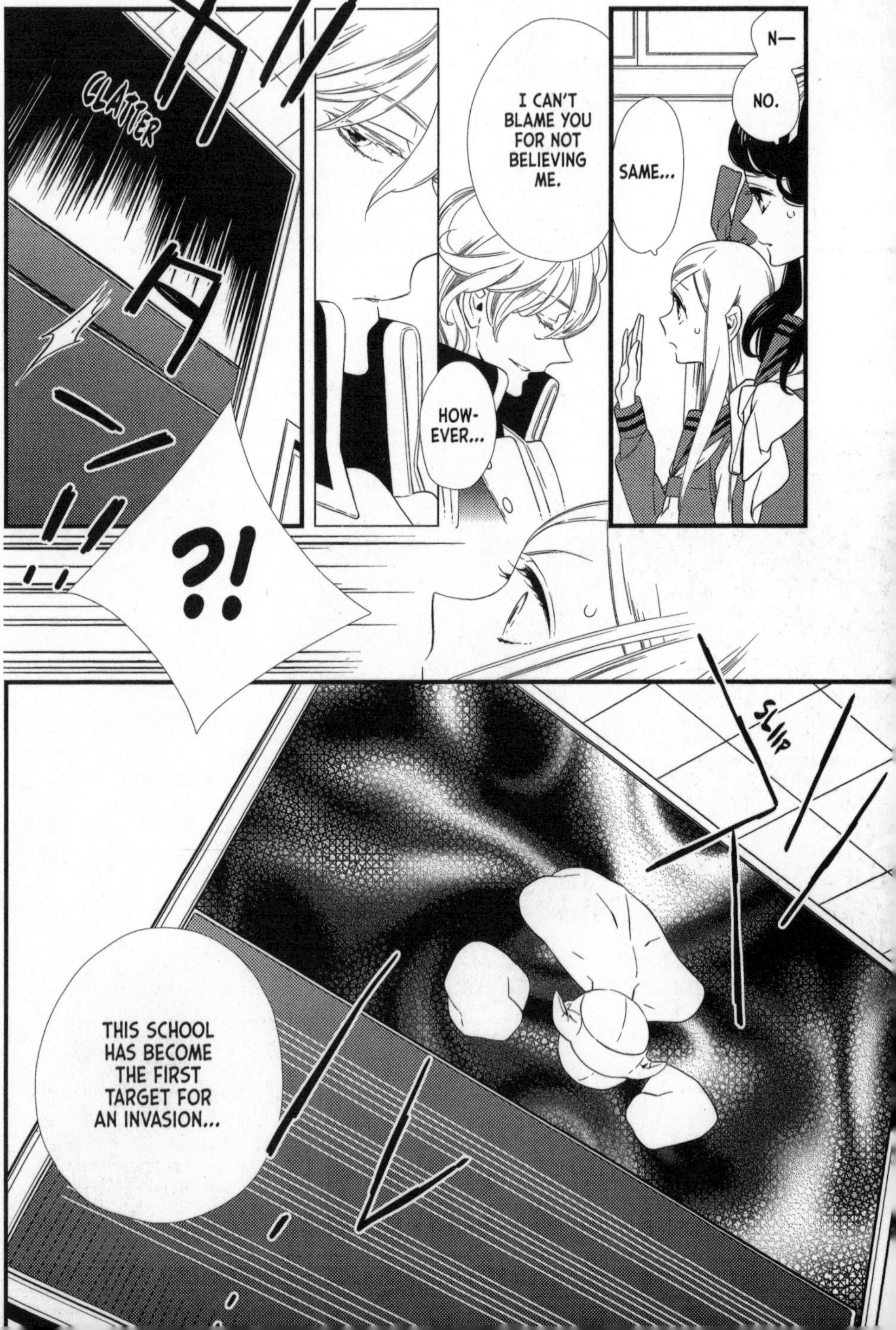

N—
NO.
SAME...
I CAN'T BLAME YOU FOR NOT BELIEVING ME.
HOW-EVER...
CLATTER
?!
SLIP
THIS SCHOOL HAS BECOME THE FIRST TARGET FOR AN INVASION...

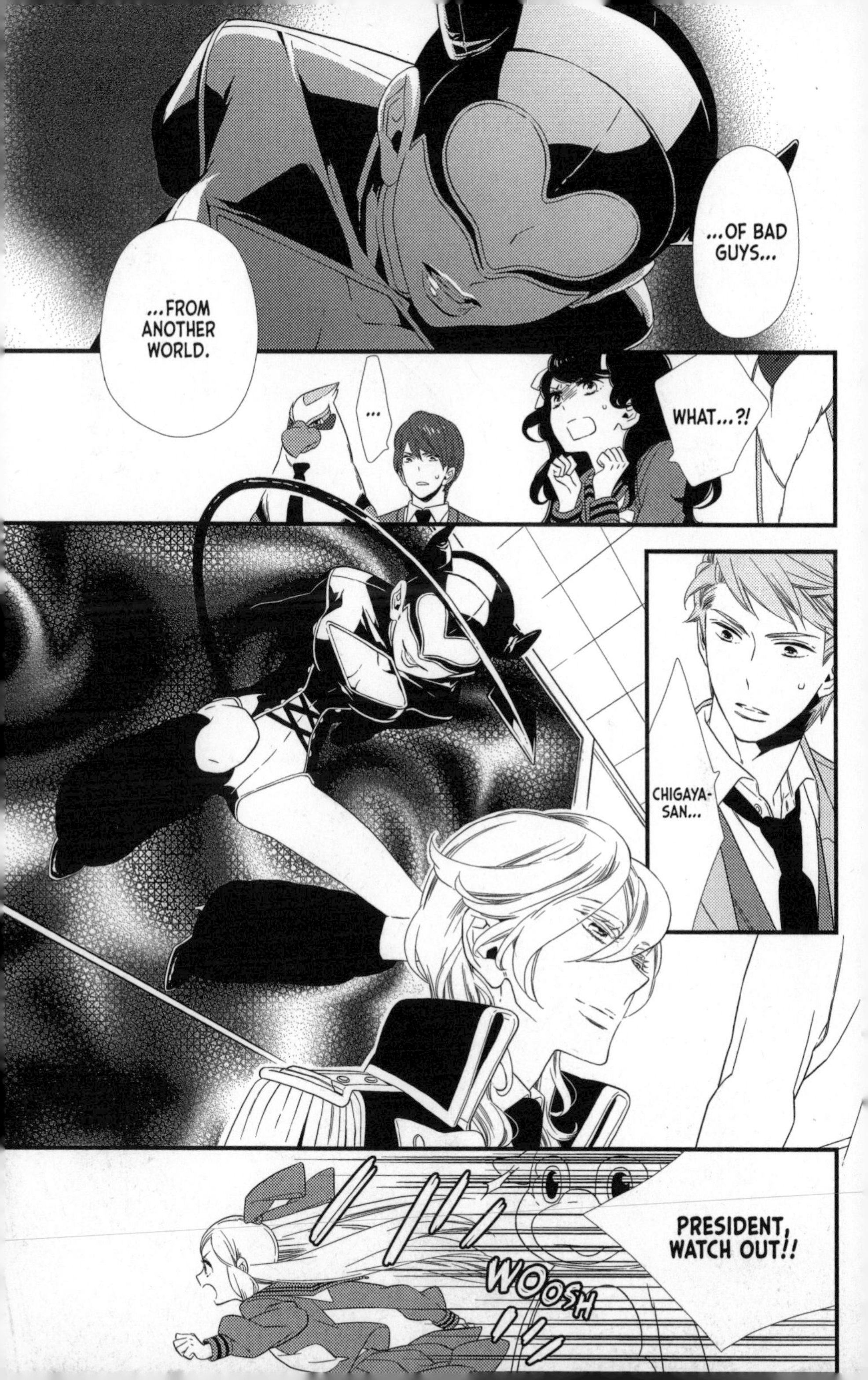
...OF BAD GUYS...
...FROM ANOTHER WORLD.
WHAT...?!
...
CHIGAYA-SAN...
PRESIDENT, WATCH OUT!!
WOOSH

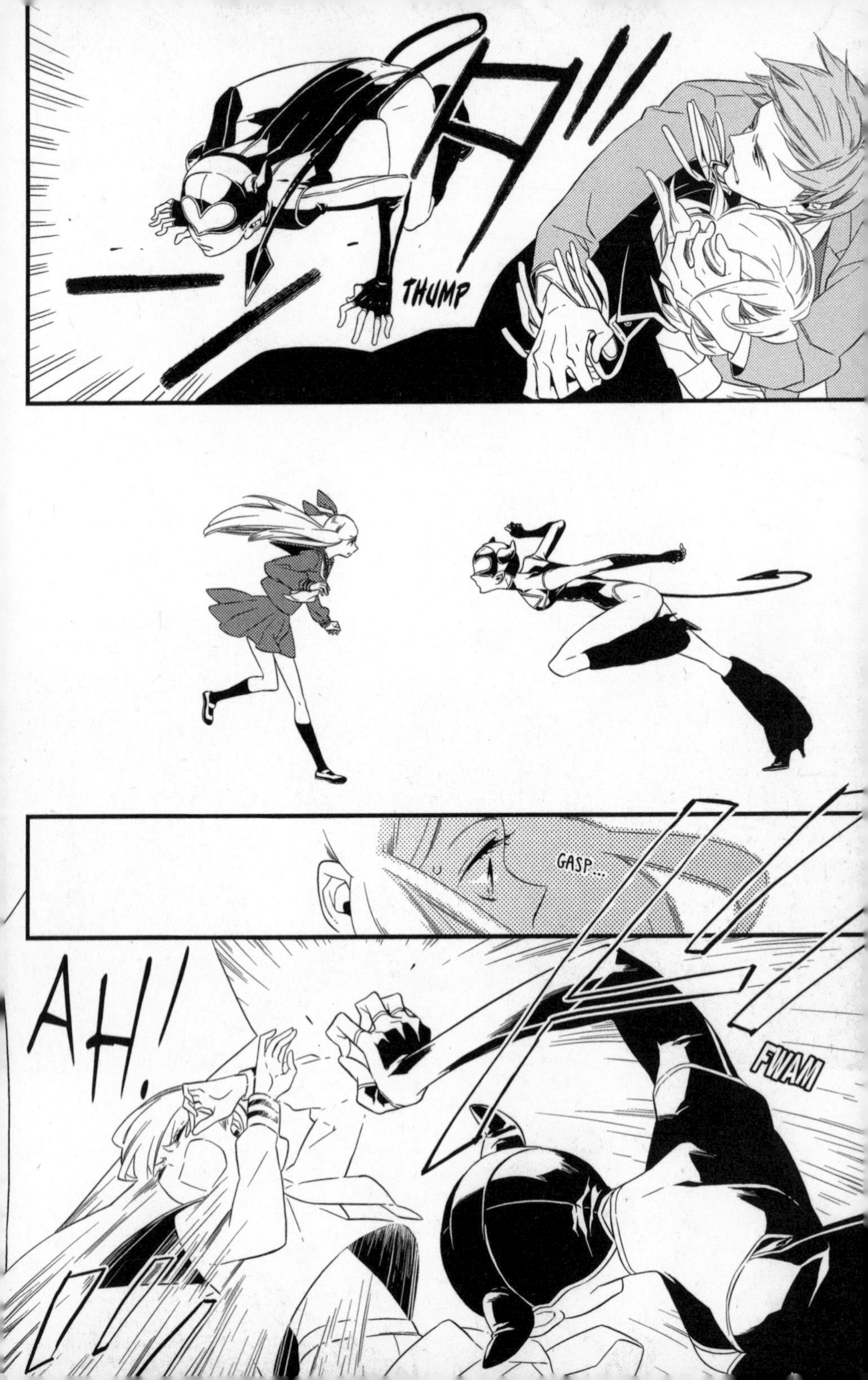
THUMP
GASP...
FWAM
AH!

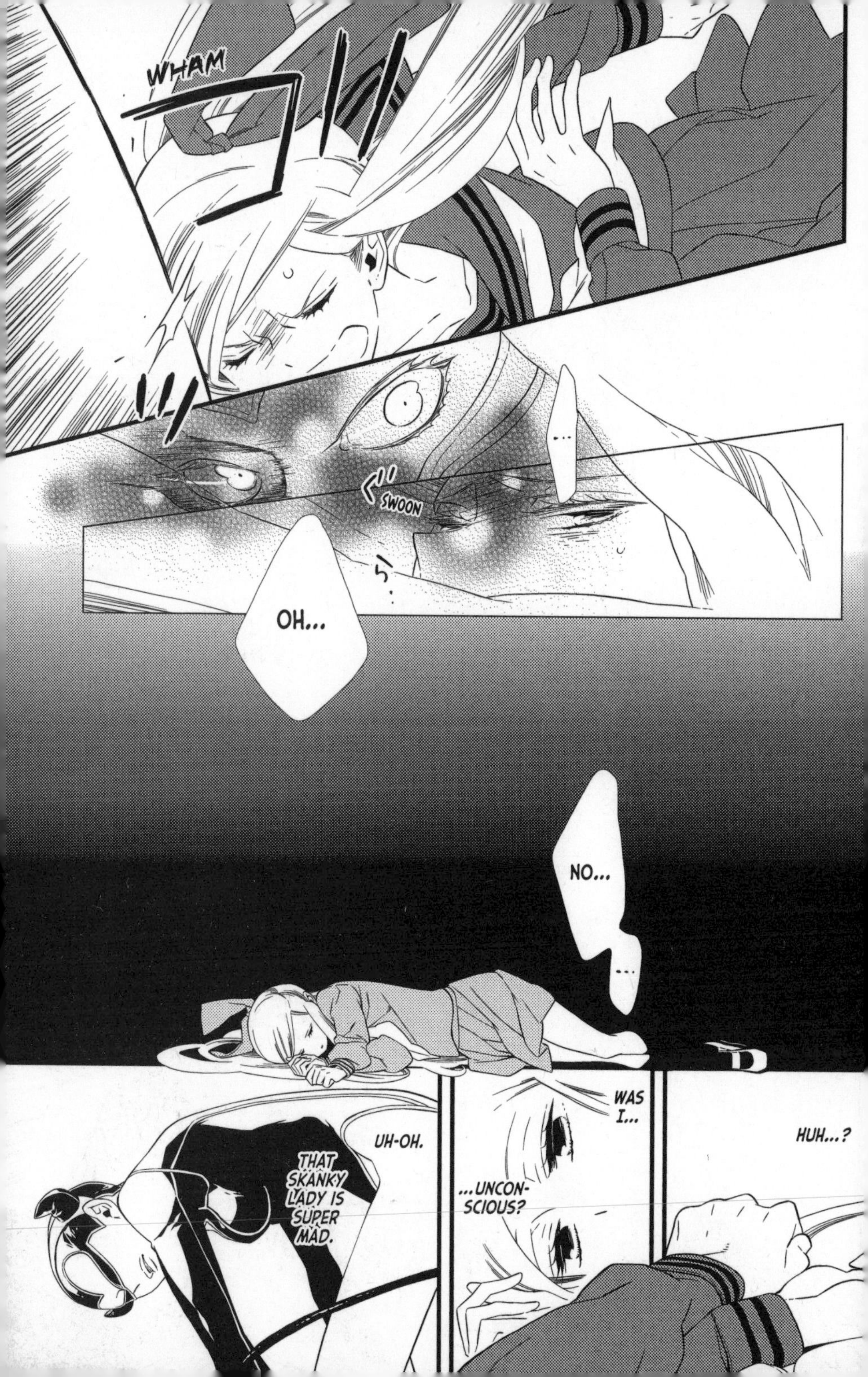
WHAM
...
SWOON
OH...
NO...
...
HUH...?
WAS I...
...UNCON-SCIOUS?
UH-OH.
THAT SKANKY LADY IS SUPER MAD.

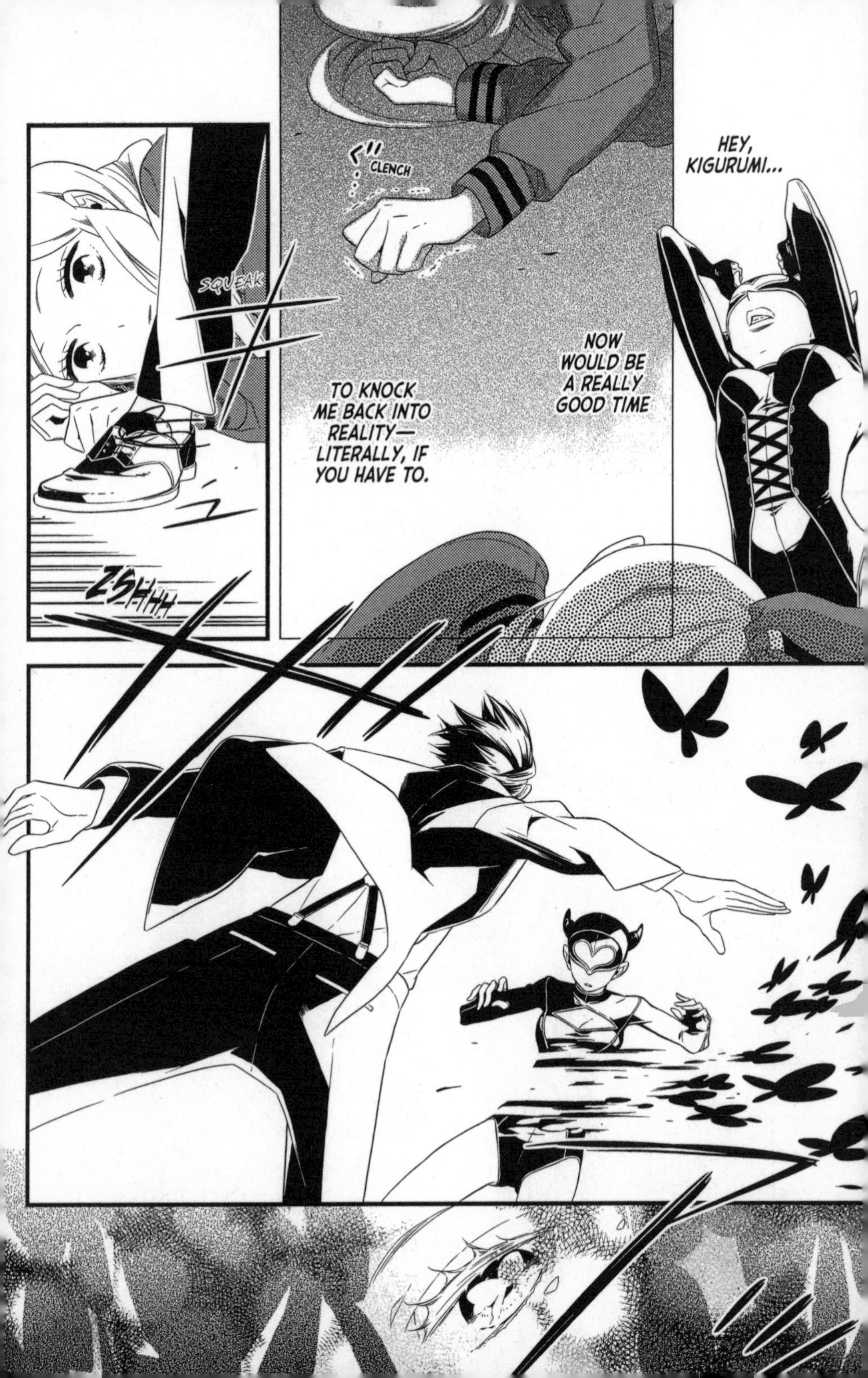
HEY, KIGURUMI...
CLENCH
NOW WOULD BE A REALLY GOOD TIME
TO KNOCK ME BACK INTO REALITY— LITERALLY, IF YOU HAVE TO.
SQUEAK
ZSHHH

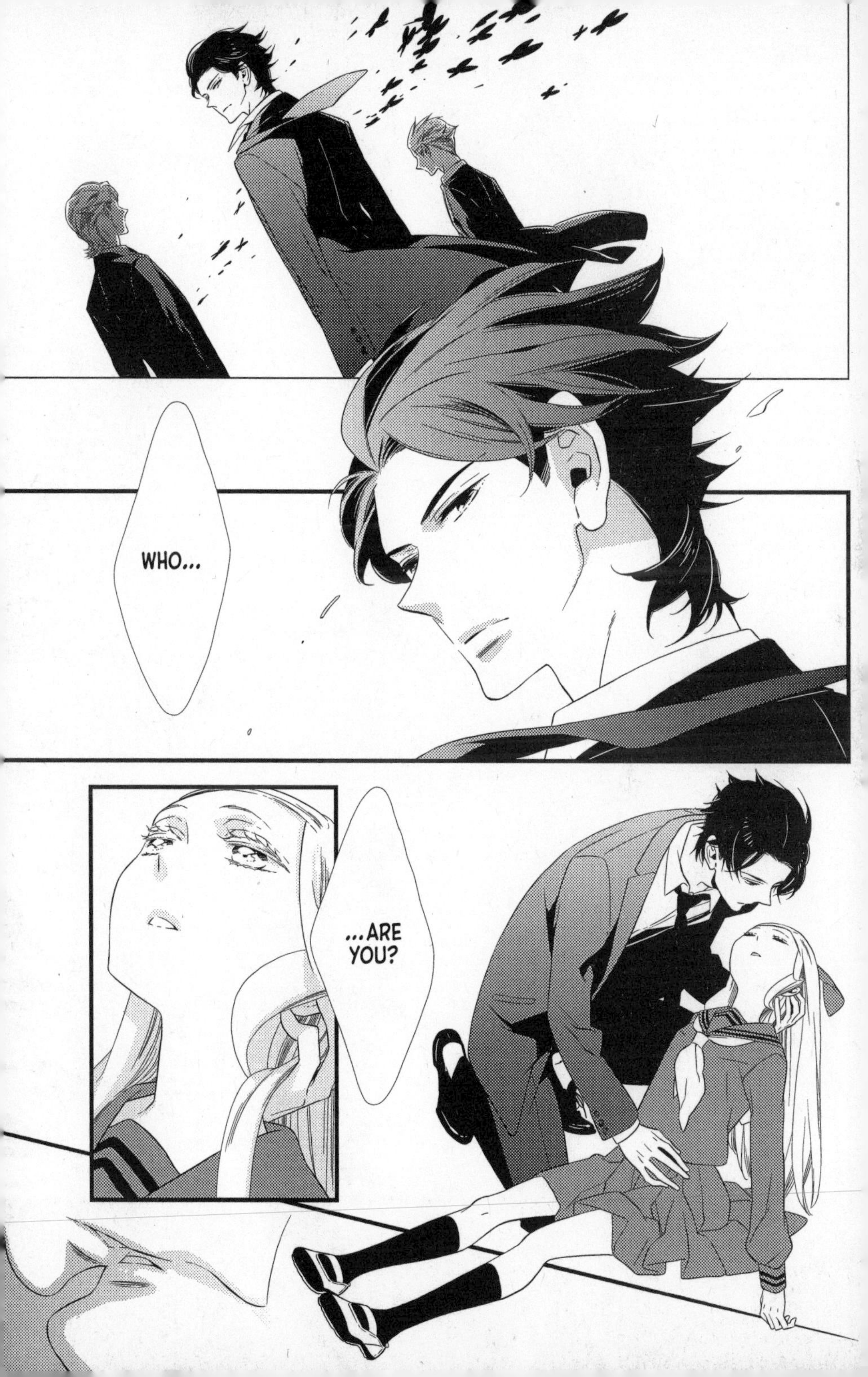
WHO...
...ARE YOU?

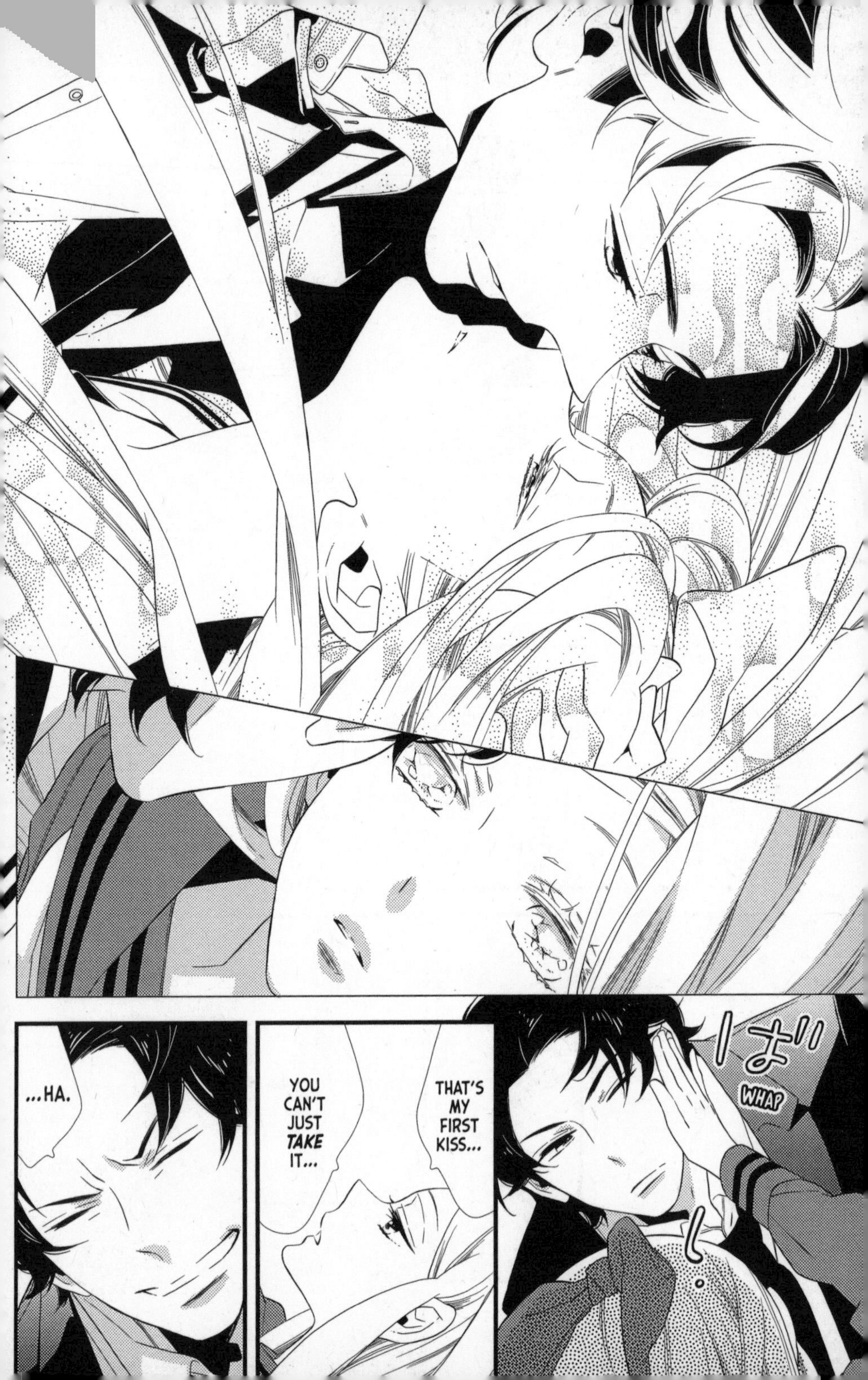
ぱし
WHAP
THAT'S MY FIRST KISS...
YOU CAN'T JUST *TAKE* IT...
...HA.

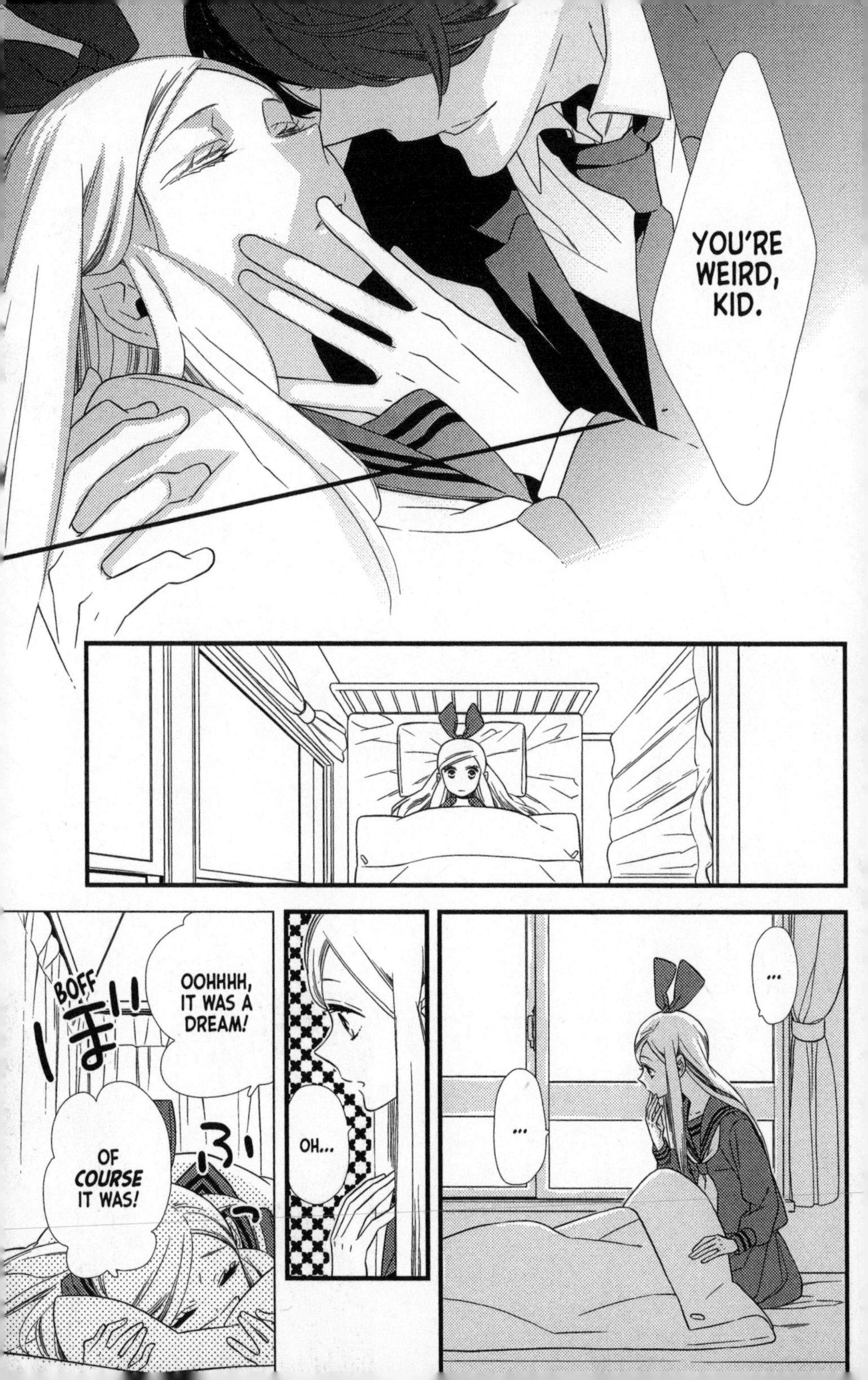
YOU'RE WEIRD, KID.
...
...
OH...
BOFF
OOHHHH, IT WAS A DREAM!
OF COURSE IT WAS!

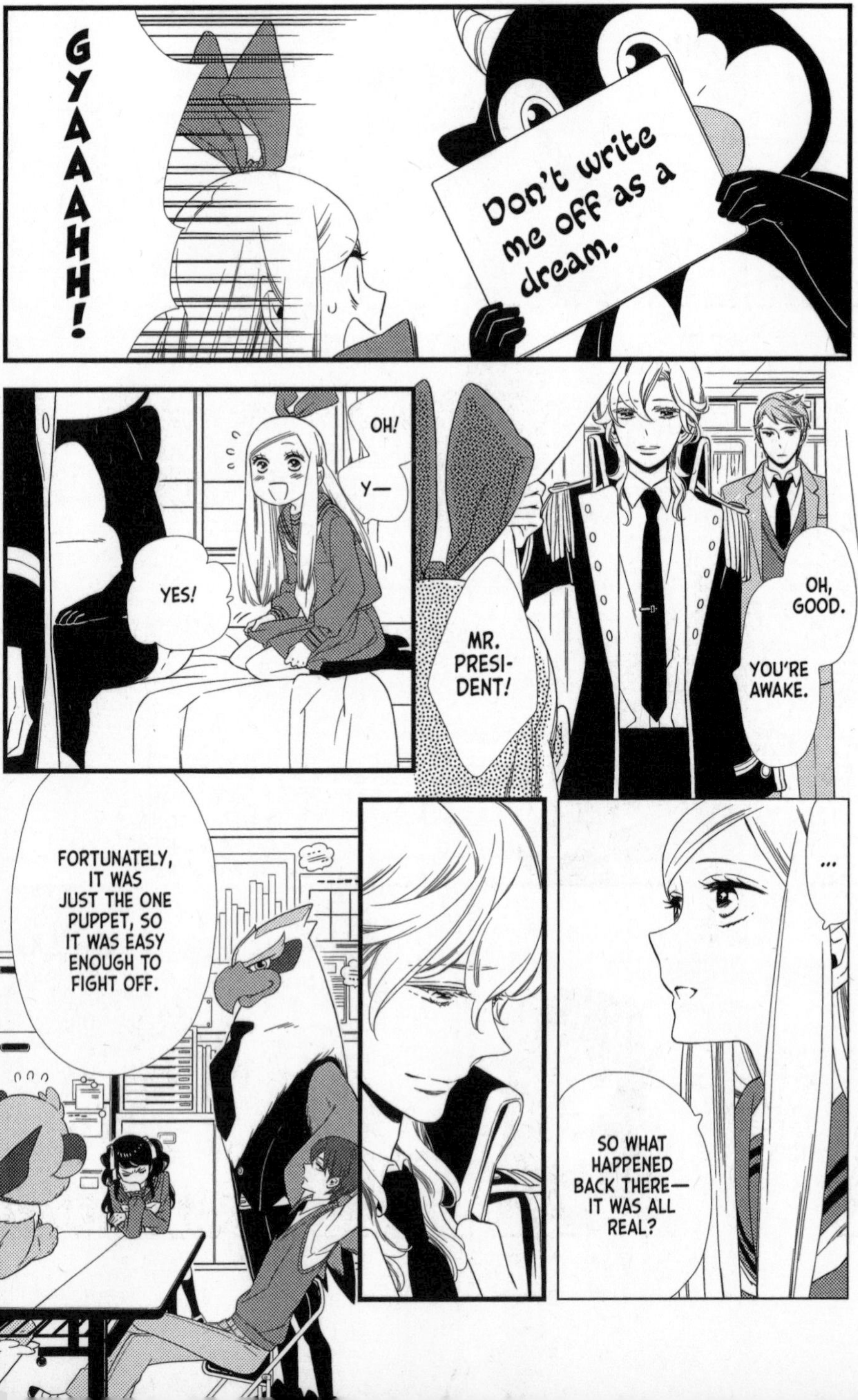
Don't write me off as a dream.
GYAAAHH!
OH, GOOD.
YOU'RE AWAKE.
MR. PRESIDENT!
OH!
Y—
YES!
...
SO WHAT HAPPENED BACK THERE— IT WAS ALL REAL?
FORTUNATELY, IT WAS JUST THE ONE PUPPET, SO IT WAS EASY ENOUGH TO FIGHT OFF.

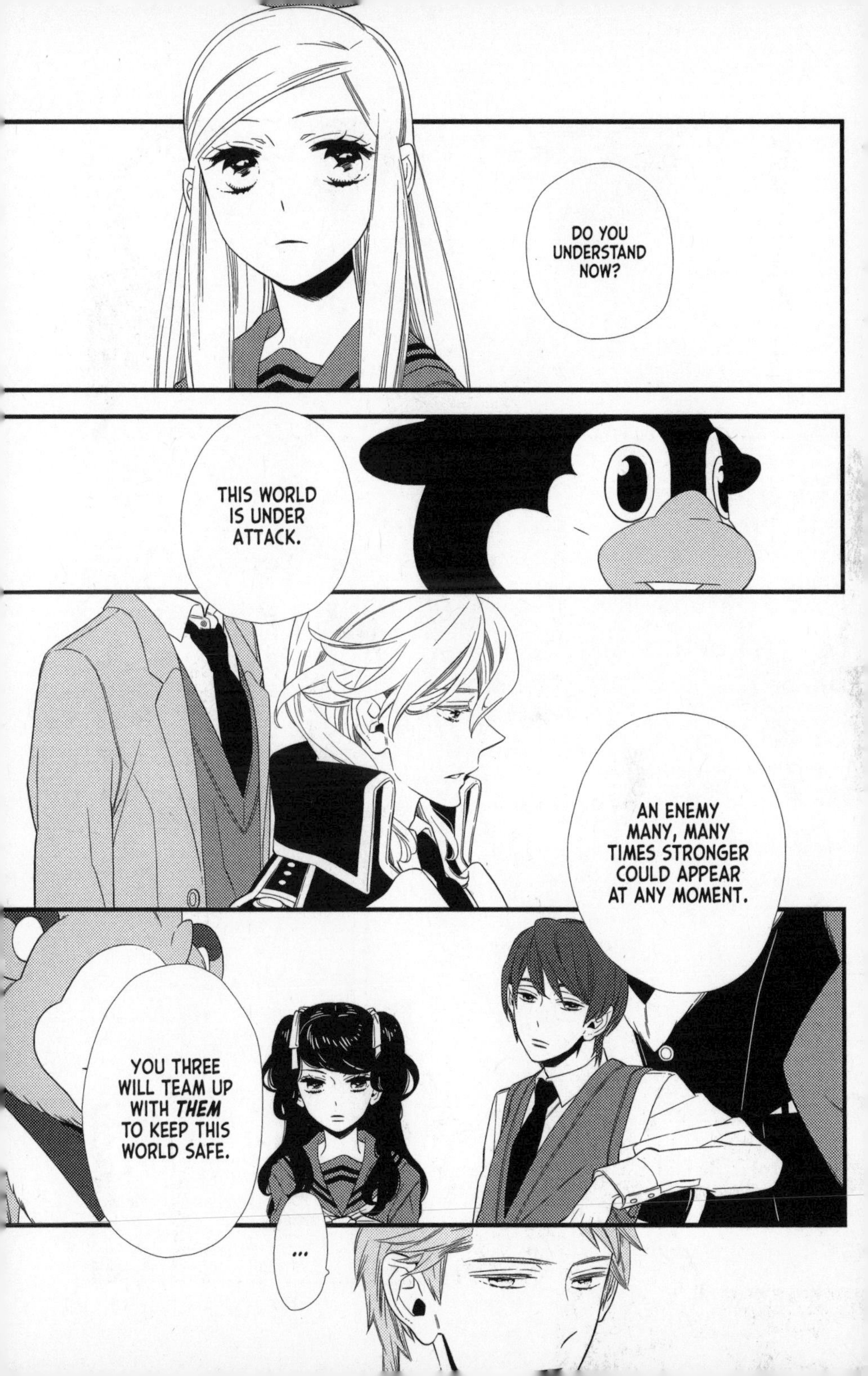
DO YOU UNDERSTAND NOW?
THIS WORLD IS UNDER ATTACK.
AN ENEMY MANY, MANY TIMES STRONGER COULD APPEAR AT ANY MOMENT.
YOU THREE WILL TEAM UP WITH *THEM* TO KEEP THIS WORLD SAFE.
...

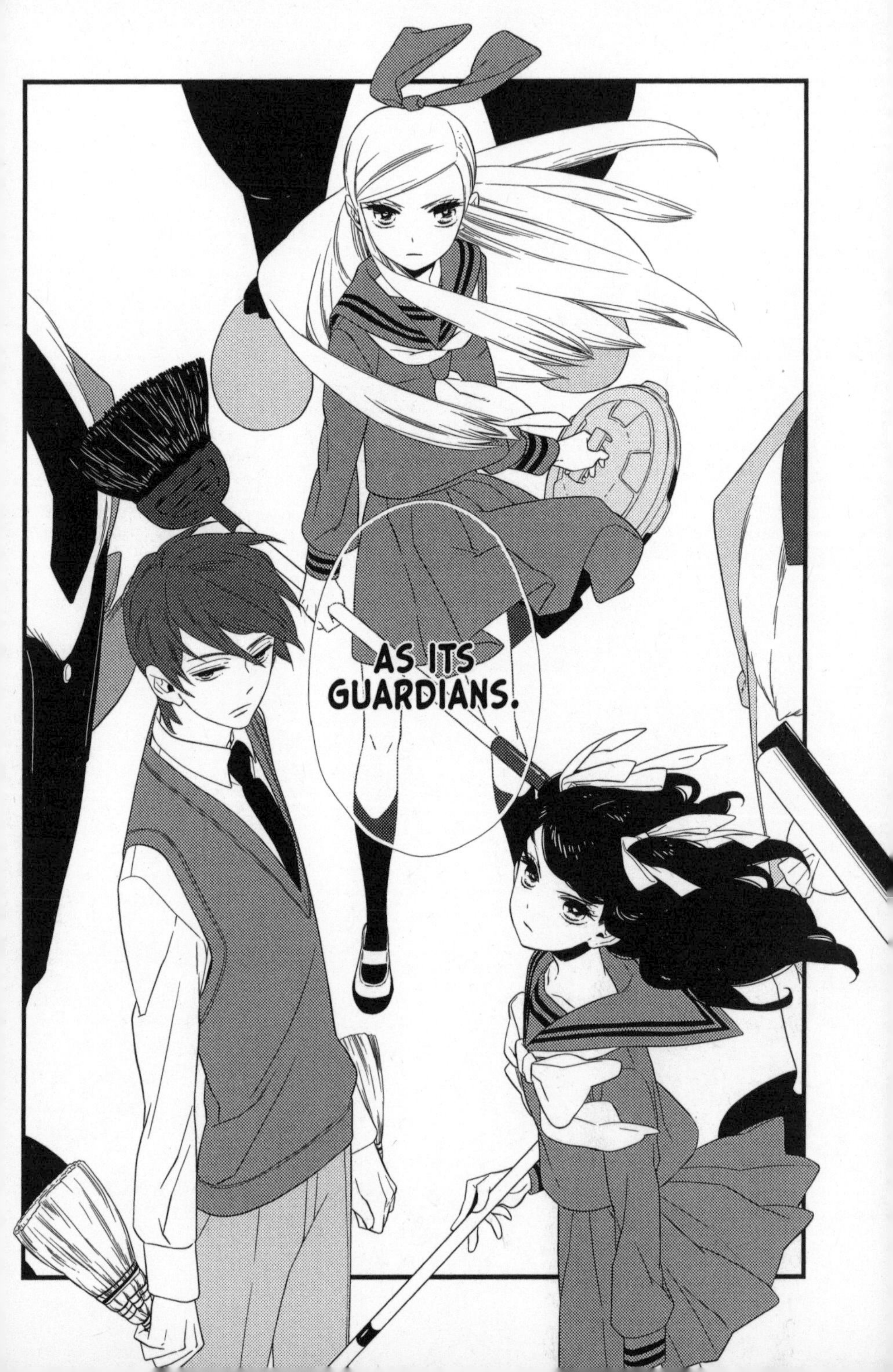
AS ITS GUARDIANS.

Look that way~~...

Kigurumi
GUARDIANS

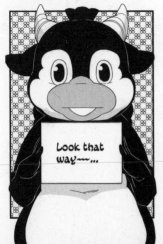

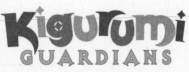

Kigurumi GUARDIANS

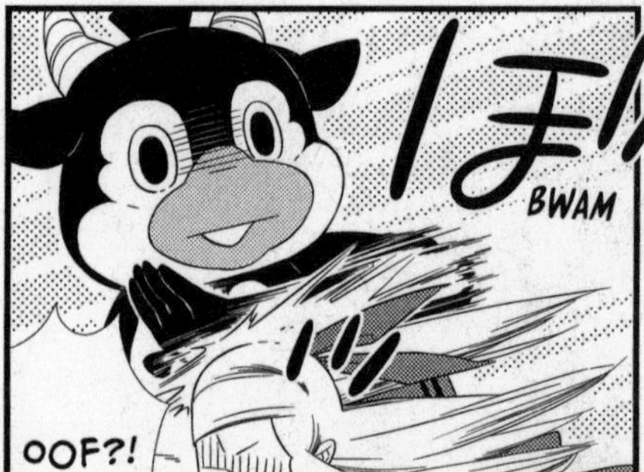
BWAM
OOF?!

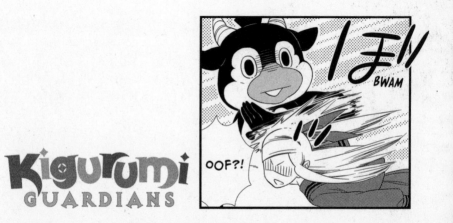

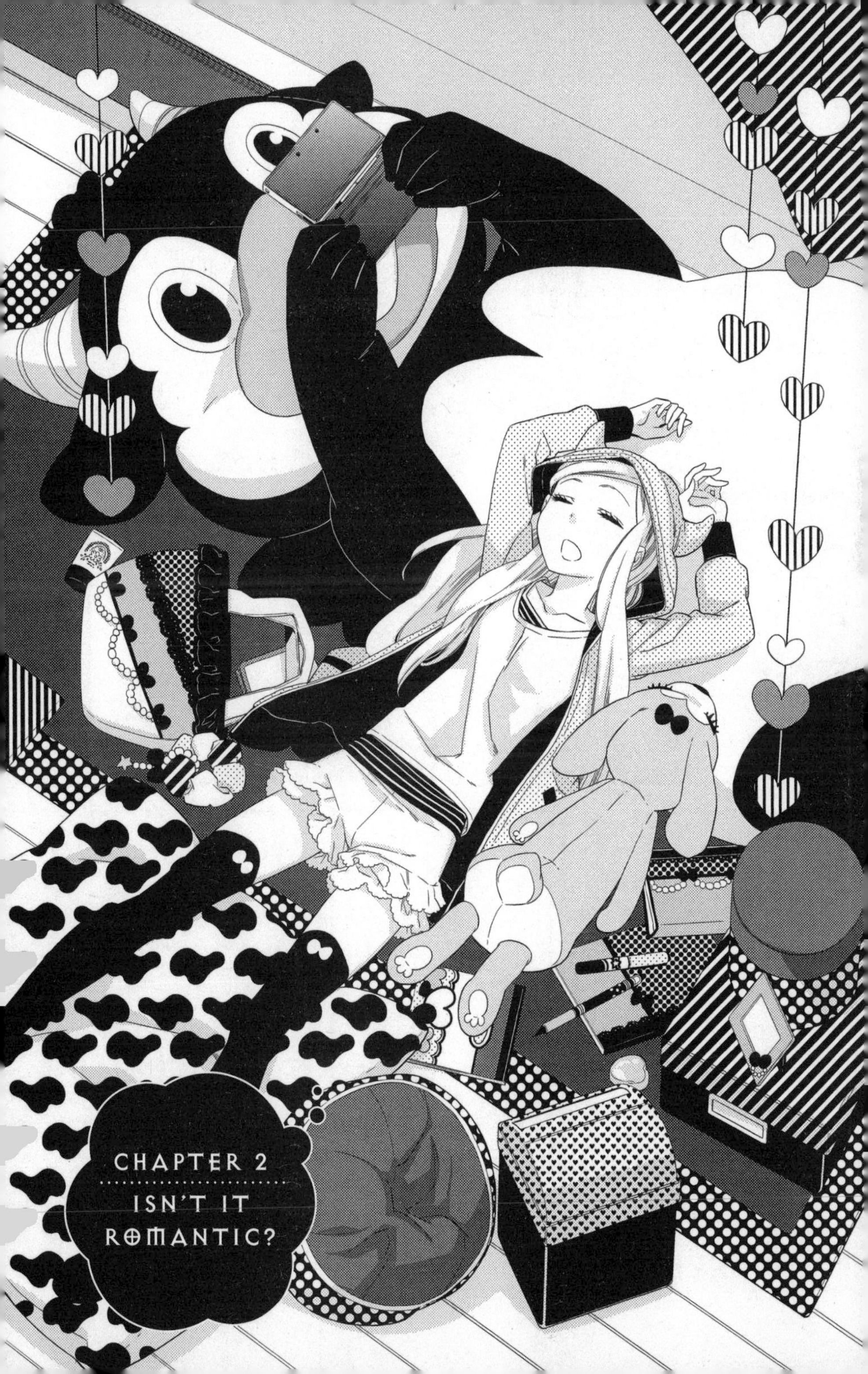
CHAPTER 2
ISN'T IT ROMANTIC?

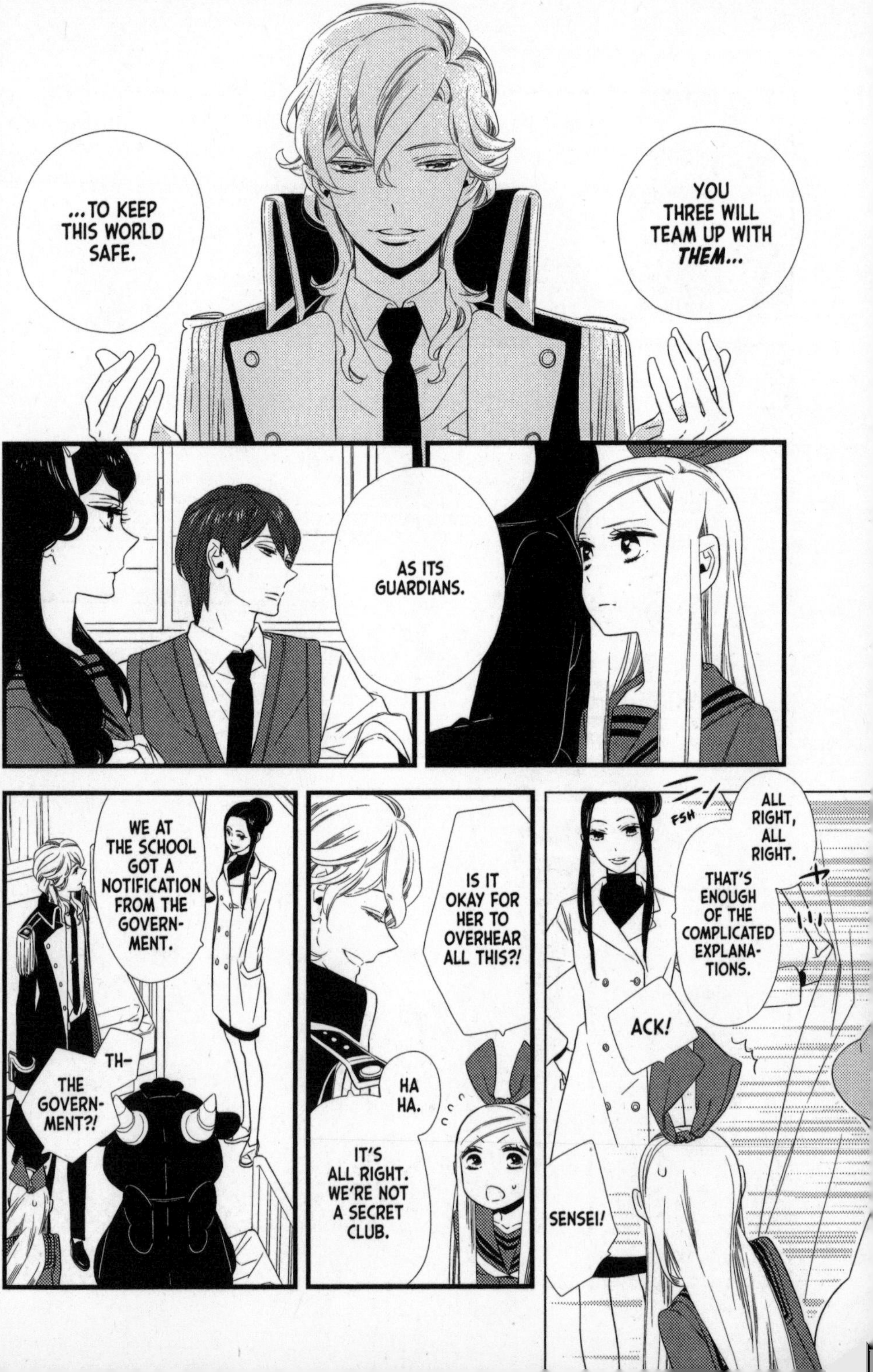
YOU THREE WILL TEAM UP WITH *THEM*...
...TO KEEP THIS WORLD SAFE.
AS ITS GUARDIANS.
FSH
ALL RIGHT, ALL RIGHT.
THAT'S ENOUGH OF THE COMPLICATED EXPLANATIONS.
ACK!
SENSEI!
IS IT OKAY FOR HER TO OVERHEAR ALL THIS?!
HA HA.
IT'S ALL RIGHT. WE'RE NOT A SECRET CLUB.
WE AT THE SCHOOL GOT A NOTIFICATION FROM THE GOVERNMENT.
TH- THE GOVERNMENT?!

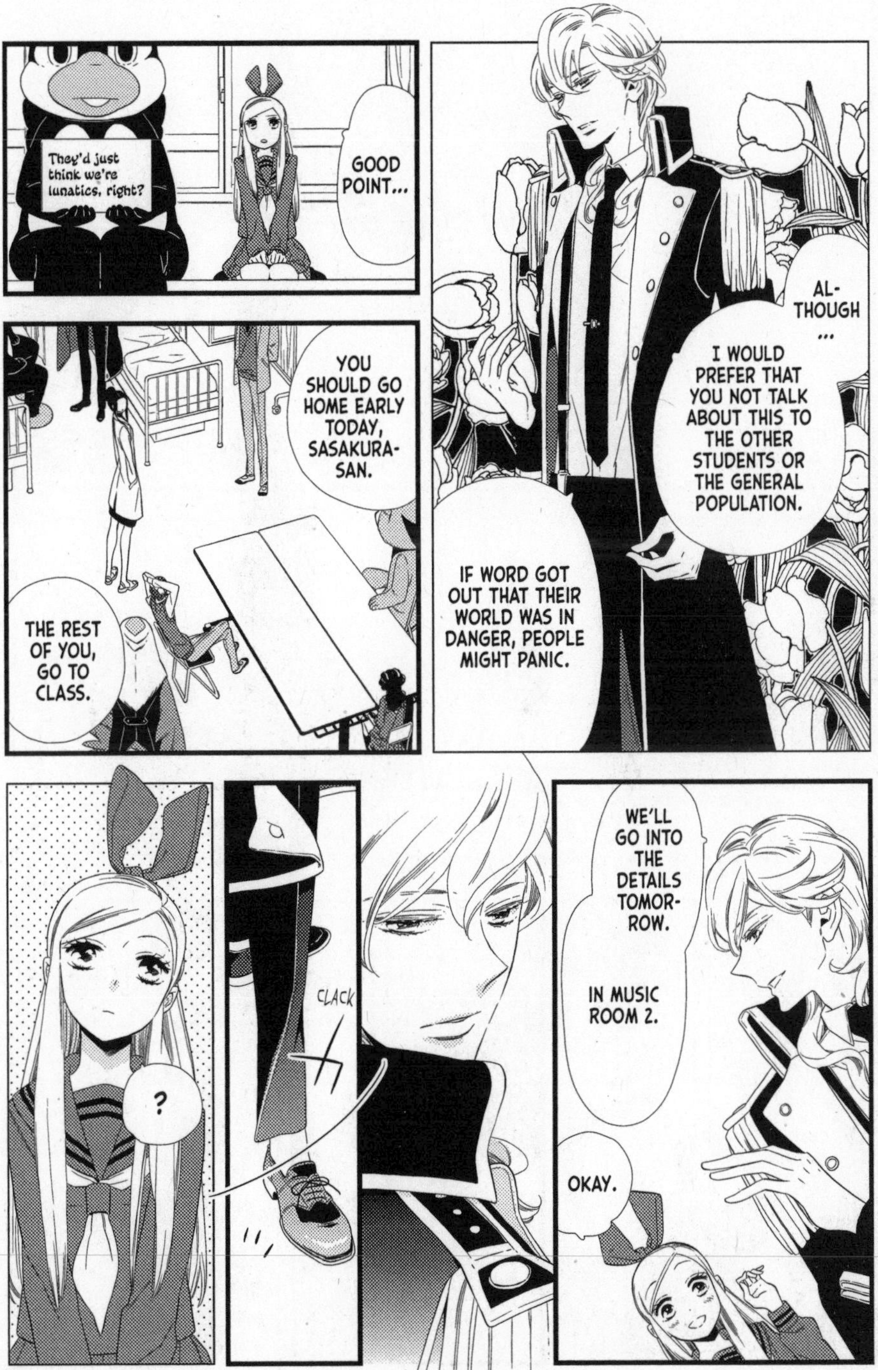
AL-THOUGH ...
I WOULD PREFER THAT YOU NOT TALK ABOUT THIS TO THE OTHER STUDENTS OR THE GENERAL POPULATION.
IF WORD GOT OUT THAT THEIR WORLD WAS IN DANGER, PEOPLE MIGHT PANIC.
They'd just think we're lunatics, right?
GOOD POINT...
YOU SHOULD GO HOME EARLY TODAY, SASAKURA-SAN.
THE REST OF YOU, GO TO CLASS.
WE'LL GO INTO THE DETAILS TOMOR-ROW.
IN MUSIC ROOM 2.
OKAY.
CLACK
?

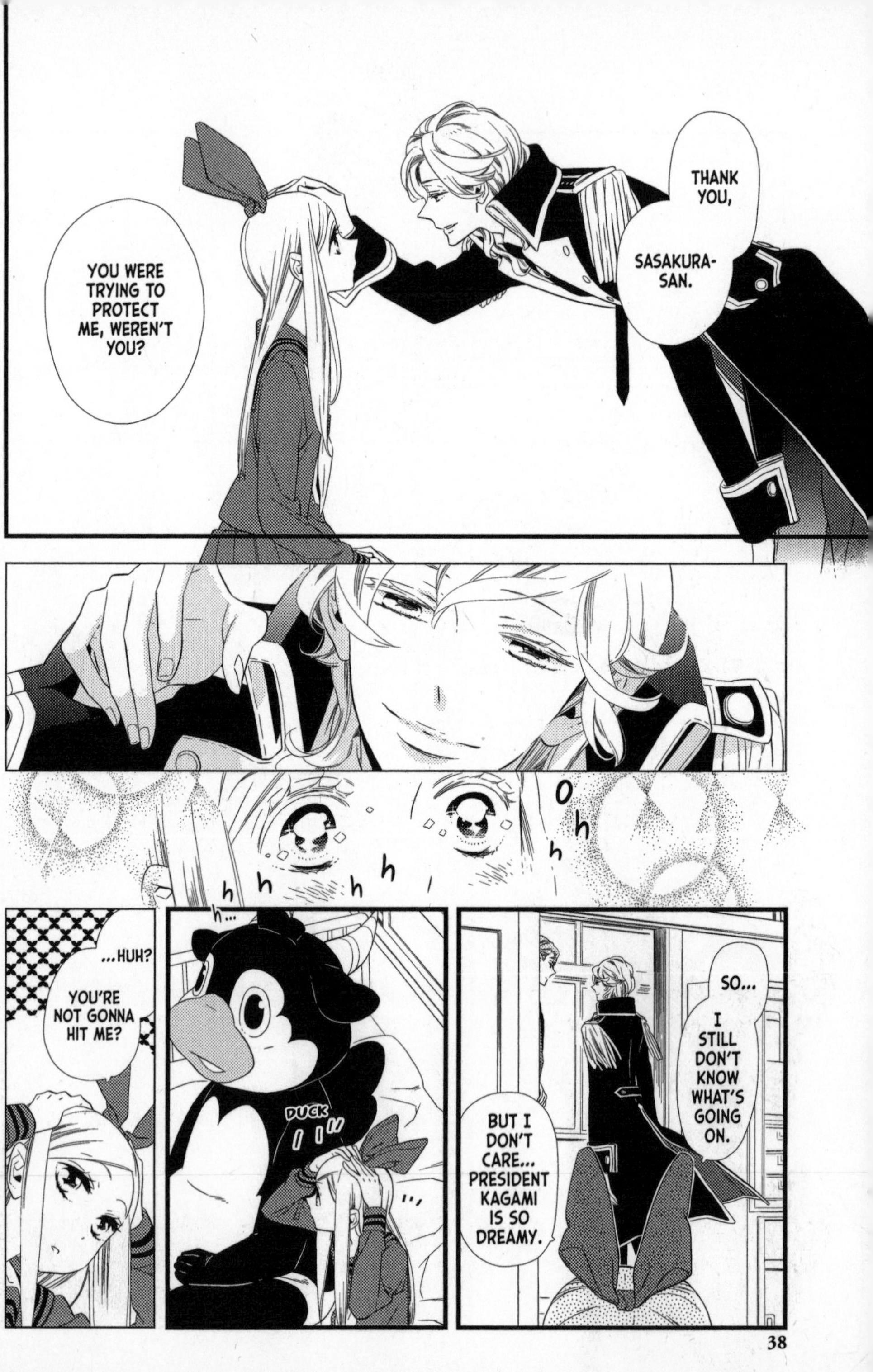
THANK YOU, SASAKURA-SAN.
YOU WERE TRYING TO PROTECT ME, WEREN'T YOU?
Ohhhhhhhhh...
SO... I STILL DON'T KNOW WHAT'S GOING ON.
BUT I DON'T CARE... PRESIDENT KAGAMI IS SO DREAMY.
DUCK
...HUH?
YOU'RE NOT GONNA HIT ME?

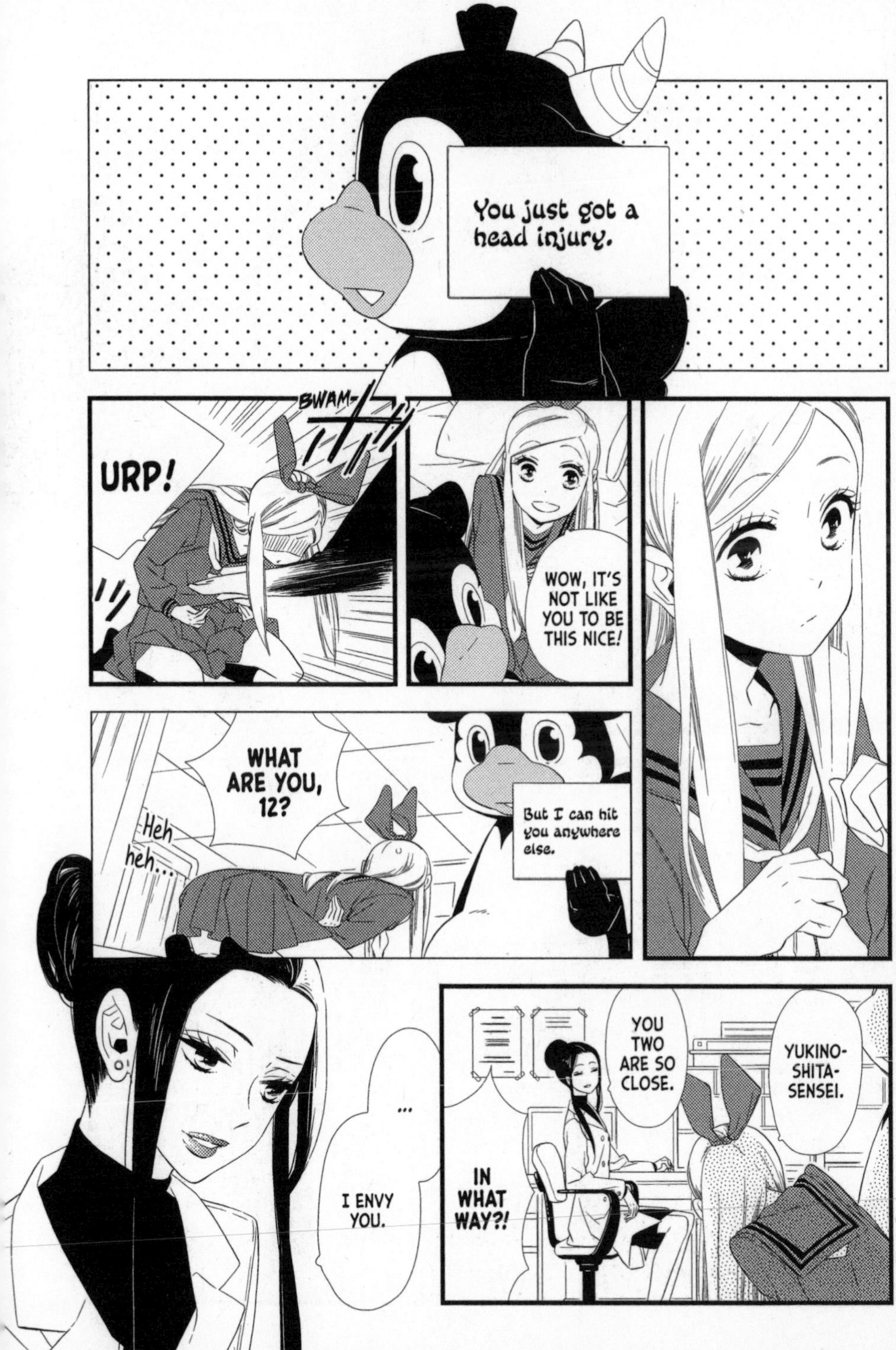
You just got a head injury.
WOW, IT'S NOT LIKE YOU TO BE THIS NICE!
BWAM-
URP!
But I can hit you anywhere else.
WHAT ARE YOU, 12?
Heh heh...
YUKINO-SHITA-SENSEI.
YOU TWO ARE SO CLOSE.
IN WHAT WAY?!
...
I ENVY YOU.

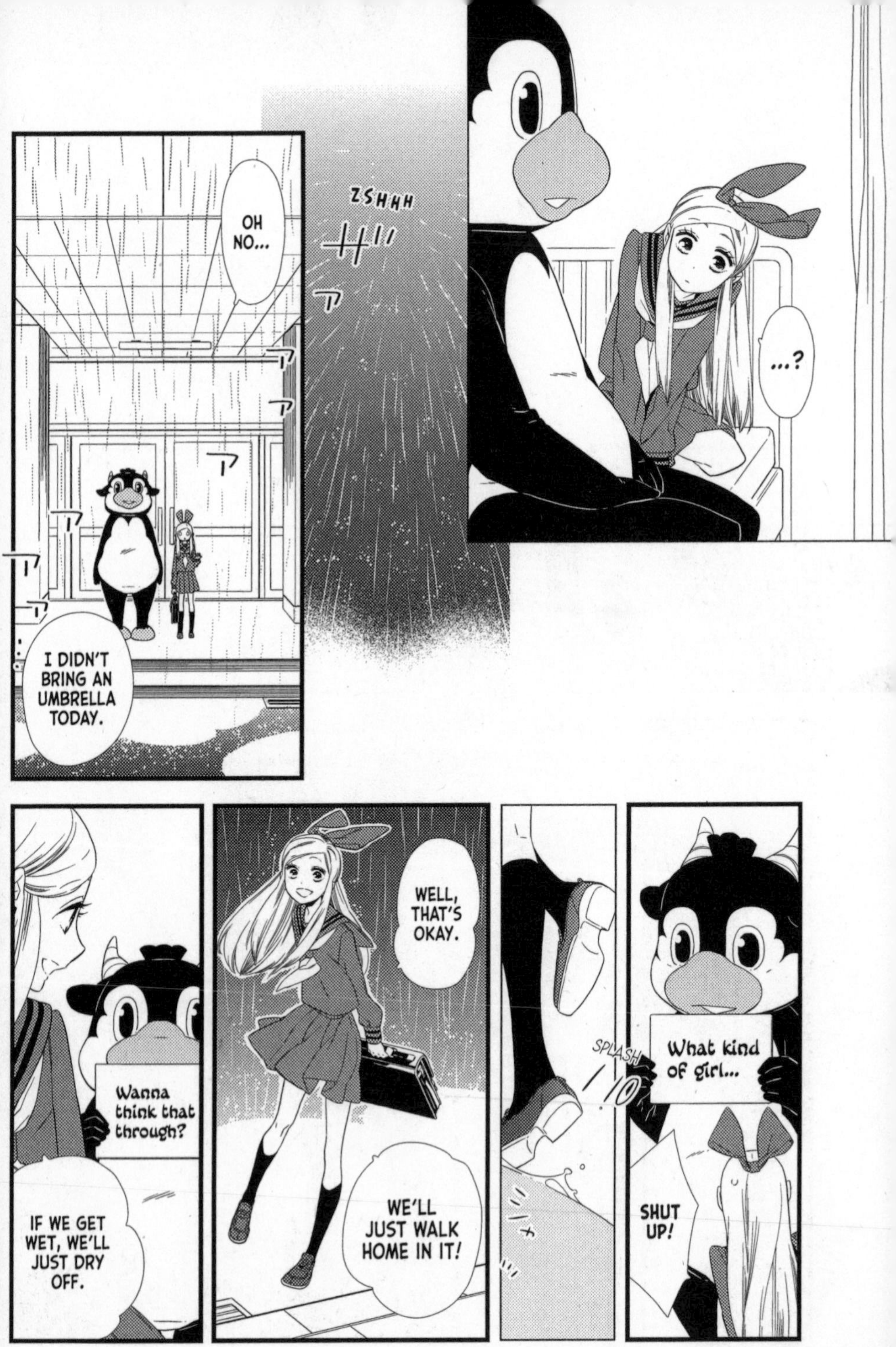
...?
ZSHHH
OH NO...
I DIDN'T BRING AN UMBRELLA TODAY.
What kind of girl...
SHUT UP!
SPLASH
WELL, THAT'S OKAY.
WE'LL JUST WALK HOME IN IT!
Wanna think that through?
IF WE GET WET, WE'LL JUST DRY OFF.

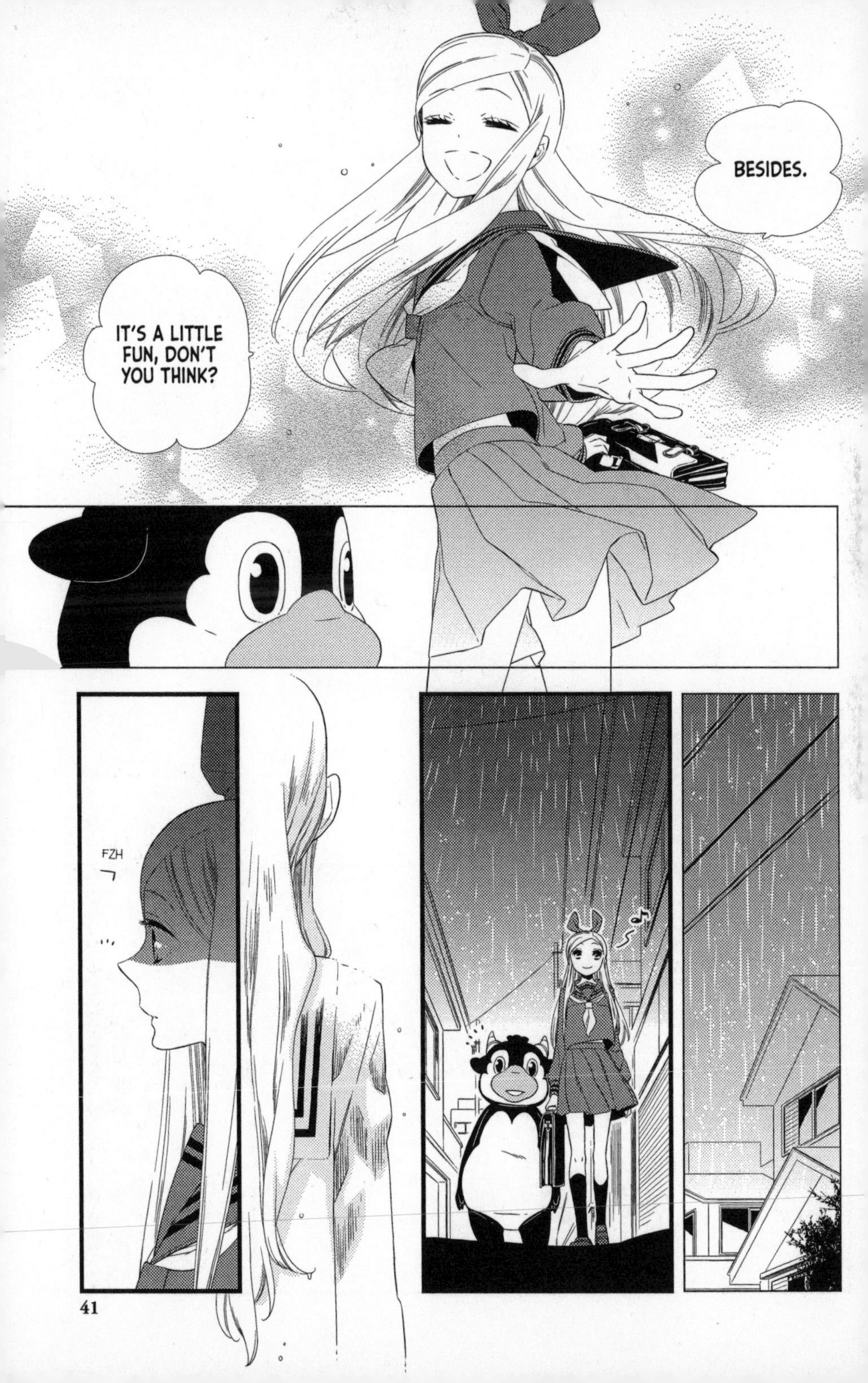
BESIDES.
IT'S A LITTLE FUN, DON'T YOU THINK?
FZH
...

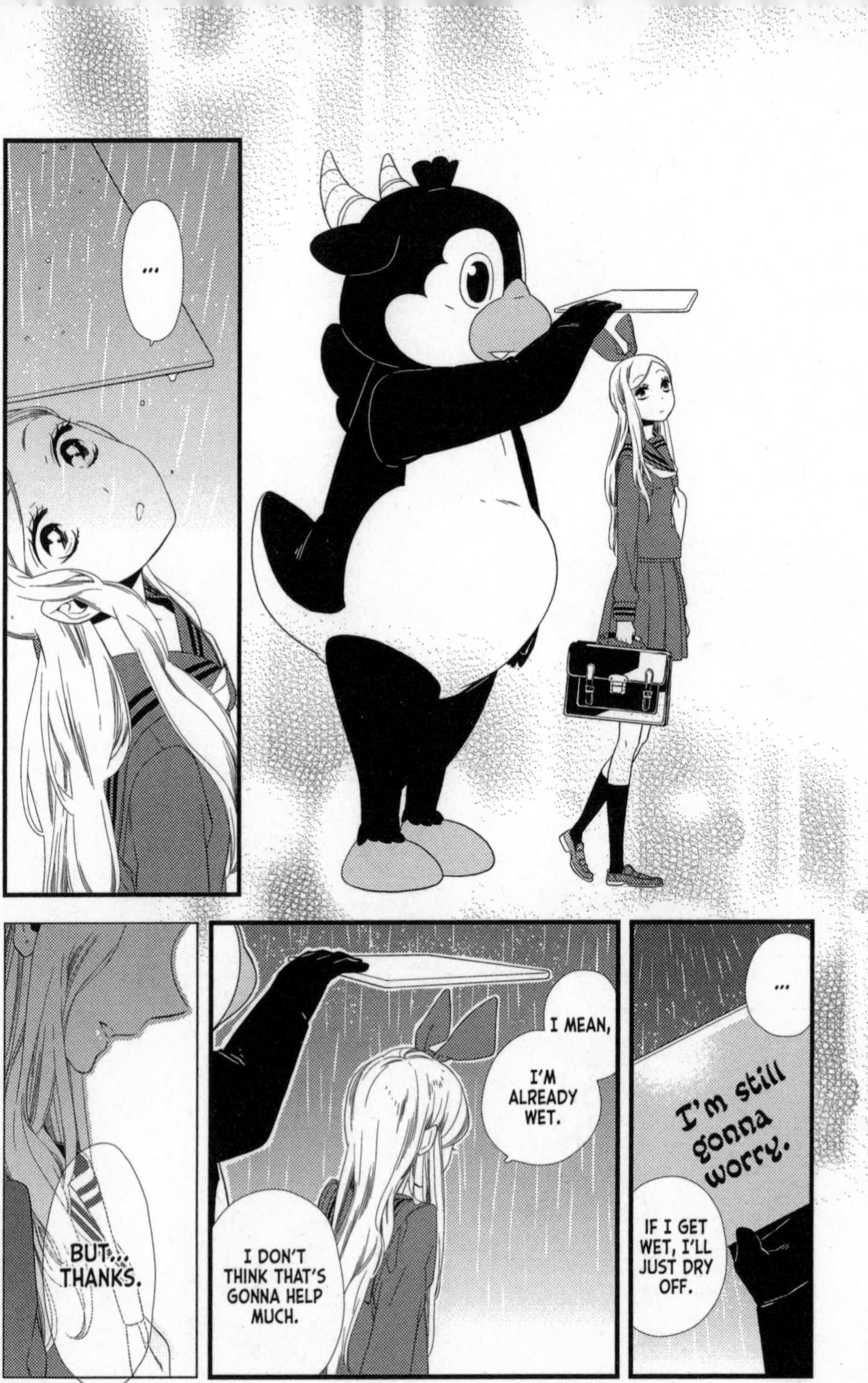
...
...
I'm still gonna worry.
IF I GET WET, I'LL JUST DRY OFF.
I MEAN,
I'M ALREADY WET.
I DON'T THINK THAT'S GONNA HELP MUCH.
BUT... THANKS.

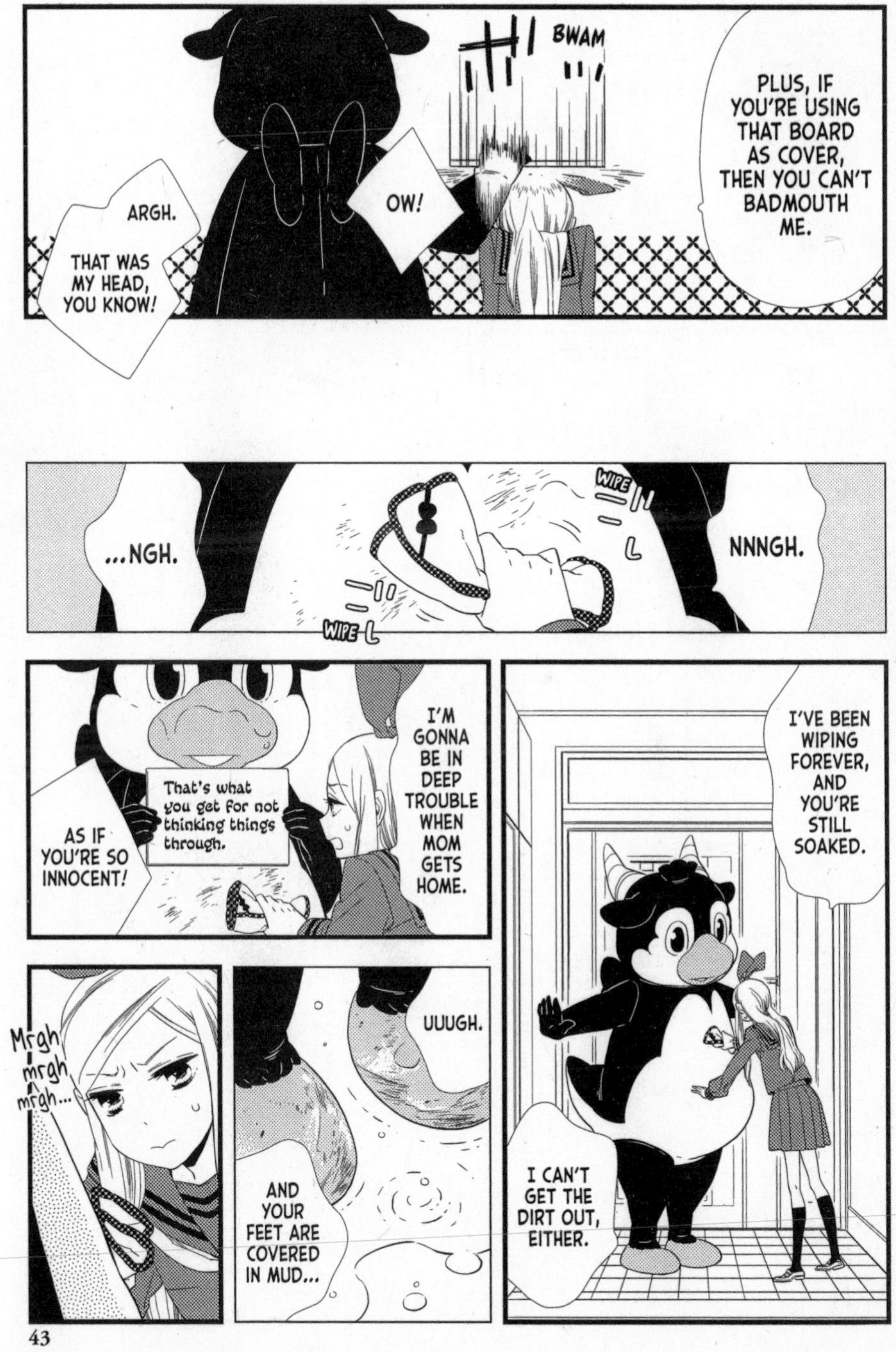
PLUS, IF YOU'RE USING THAT BOARD AS COVER, THEN YOU CAN'T BADMOUTH ME.
BWAM
OW!
ARGH.
THAT WAS MY HEAD, YOU KNOW!
NNNGH.
WIPE
WIPE
...NGH.
I'VE BEEN WIPING FOREVER, AND YOU'RE STILL SOAKED.
I CAN'T GET THE DIRT OUT, EITHER.
I'M GONNA BE IN DEEP TROUBLE WHEN MOM GETS HOME.
That's what you get for not thinking things through.
AS IF YOU'RE SO INNOCENT!
UUUGH.
AND YOUR FEET ARE COVERED IN MUD...
Mrgh mrgh mrgh...

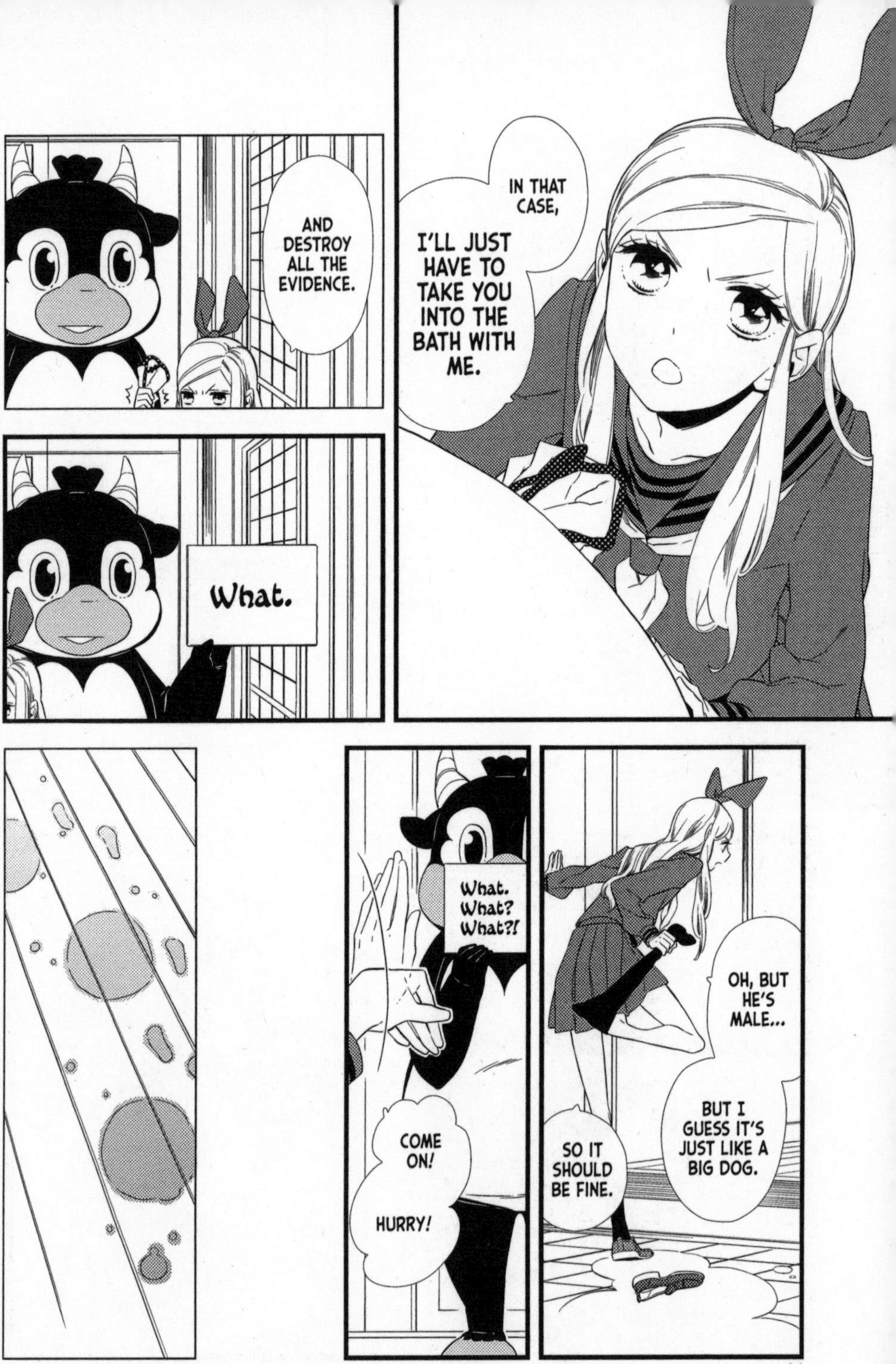
IN THAT CASE,
I'LL JUST HAVE TO TAKE YOU INTO THE BATH WITH ME.
AND DESTROY ALL THE EVIDENCE.
What.
OH, BUT HE'S MALE...
BUT I GUESS IT'S JUST LIKE A BIG DOG.
SO IT SHOULD BE FINE.
What. What? What?!
COME ON!
HURRY!

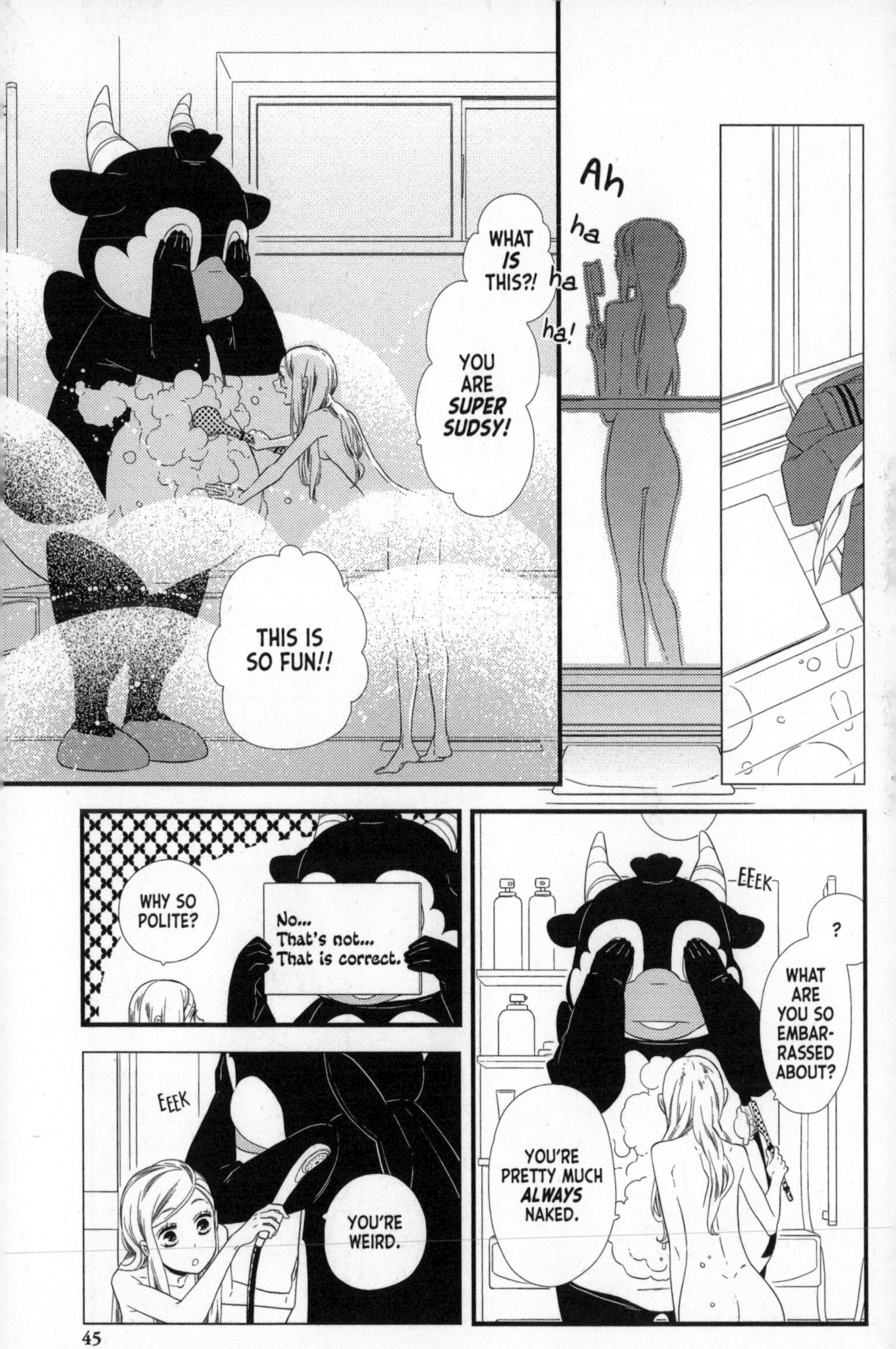
Ah
ha
ha
ha!
WHAT IS THIS?!
YOU ARE SUPER SUDSY!
THIS IS SO FUN!!
EEEK
?
WHAT ARE YOU SO EMBAR-RASSED ABOUT?
YOU'RE PRETTY MUCH ALWAYS NAKED.
No... That's not... That is correct.
WHY SO POLITE?
EEEK
YOU'RE WEIRD.

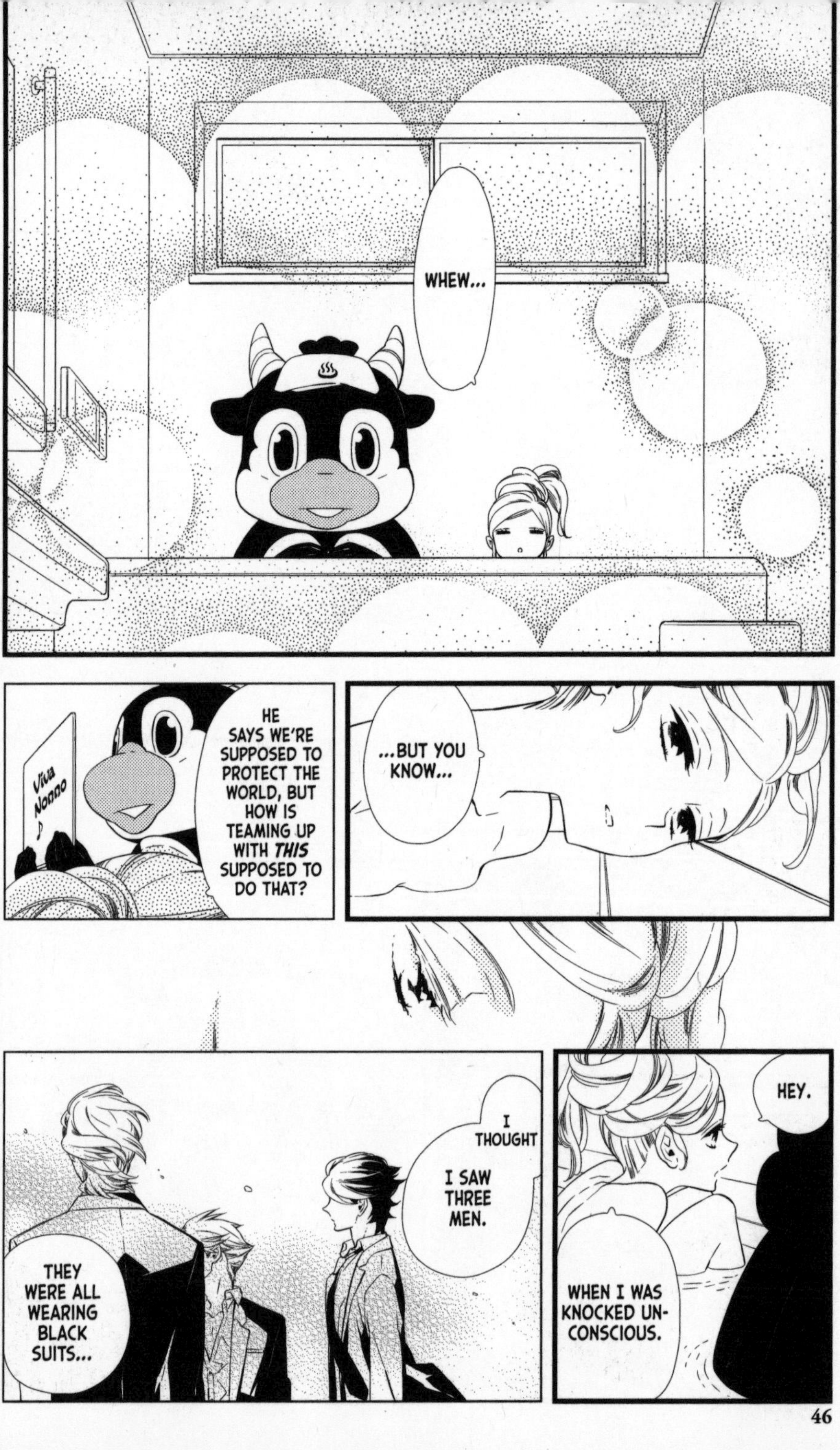
WHEW...
...BUT YOU KNOW...
HE SAYS WE'RE SUPPOSED TO PROTECT THE WORLD, BUT HOW IS TEAMING UP WITH *THIS* SUPPOSED TO DO THAT?
Viva Nonno ♪
HEY.
WHEN I WAS KNOCKED UN-CONSCIOUS.
I THOUGHT I SAW THREE MEN.
THEY WERE ALL WEARING BLACK SUITS...

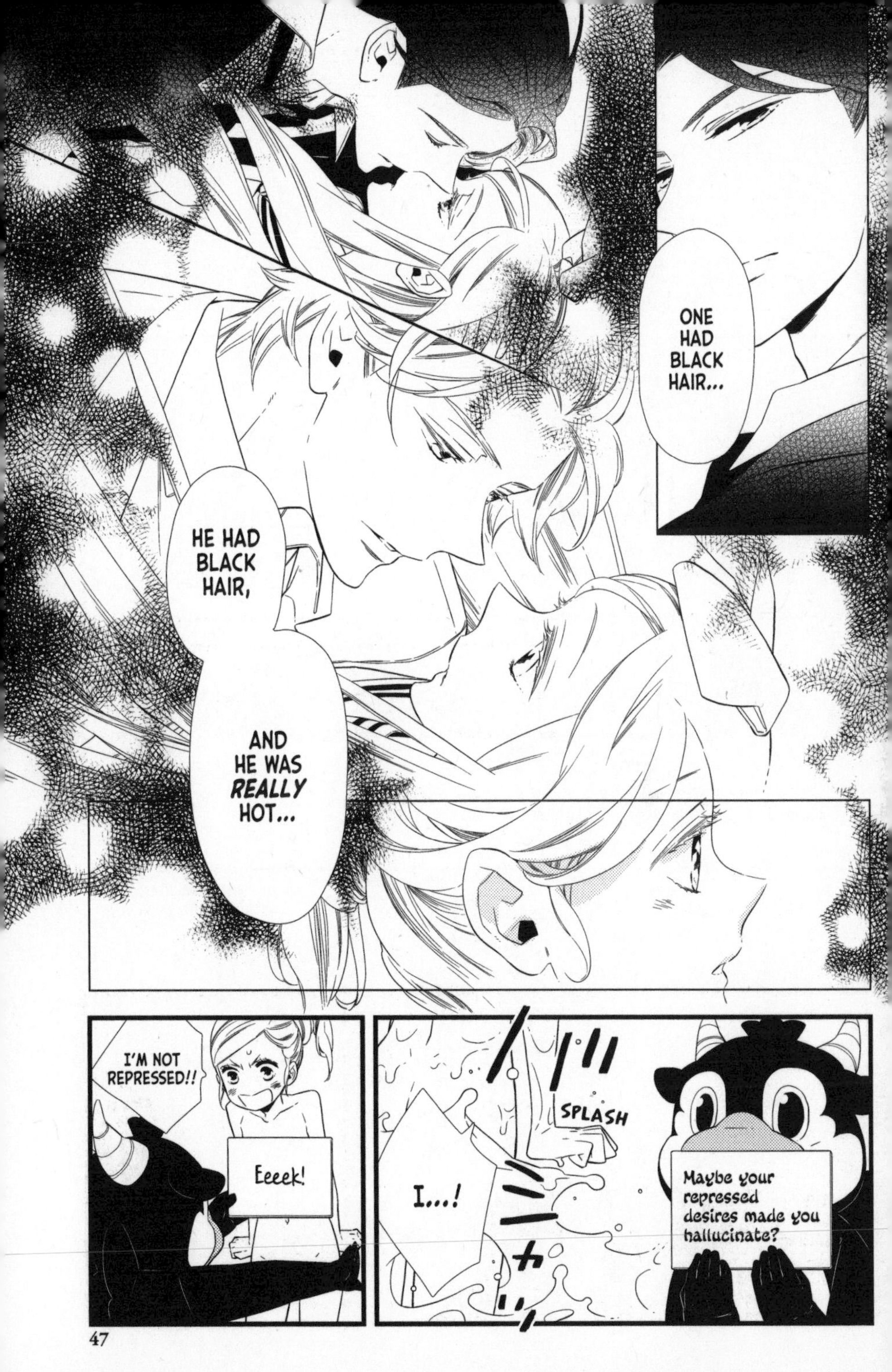

ONE HAD BLACK HAIR...
HE HAD BLACK HAIR,
AND HE WAS *REALLY* HOT...
Maybe your repressed desires made you hallucinate?
SPLASH
I...!
I'M NOT REPRESSED!!
Eeeek!

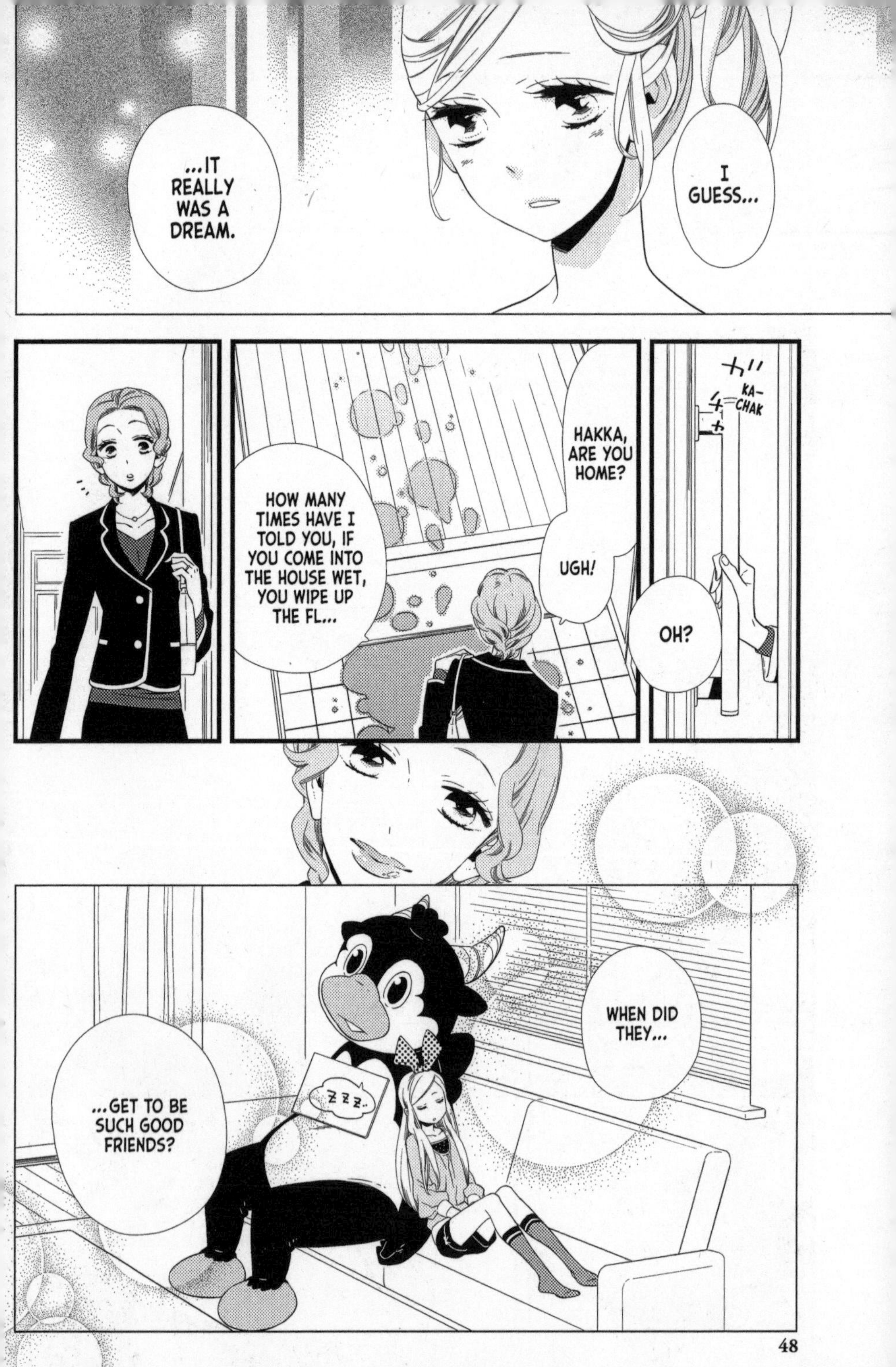
I GUESS...
...IT REALLY WAS A DREAM.
KA-CHAK
OH?
HAKKA, ARE YOU HOME?
UGH!
HOW MANY TIMES HAVE I TOLD YOU, IF YOU COME INTO THE HOUSE WET, YOU WIPE UP THE FL...
WHEN DID THEY...
ZZZ..
...GET TO BE SUCH GOOD FRIENDS?

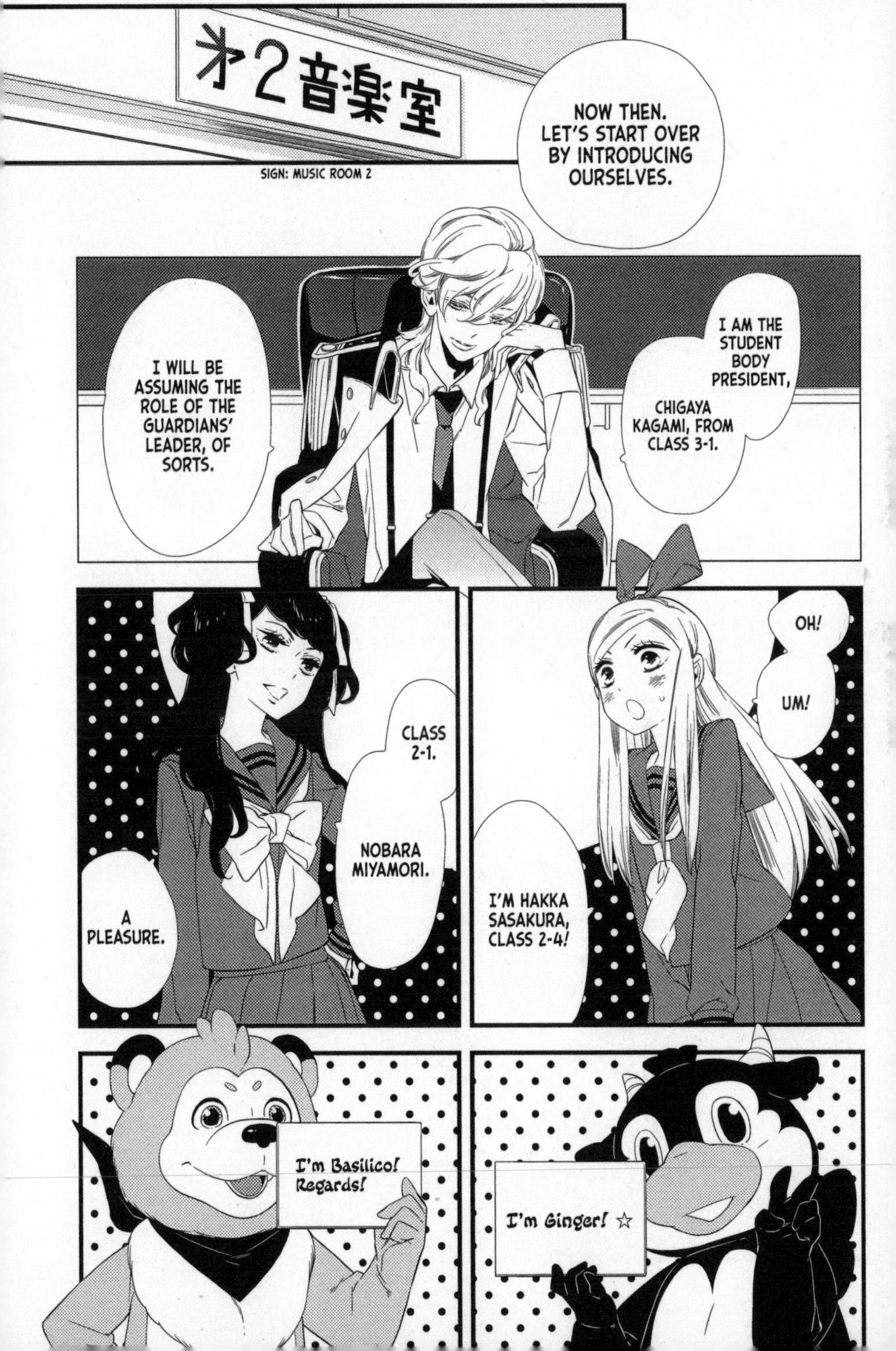
第2音楽室
SIGN: MUSIC ROOM 2
NOW THEN. LET'S START OVER BY INTRODUCING OURSELVES.
I AM THE STUDENT BODY PRESIDENT,
CHIGAYA KAGAMI, FROM CLASS 3-1.
I WILL BE ASSUMING THE ROLE OF THE GUARDIANS' LEADER, OF SORTS.
OH!
UM!
I'M HAKKA SASAKURA, CLASS 2-4!
CLASS 2-1.
NOBARA MIYAMORI.
A PLEASURE.
I'm Ginger! ☆
I'm Basilico! Regards!

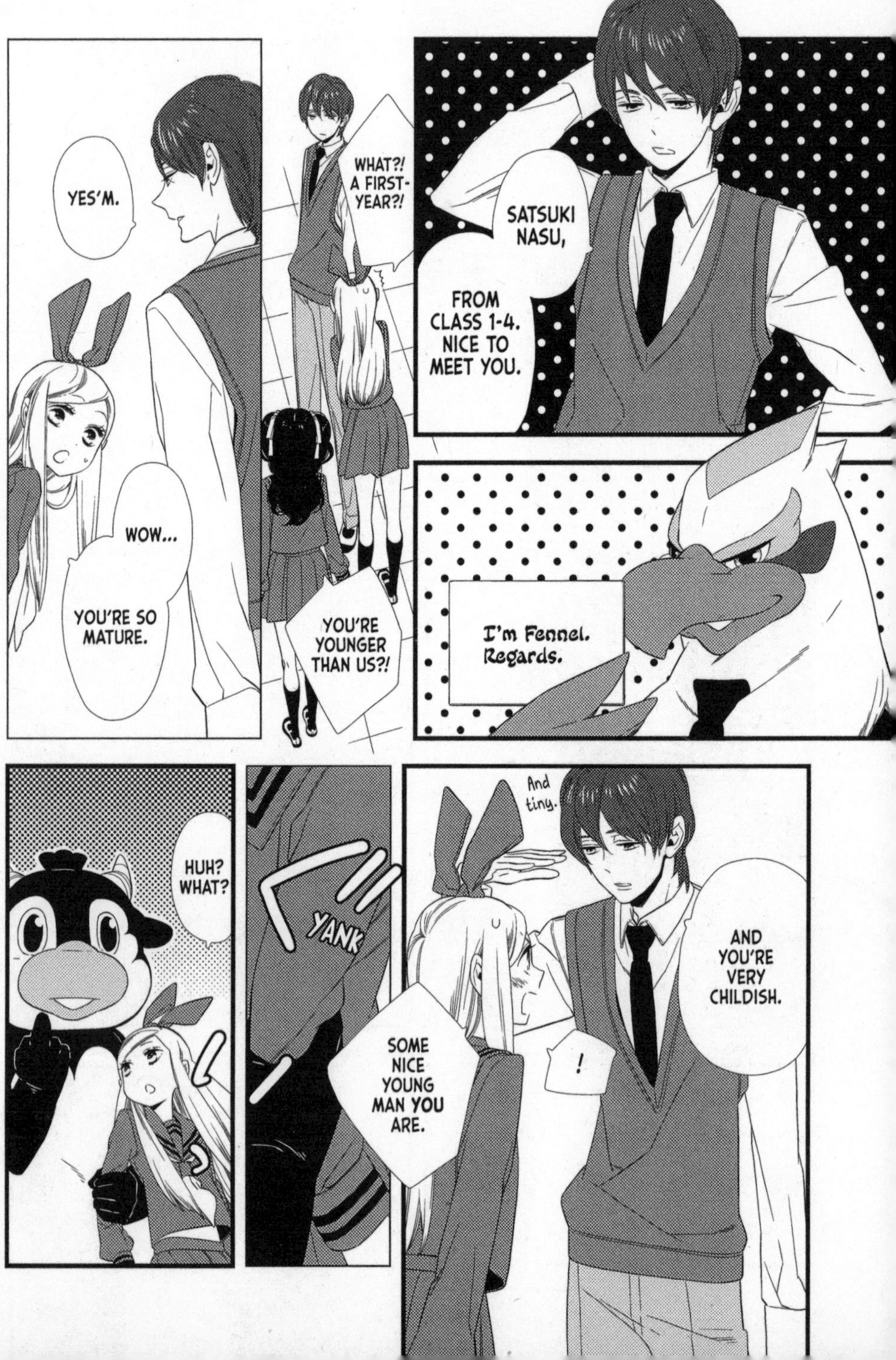
SATSUKI NASU,
FROM CLASS 1-4. NICE TO MEET YOU.
I'm Fennel. Regards.
WHAT?! A FIRST-YEAR?!
YOU'RE YOUNGER THAN US?!
YES'M.
WOW...
YOU'RE SO MATURE.
And tiny.
AND YOU'RE VERY CHILDISH.
!
SOME NICE YOUNG MAN YOU ARE.
YANK
HUH? WHAT?

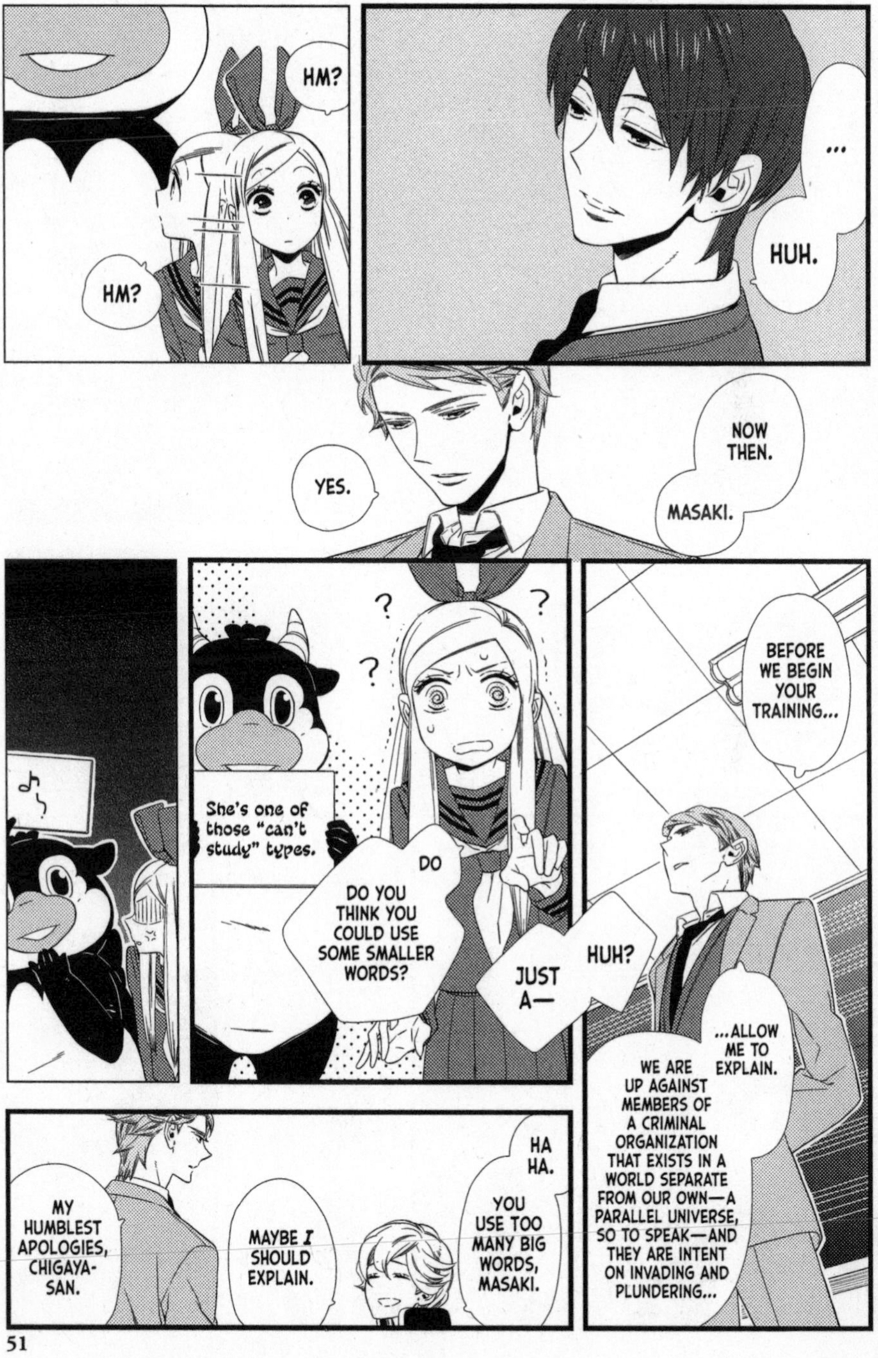
...
HUH.
HM?
HM?
NOW THEN.
MASAKI.
YES.
BEFORE WE BEGIN YOUR TRAINING...
...ALLOW ME TO EXPLAIN.
WE ARE UP AGAINST MEMBERS OF A CRIMINAL ORGANIZATION THAT EXISTS IN A WORLD SEPARATE FROM OUR OWN—A PARALLEL UNIVERSE, SO TO SPEAK—AND THEY ARE INTENT ON INVADING AND PLUNDERING...
HUH?
JUST A—
DO
DO YOU THINK YOU COULD USE SOME SMALLER WORDS?
She's one of those "can't study" types.
HA HA.
YOU USE TOO MANY BIG WORDS, MASAKI.
MAYBE I SHOULD EXPLAIN.
MY HUMBLEST APOLOGIES, CHIGAYA-SAN.

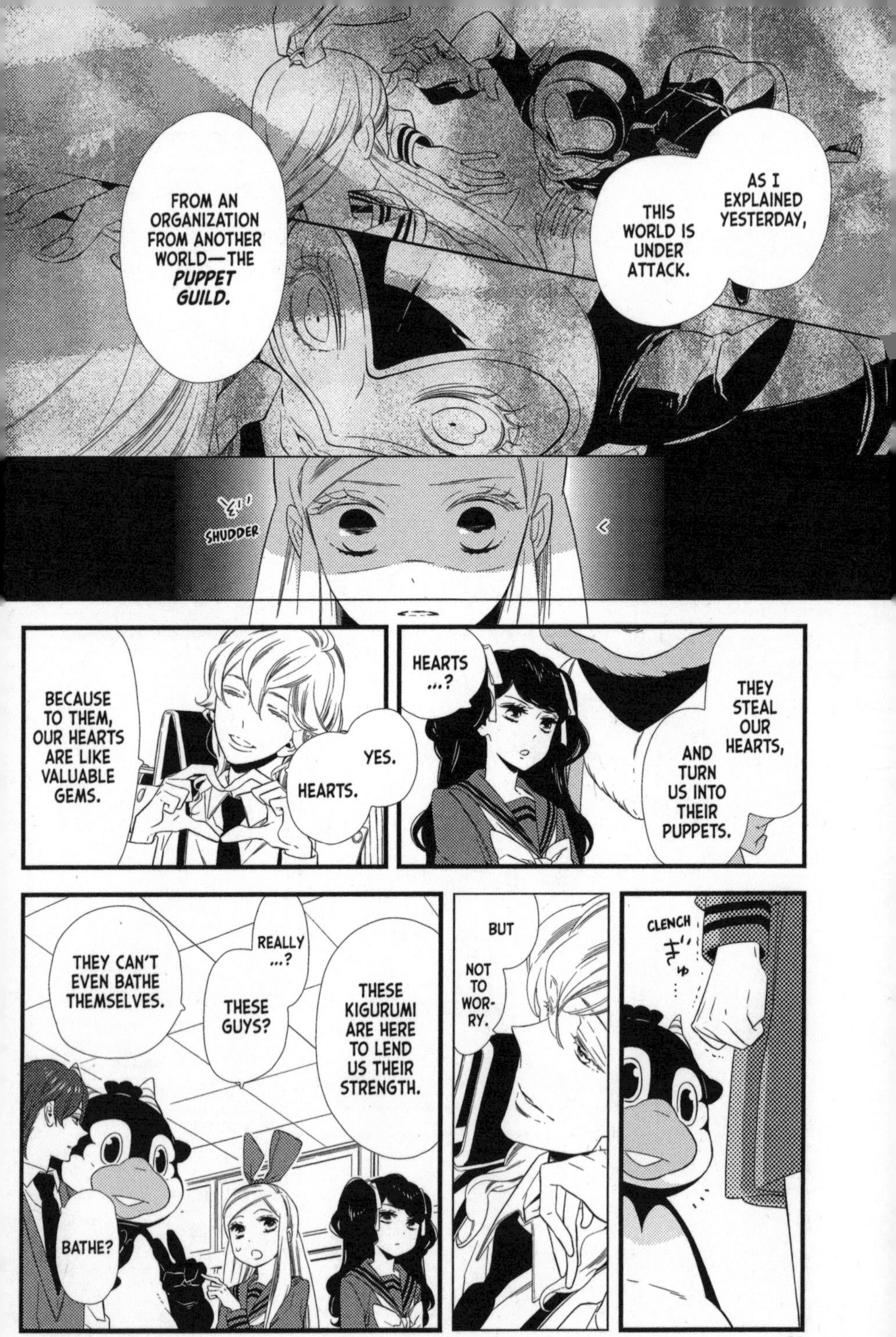
AS I EXPLAINED YESTERDAY,
THIS WORLD IS UNDER ATTACK.
FROM AN ORGANIZATION FROM ANOTHER WORLD—THE *PUPPET GUILD.*
SHUDDER
THEY STEAL OUR HEARTS,
AND TURN US INTO THEIR PUPPETS.
HEARTS ...?
YES.
HEARTS.
BECAUSE TO THEM, OUR HEARTS ARE LIKE VALUABLE GEMS.
CLENCH
BUT
NOT TO WOR-RY.
THESE KIGURUMI ARE HERE TO LEND US THEIR STRENGTH.
REALLY ...?
THESE GUYS?
THEY CAN'T EVEN BATHE THEMSELVES.
BATHE?

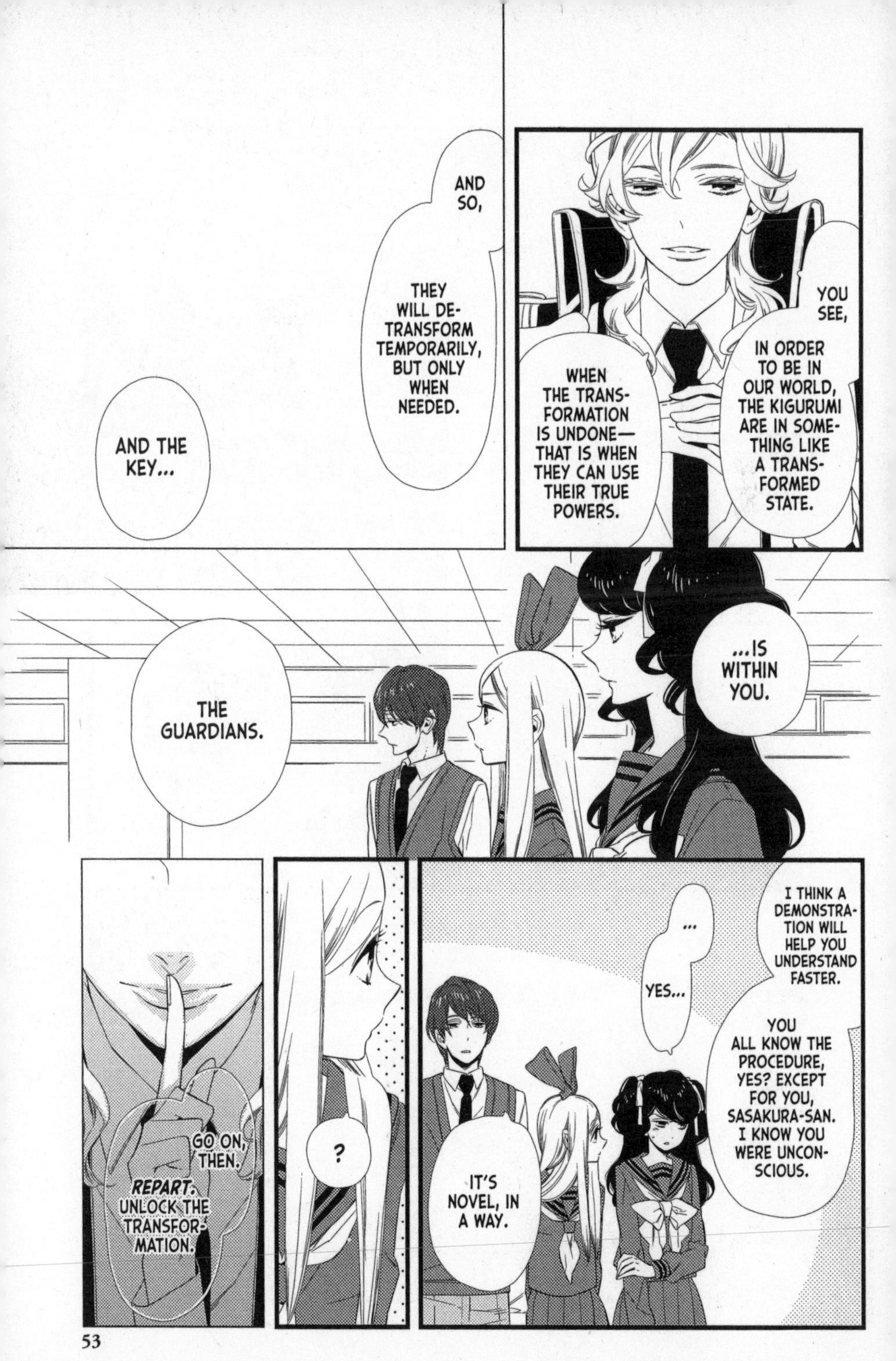
YOU SEE,
IN ORDER TO BE IN OUR WORLD, THE KIGURUMI ARE IN SOMETHING LIKE A TRANSFORMED STATE.
WHEN THE TRANSFORMATION IS UNDONE—THAT IS WHEN THEY CAN USE THEIR TRUE POWERS.
AND SO,
THEY WILL DE-TRANSFORM TEMPORARILY, BUT ONLY WHEN NEEDED.
AND THE KEY...
...IS WITHIN YOU.
THE GUARDIANS.
I THINK A DEMONSTRATION WILL HELP YOU UNDERSTAND FASTER.
YOU ALL KNOW THE PROCEDURE, YES? EXCEPT FOR YOU, SASAKURA-SAN. I KNOW YOU WERE UNCONSCIOUS.
...
YES...
IT'S NOVEL, IN A WAY.
?
GO ON, THEN.
REPART. UNLOCK THE TRANSFORMATION.

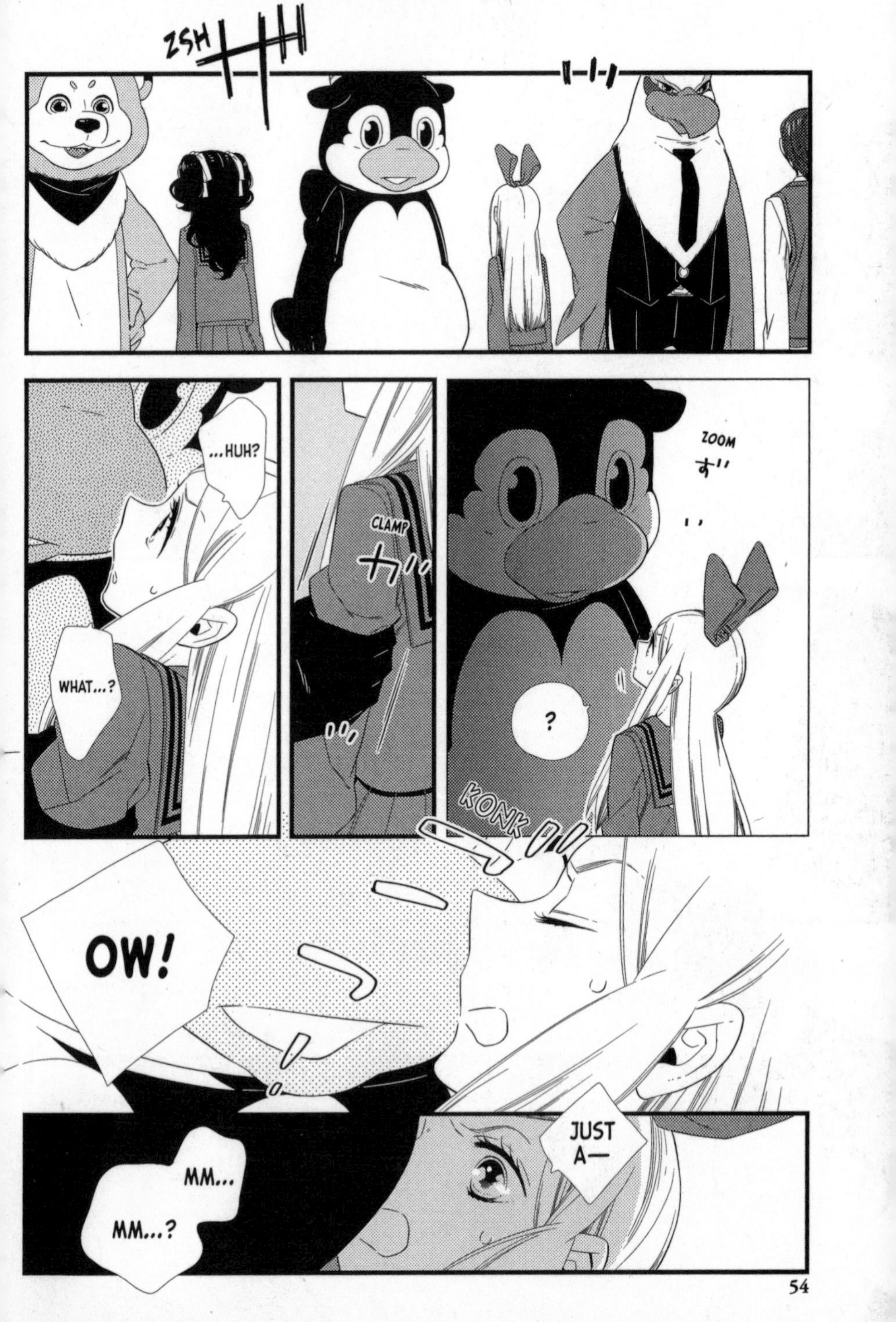
ZSH
ZOOM
?
KONK
CLAMP
...HUH?
WHAT...?
OW!
JUST A—
MM...
MM...?

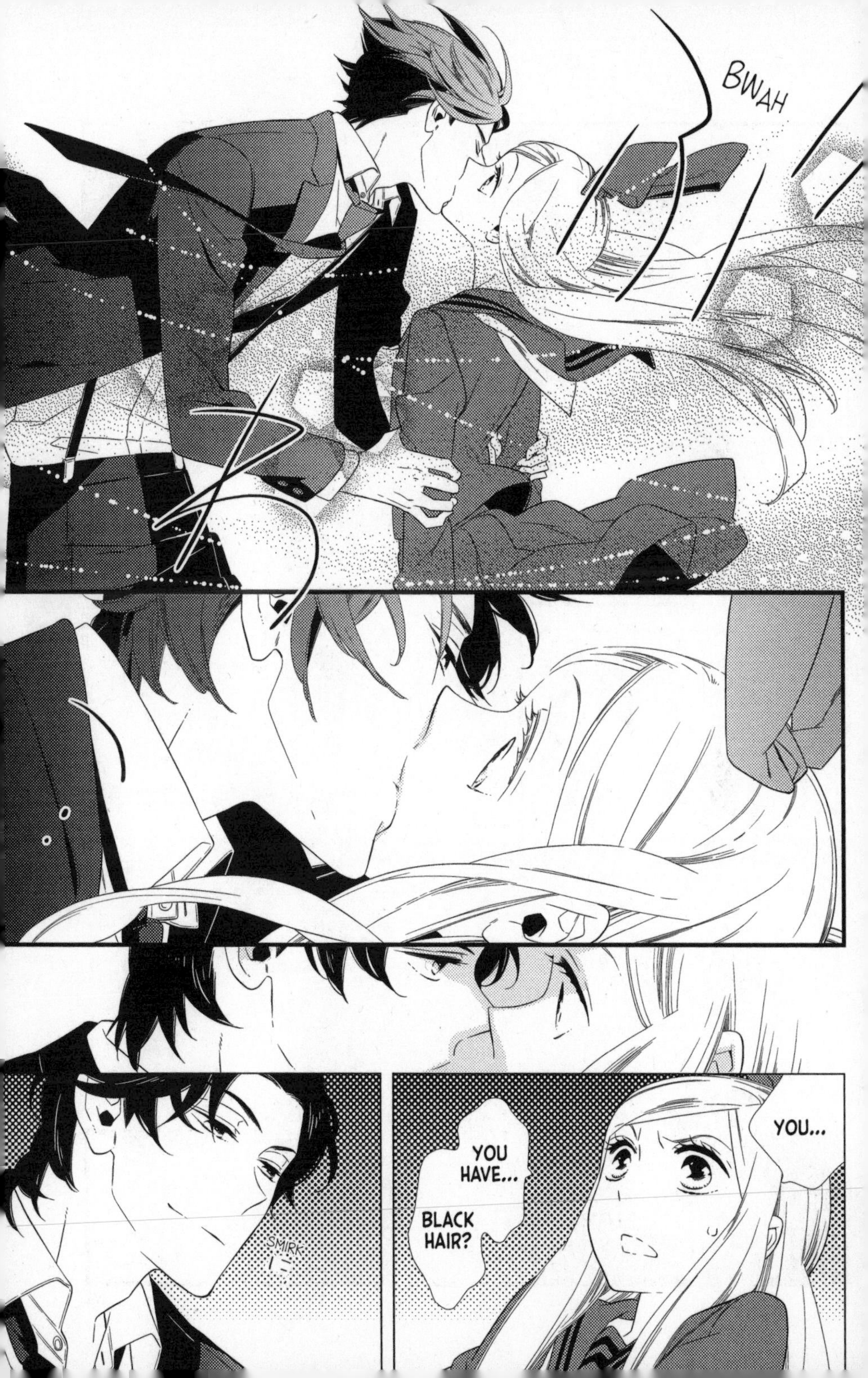
BWAH
YOU...
YOU HAVE...
BLACK HAIR?
SMIRK

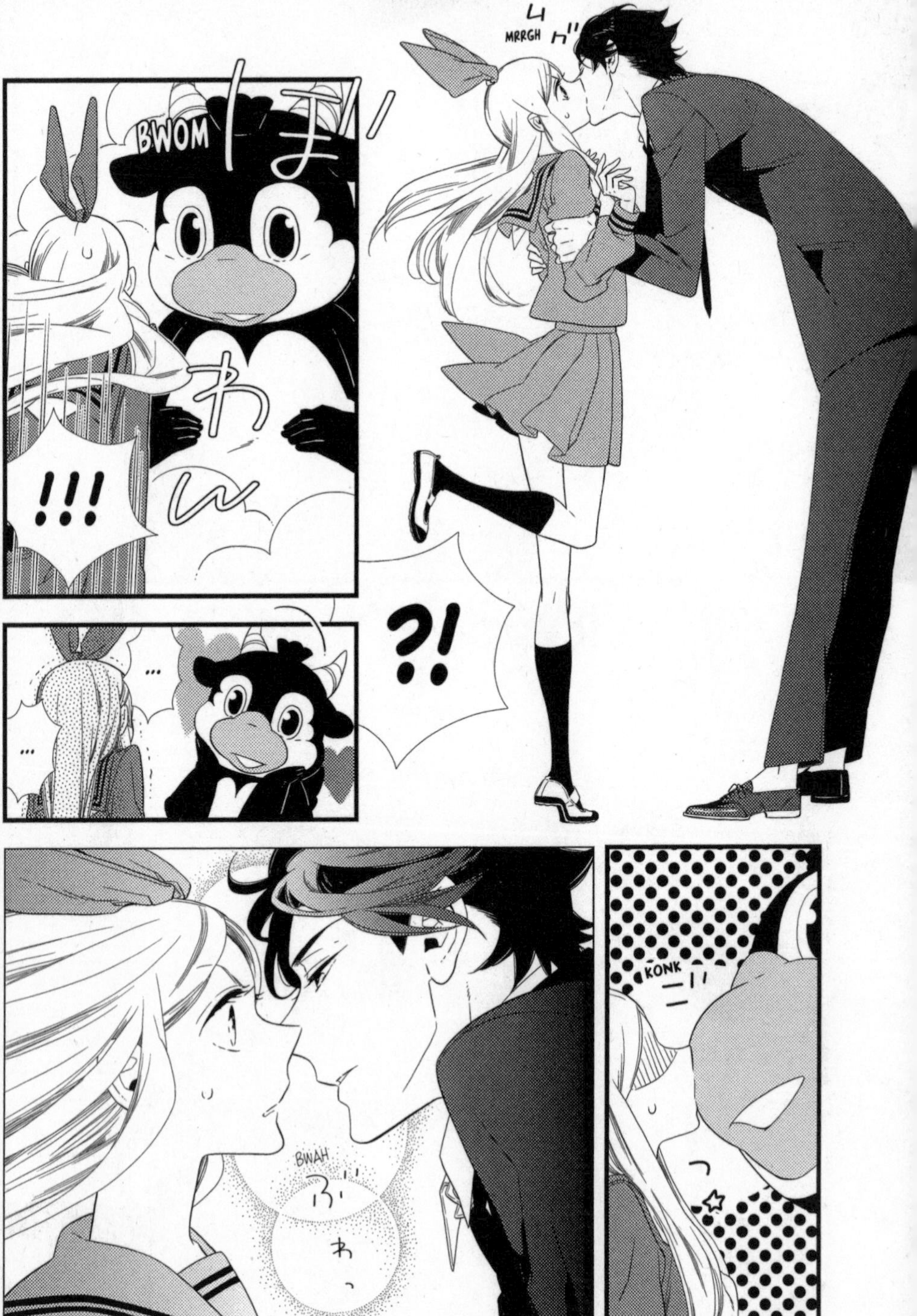
MRRGH
?!
BWOM
!!!
...
...
KONK
BWAH
ぶわっ

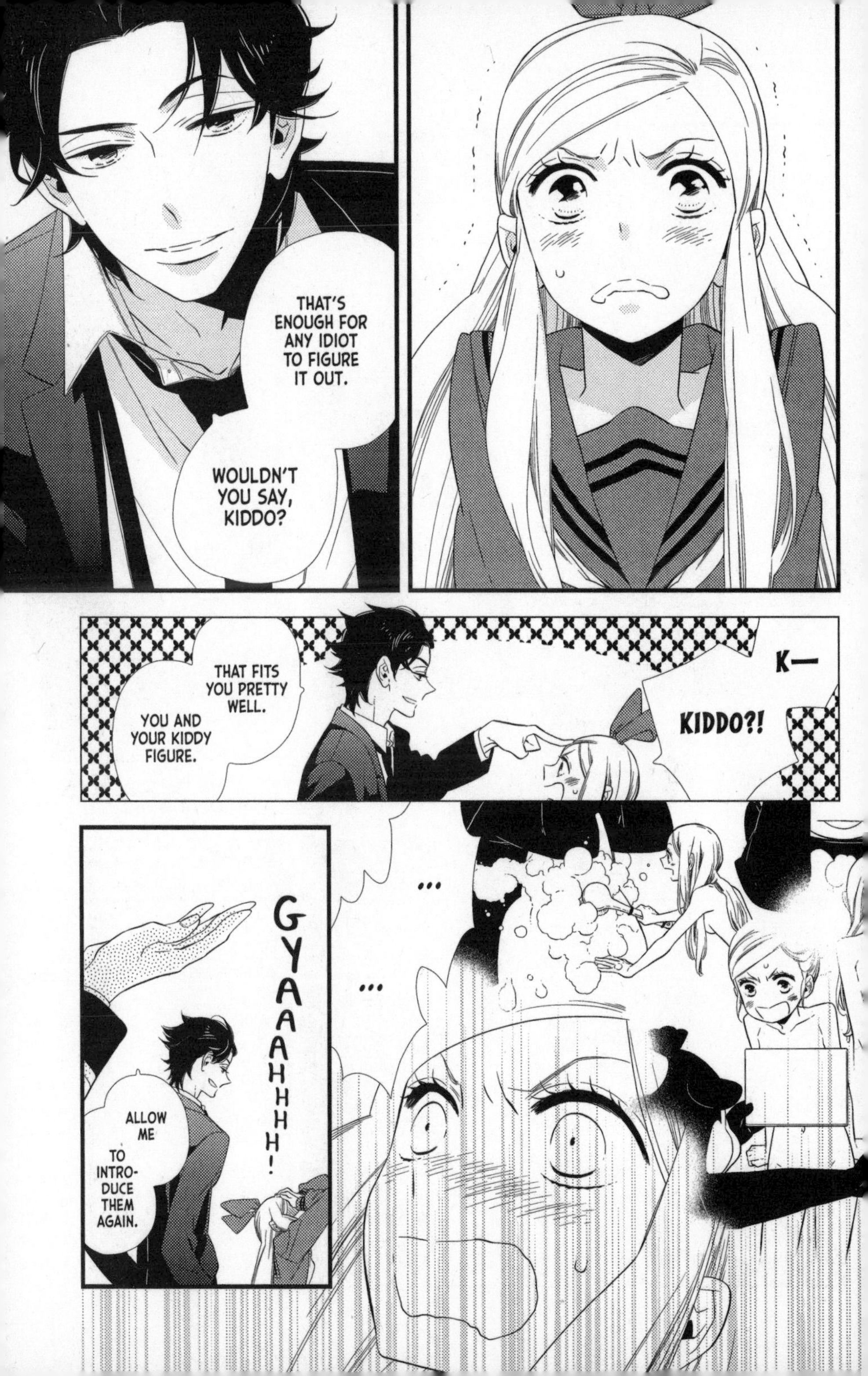
THAT'S ENOUGH FOR ANY IDIOT TO FIGURE IT OUT.
WOULDN'T YOU SAY, KIDDO?
K—
KIDDO?!
THAT FITS YOU PRETTY WELL.
YOU AND YOUR KIDDY FIGURE.
...
...
GYAAAHHHH!
ALLOW ME TO INTRO-DUCE THEM AGAIN.

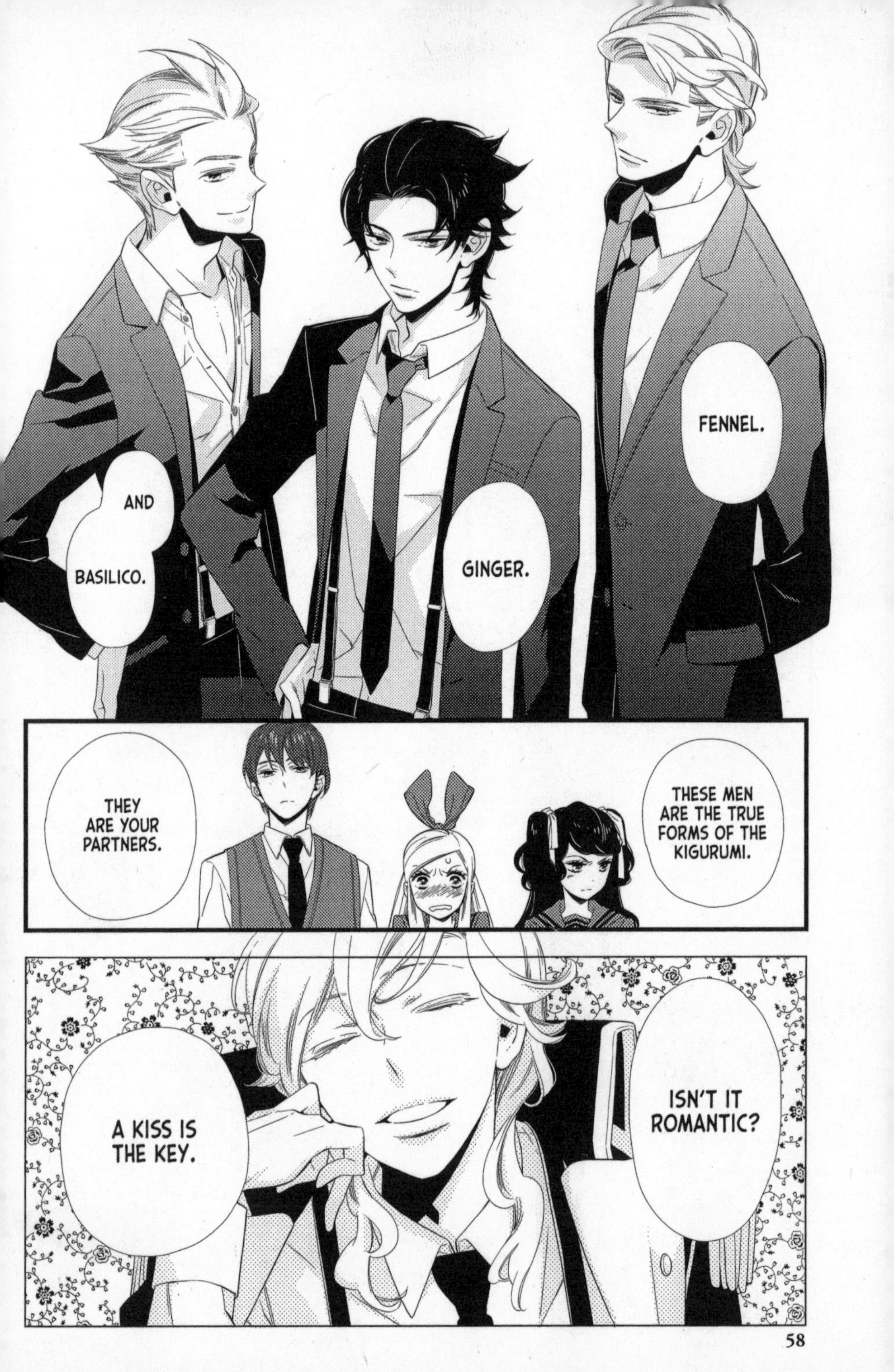
FENNEL.
GINGER.
AND BASILICO.
THESE MEN ARE THE TRUE FORMS OF THE KIGURUMI.
THEY ARE YOUR PARTNERS.
ISN'T IT ROMANTIC?
A KISS IS THE KEY.

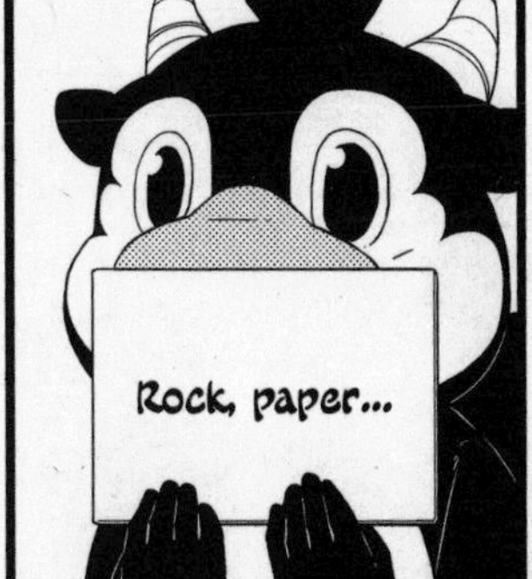
Rock, paper...

Kigurumi
GUARDIANS

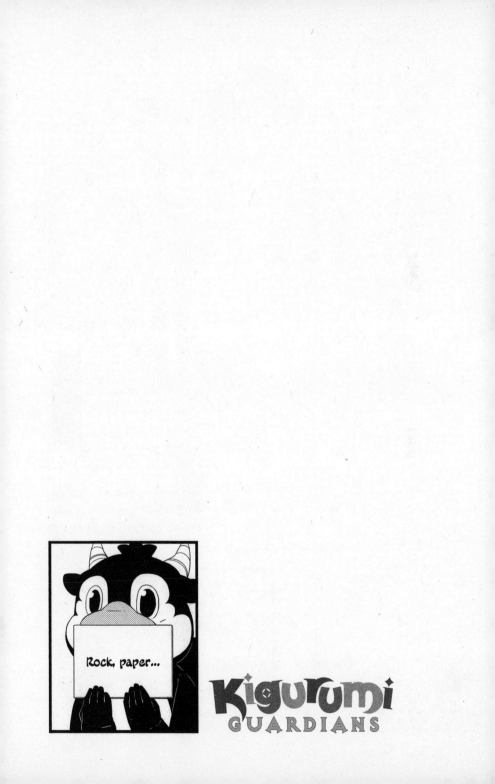

Kigurumi
GUARDIANS

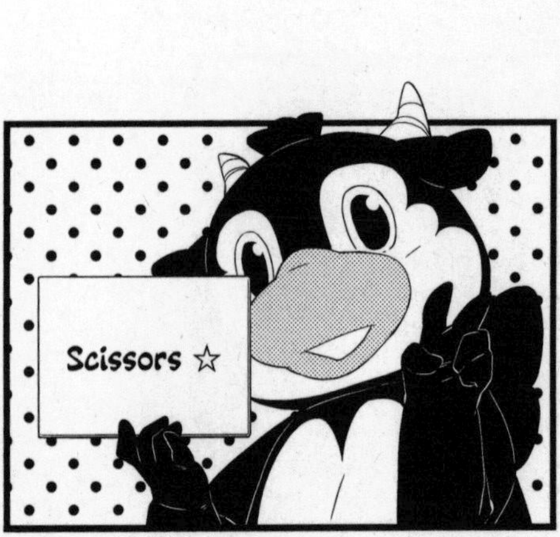
Scissors ☆

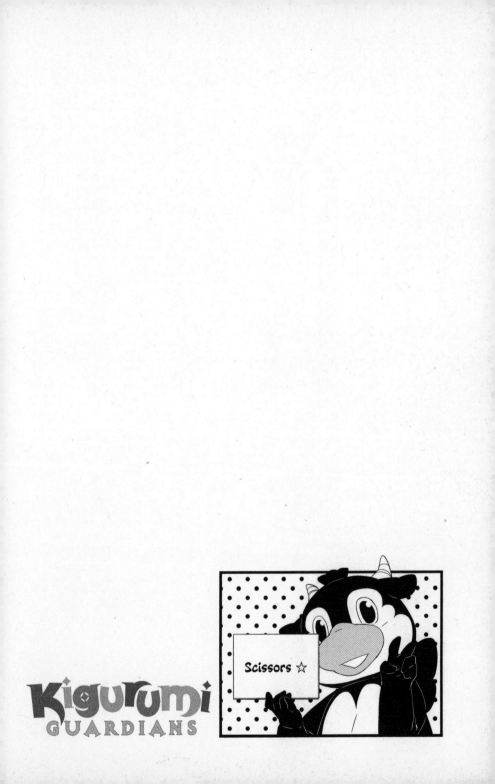

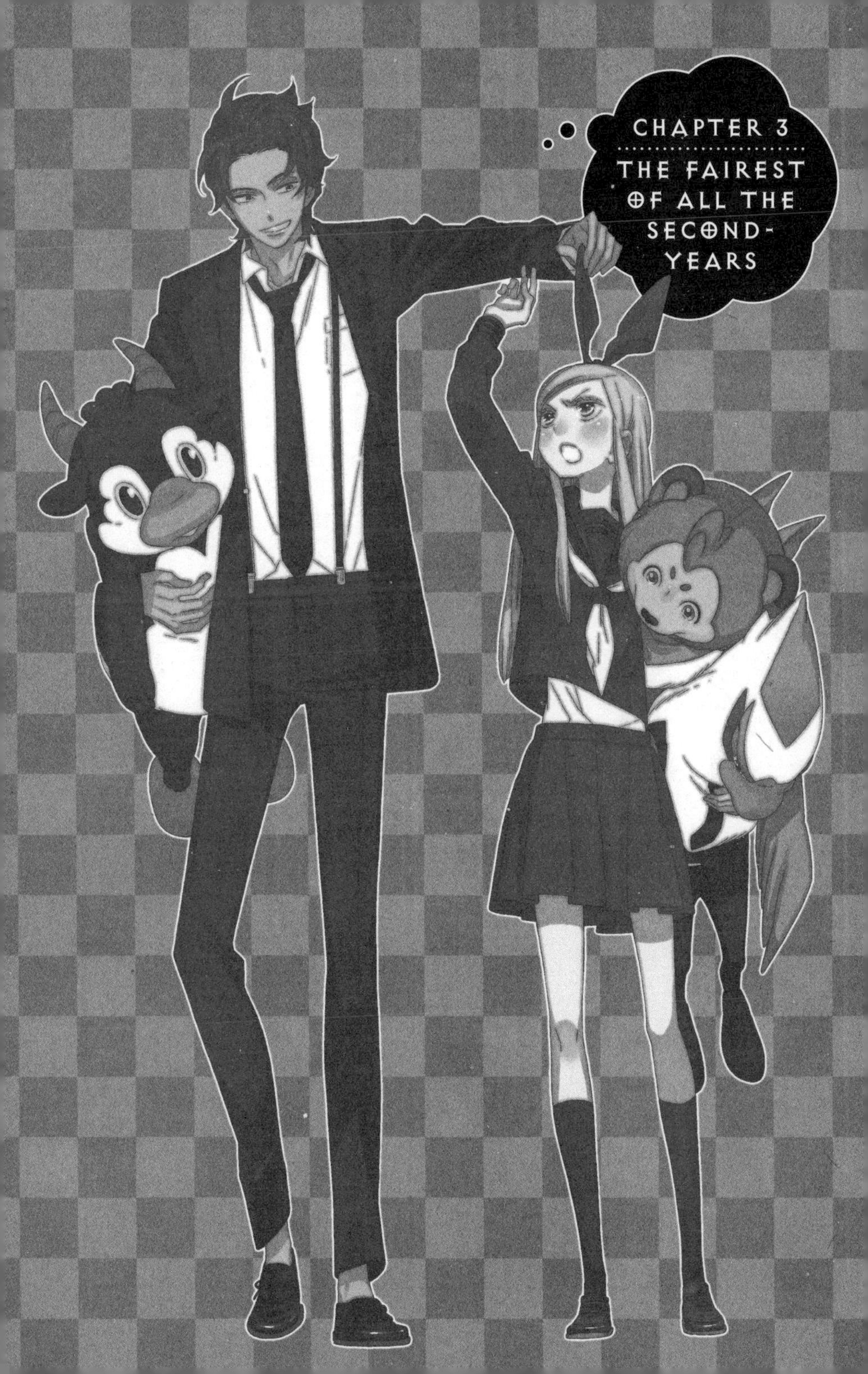
CHAPTER 3
THE FAIREST OF ALL THE SECOND-YEARS

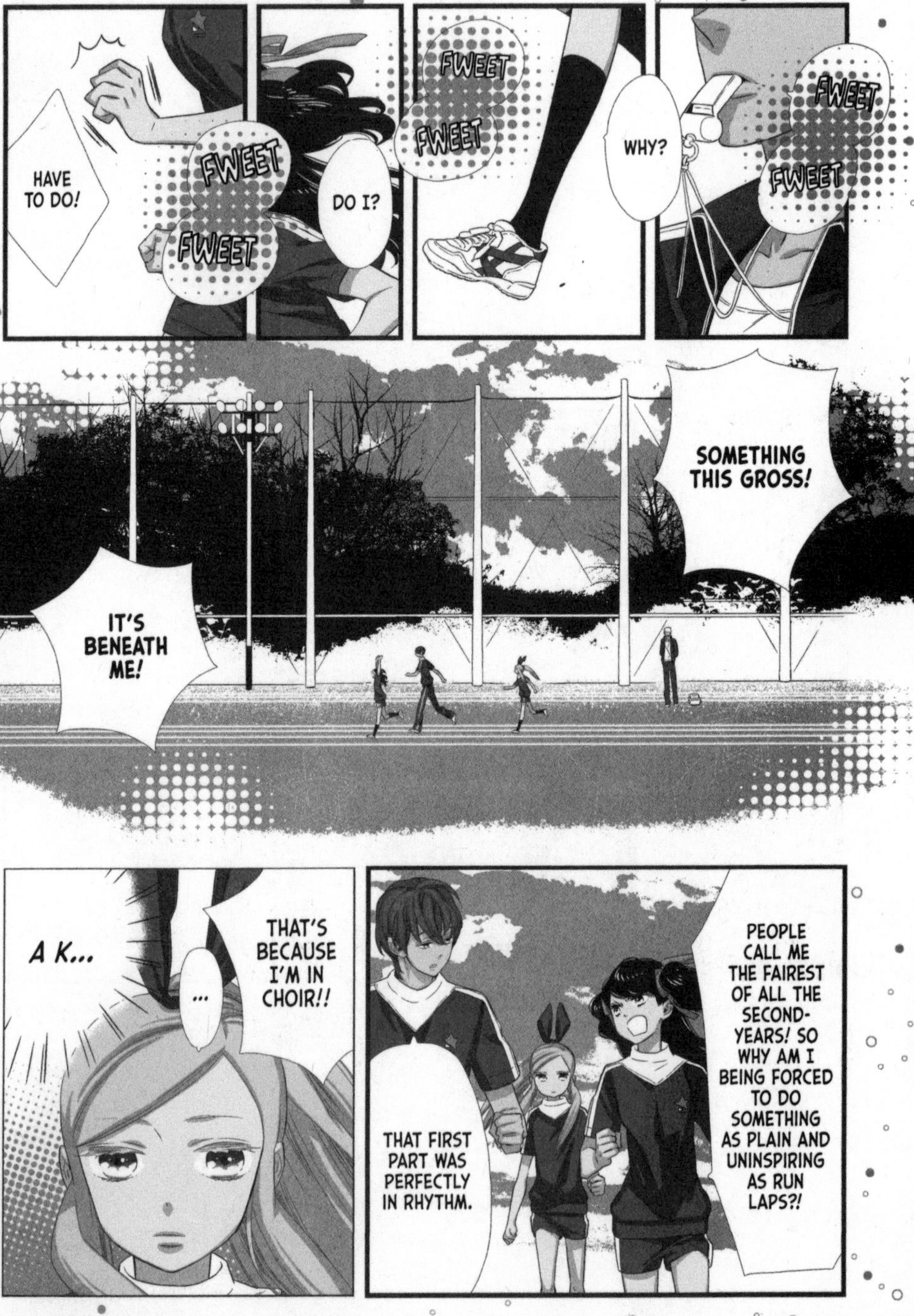
WHY?
FWEET
FWEET
FWEET
FWEET
DO I?
FWEET
FWEET
HAVE TO DO!
SOMETHING THIS GROSS!
IT'S BENEATH ME!
PEOPLE CALL ME THE FAIREST OF ALL THE SECOND-YEARS! SO WHY AM I BEING FORCED TO DO SOMETHING AS PLAIN AND UNINSPIRING AS RUN LAPS?!
THAT FIRST PART WAS PERFECTLY IN RHYTHM.
THAT'S BECAUSE I'M IN CHOIR!!
...
A K...

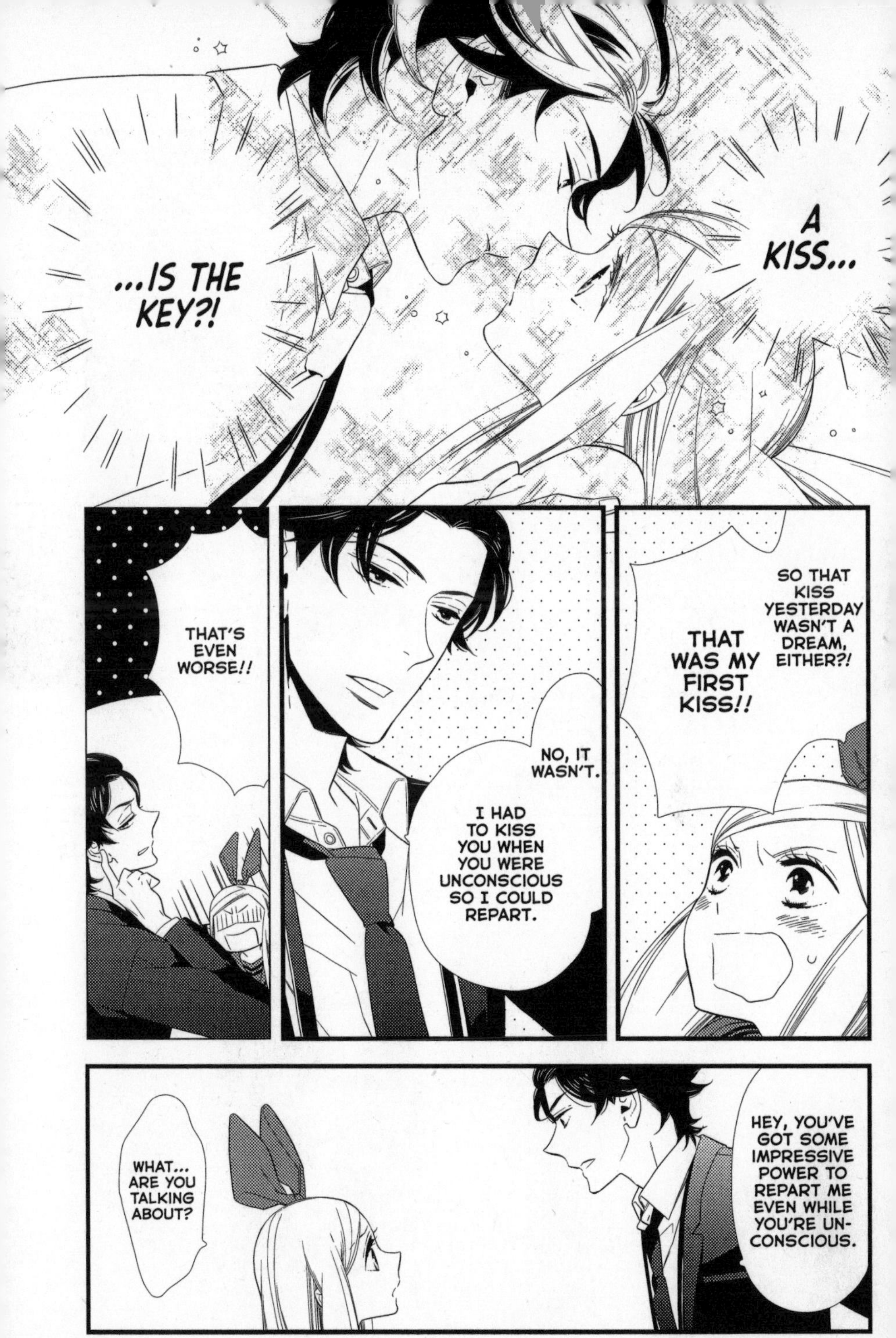
A KISS...
...IS THE KEY?!
SO THAT KISS YESTERDAY WASN'T A DREAM, EITHER?!
THAT WAS MY FIRST KISS!!
NO, IT WASN'T.
I HAD TO KISS YOU WHEN YOU WERE UNCONSCIOUS SO I COULD REPART.
THAT'S EVEN WORSE!!
HEY, YOU'VE GOT SOME IMPRESSIVE POWER TO REPART ME EVEN WHILE YOU'RE UN-CONSCIOUS.
WHAT... ARE YOU TALKING ABOUT?

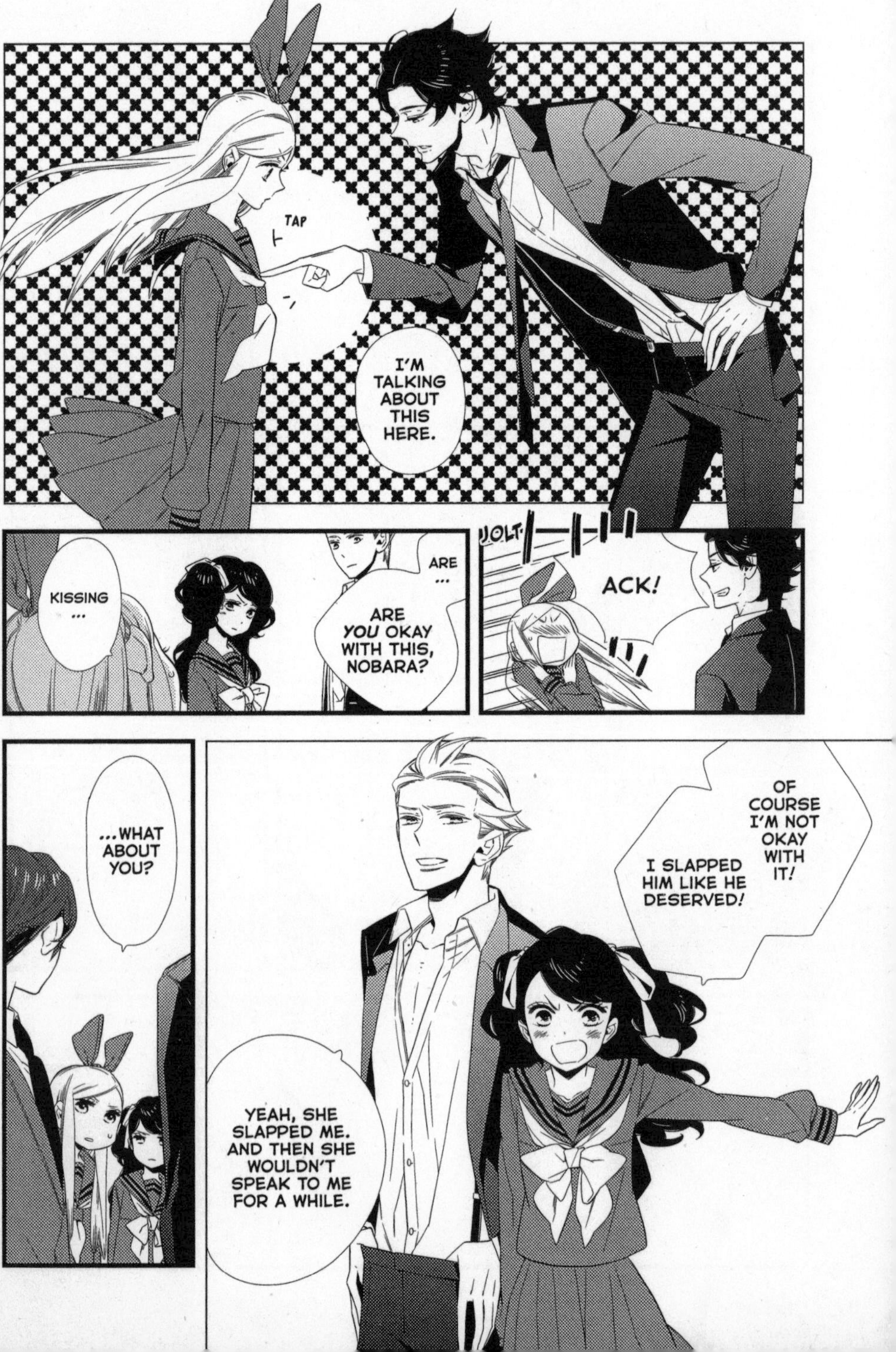
TAP
I'M TALKING ABOUT THIS HERE.
JOLT
ACK!
ARE ...
ARE *YOU* OKAY WITH THIS, NOBARA?
KISSING ...
OF COURSE I'M NOT OKAY WITH IT!
I SLAPPED HIM LIKE HE DESERVED!
YEAH, SHE SLAPPED ME. AND THEN SHE WOULDN'T SPEAK TO ME FOR A WHILE.
...WHAT ABOUT YOU?

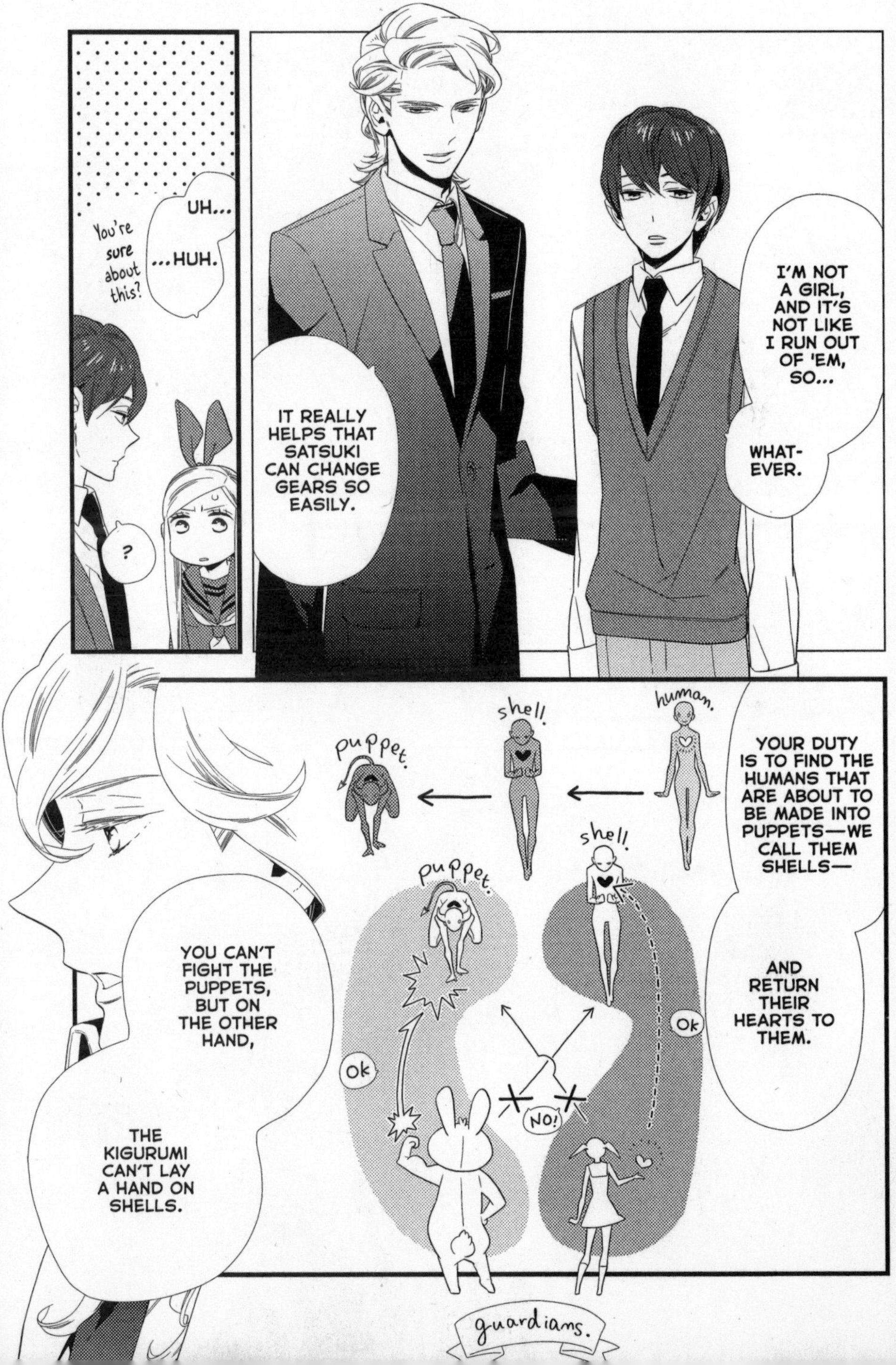
I'M NOT A GIRL, AND IT'S NOT LIKE I RUN OUT OF 'EM, SO...
WHAT-EVER.
IT REALLY HELPS THAT SATSUKI CAN CHANGE GEARS SO EASILY.
UH...
...HUH.
You're sure about this?
?
YOUR DUTY IS TO FIND THE HUMANS THAT ARE ABOUT TO BE MADE INTO PUPPETS—WE CALL THEM SHELLS—
AND RETURN THEIR HEARTS TO THEM.
human.
shell.
puppet.
shell.
puppet.
Ok
Ok
NO!
YOU CAN'T FIGHT THE PUPPETS, BUT ON THE OTHER HAND,
THE KIGURUMI CAN'T LAY A HAND ON SHELLS.
guardians.

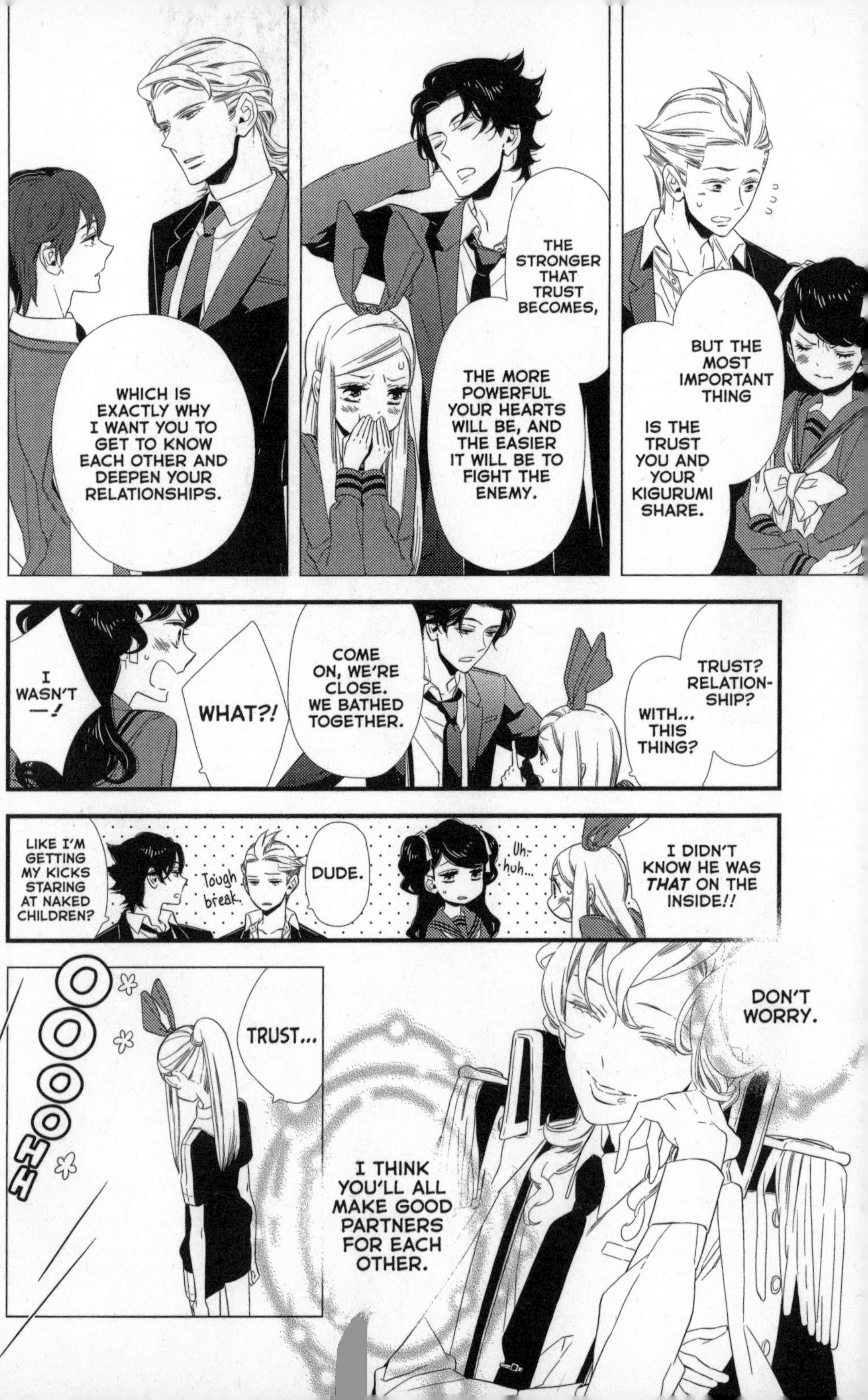
BUT THE MOST IMPORTANT THING
IS THE TRUST YOU AND YOUR KIGURUMI SHARE.
THE STRONGER THAT TRUST BECOMES,
THE MORE POWERFUL YOUR HEARTS WILL BE, AND THE EASIER IT WILL BE TO FIGHT THE ENEMY.
WHICH IS EXACTLY WHY I WANT YOU TO GET TO KNOW EACH OTHER AND DEEPEN YOUR RELATIONSHIPS.
TRUST? RELATIONSHIP?
WITH... THIS THING?
COME ON, WE'RE CLOSE. WE BATHED TOGETHER.
WHAT?!
I WASN'T—!
I DIDN'T KNOW HE WAS *THAT* ON THE INSIDE!!
Uh-huh...
DUDE.
Tough break.
LIKE I'M GETTING MY KICKS STARING AT NAKED CHILDREN?
DON'T WORRY.
I THINK YOU'LL ALL MAKE GOOD PARTNERS FOR EACH OTHER.
TRUST...
OOOOOHH

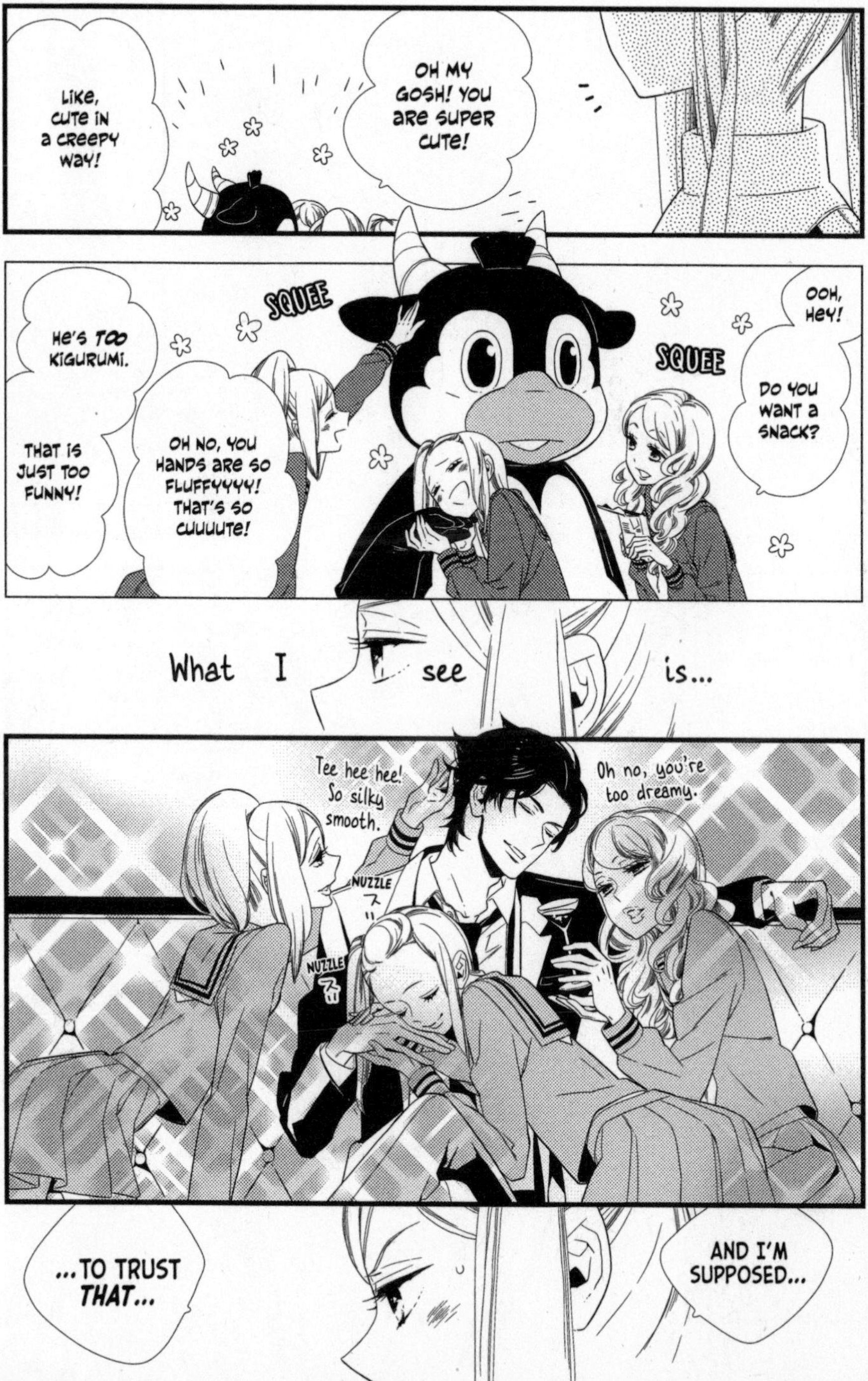
OH MY GOSH! YOU ARE SUPER CUTE!
LIKE, CUTE IN A CREEPY WAY!
OOH, HEY!
DO YOU WANT A SNACK?
SQUEE
SQUEE
OH NO, YOU HANDS ARE SO FLUFFYYYY! THAT'S SO CUUUUTE!
HE'S TOO KIGURUMI.
THAT IS JUST TOO FUNNY!
What I see is...
Oh no, you're too dreamy.
Tee hee hee! So silky smooth.
NUZZLE
NUZZLE
AND I'M SUPPOSED...
...TO TRUST THAT...

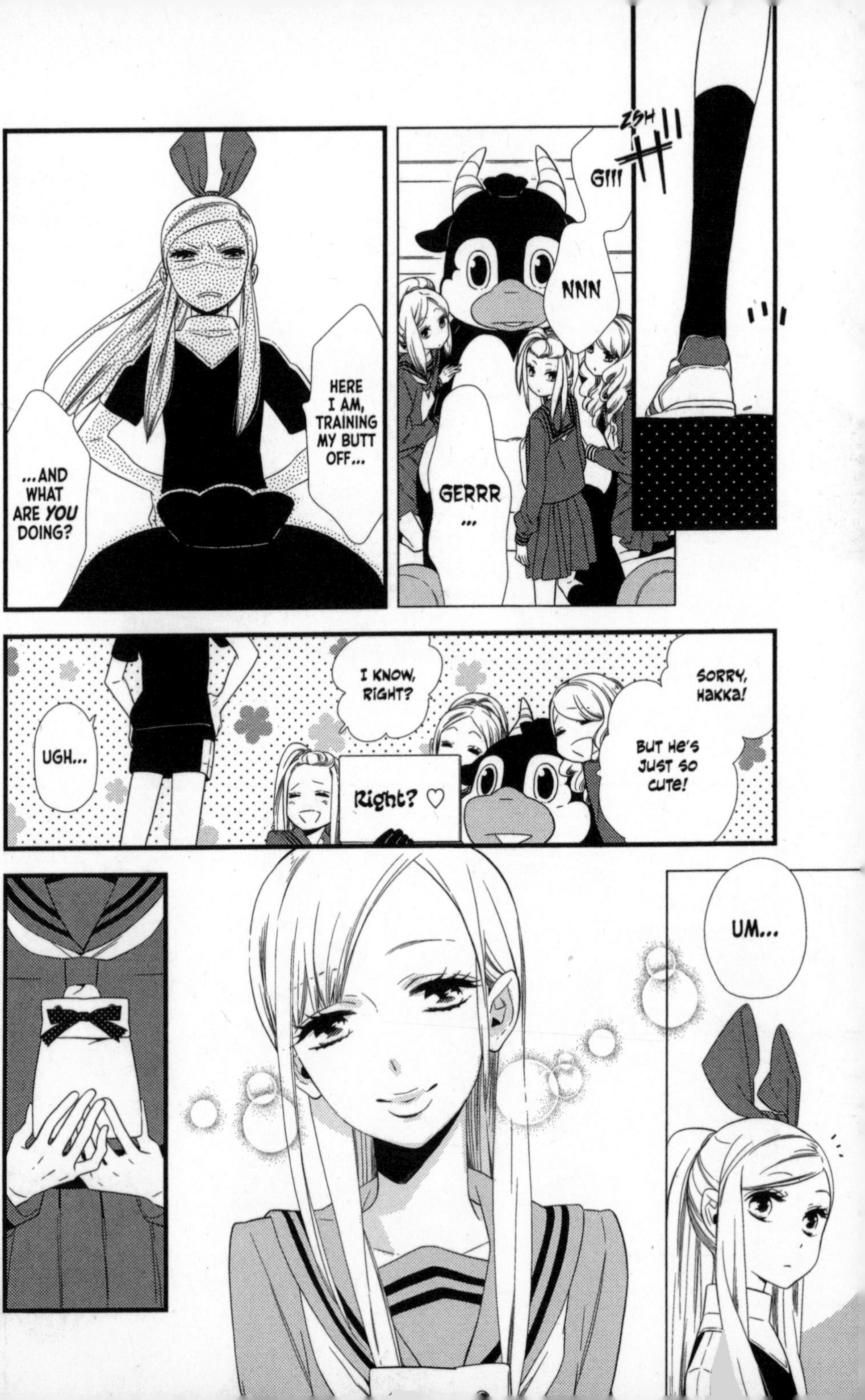
ZSH
GIII
NNN
GERRR...
HERE I AM, TRAINING MY BUTT OFF...
...AND WHAT ARE *YOU* DOING?
SORRY, HAKKA!
BUT HE'S JUST SO CUTE!
I KNOW, RIGHT?
Right? ♡
UGH...
UM...

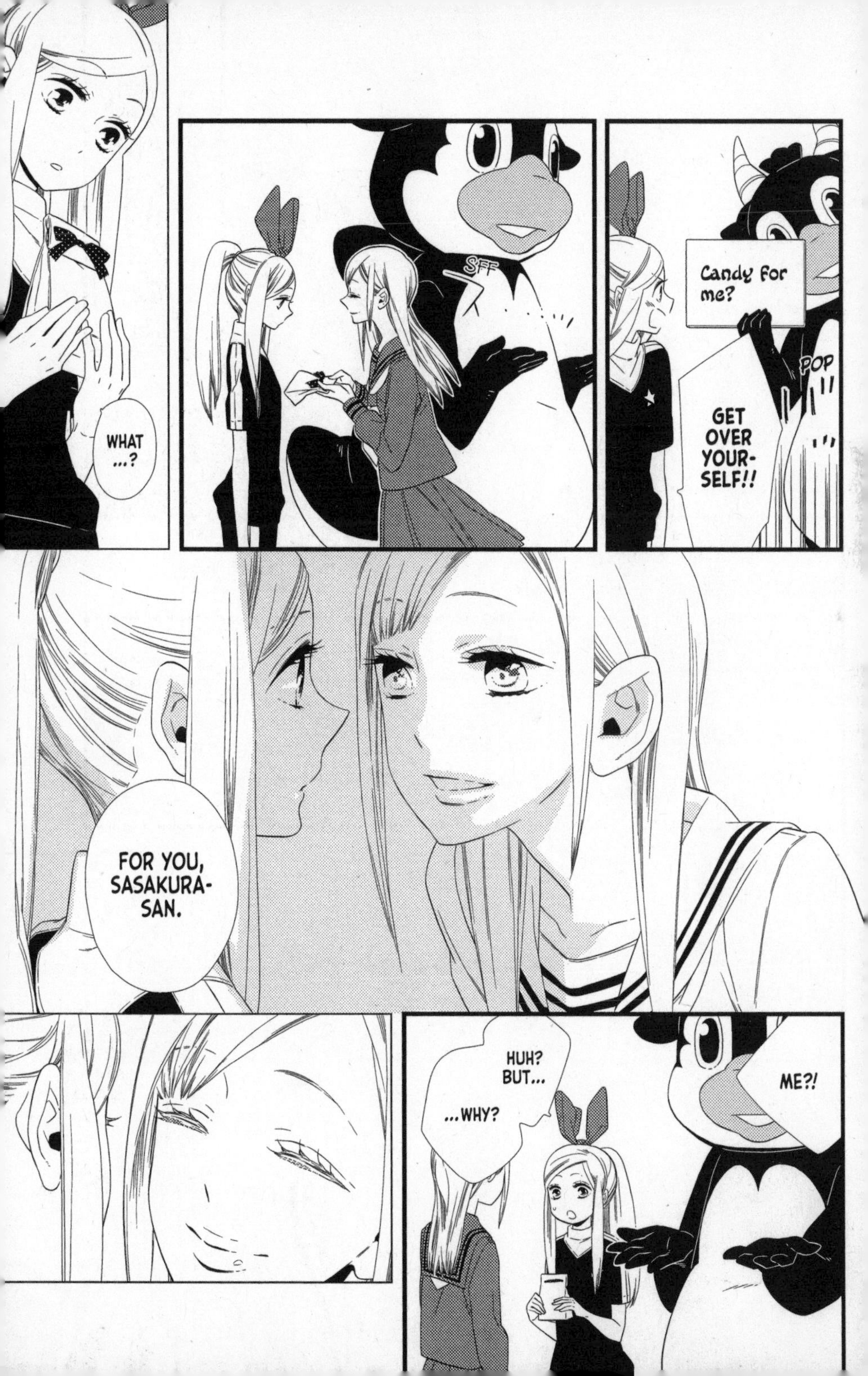
Candy for me?
POP
GET OVER YOURSELF!!
SFF
WHAT ...?
FOR YOU, SASAKURA-SAN.
ME?!
HUH? BUT...
...WHY?

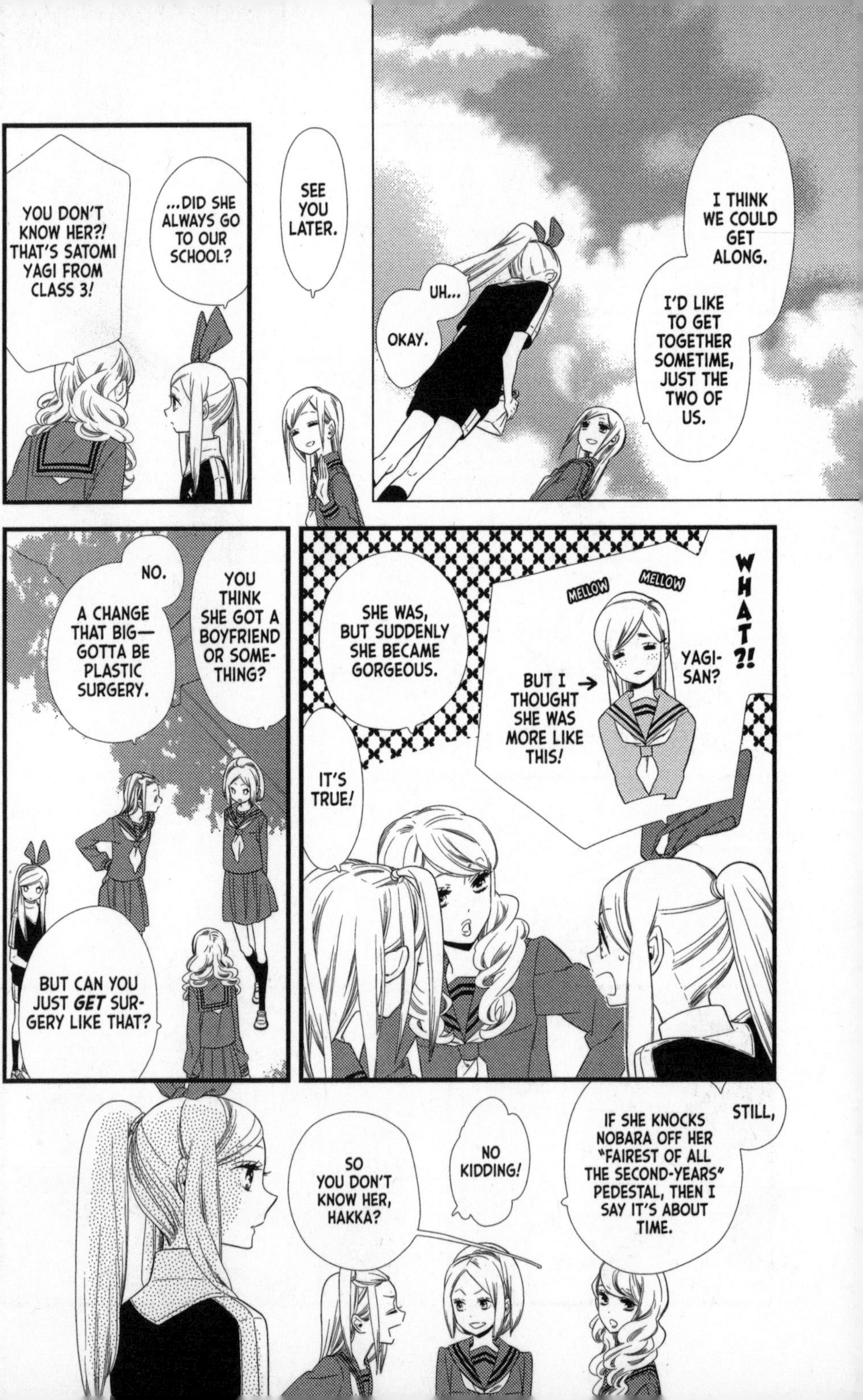

I THINK WE COULD GET ALONG.
I'D LIKE TO GET TOGETHER SOMETIME, JUST THE TWO OF US.
UH...
OKAY.
SEE YOU LATER.
...DID SHE ALWAYS GO TO OUR SCHOOL?
YOU DON'T KNOW HER?! THAT'S SATOMI YAGI FROM CLASS 3!
WHAT?!
YAGI-SAN?
MELLOW
MELLOW
BUT I THOUGHT SHE WAS MORE LIKE THIS!
SHE WAS, BUT SUDDENLY SHE BECAME GORGEOUS.
IT'S TRUE!
YOU THINK SHE GOT A BOYFRIEND OR SOME-THING?
NO.
A CHANGE THAT BIG—GOTTA BE PLASTIC SURGERY.
BUT CAN YOU JUST *GET* SUR-GERY LIKE THAT?
STILL,
IF SHE KNOCKS NOBARA OFF HER "FAIREST OF ALL THE SECOND-YEARS" PEDESTAL, THEN I SAY IT'S ABOUT TIME.
NO KIDDING!
SO YOU DON'T KNOW HER, HAKKA?

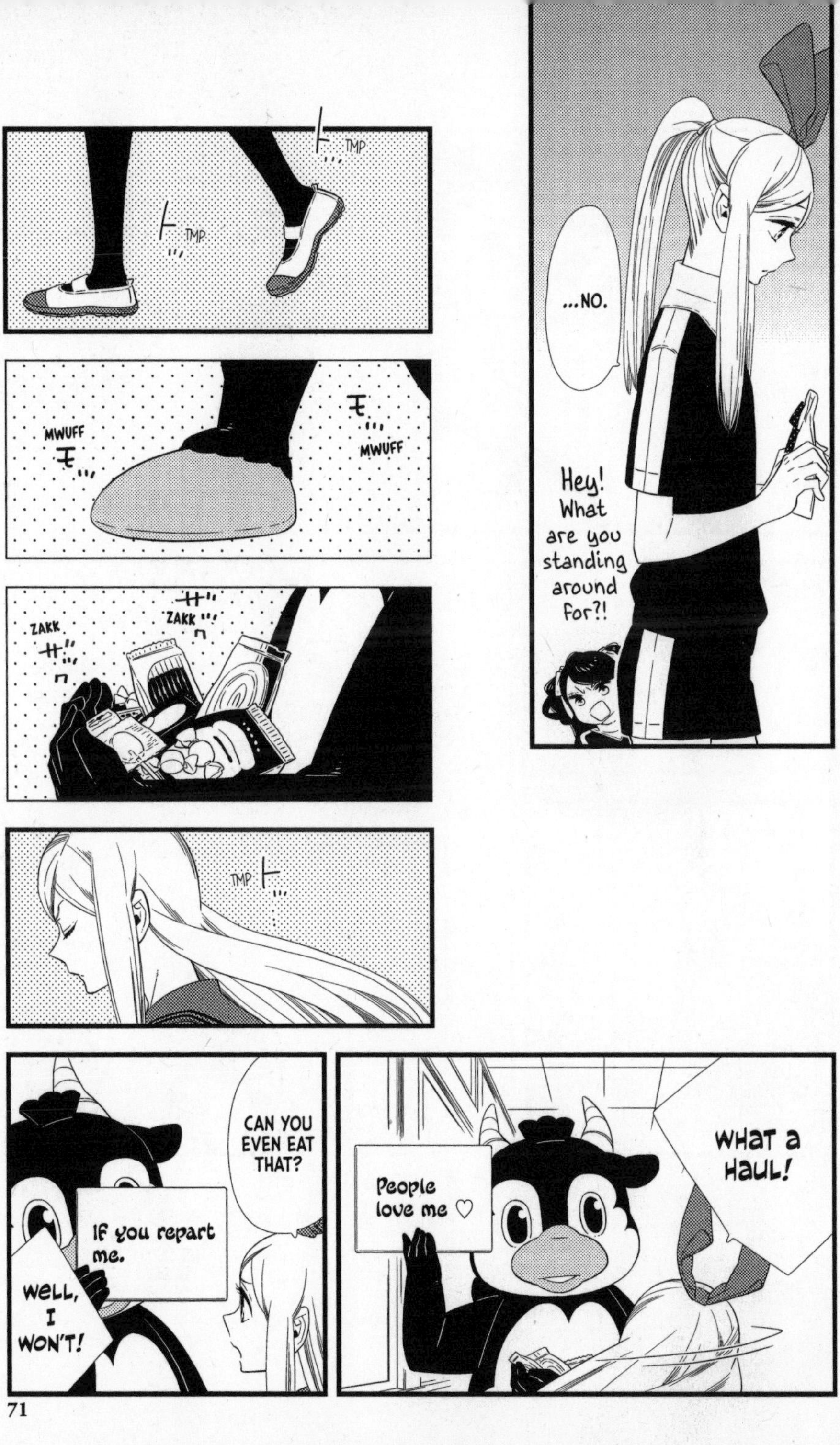
...NO.
Hey! What are you standing around for?!
TMP
TMP
MWUFF
MWUFF
ZAKK
ZAKK
TMP
WHAT a HAUL!
People love me ♡
CAN YOU EVEN EAT THAT?
If you repart me.
WELL, I WON'T!

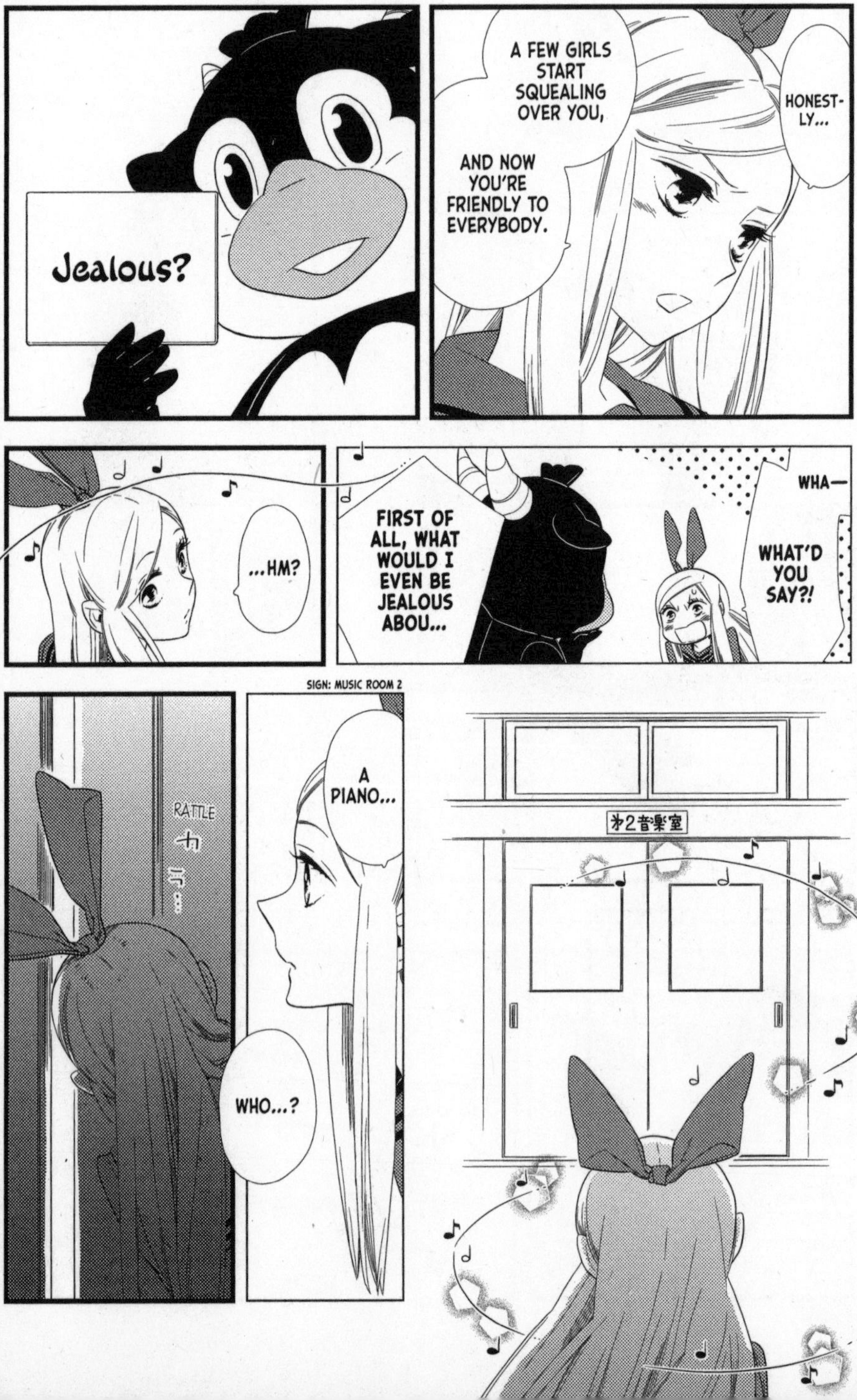
HONESTLY...
A FEW GIRLS START SQUEALING OVER YOU,
AND NOW YOU'RE FRIENDLY TO EVERYBODY.
Jealous?
WHA—
WHAT'D YOU SAY?!
FIRST OF ALL, WHAT WOULD I EVEN BE JEALOUS ABOU...
...HM?
SIGN: MUSIC ROOM 2
第2音楽室
A PIANO...
WHO...?
RATTLE

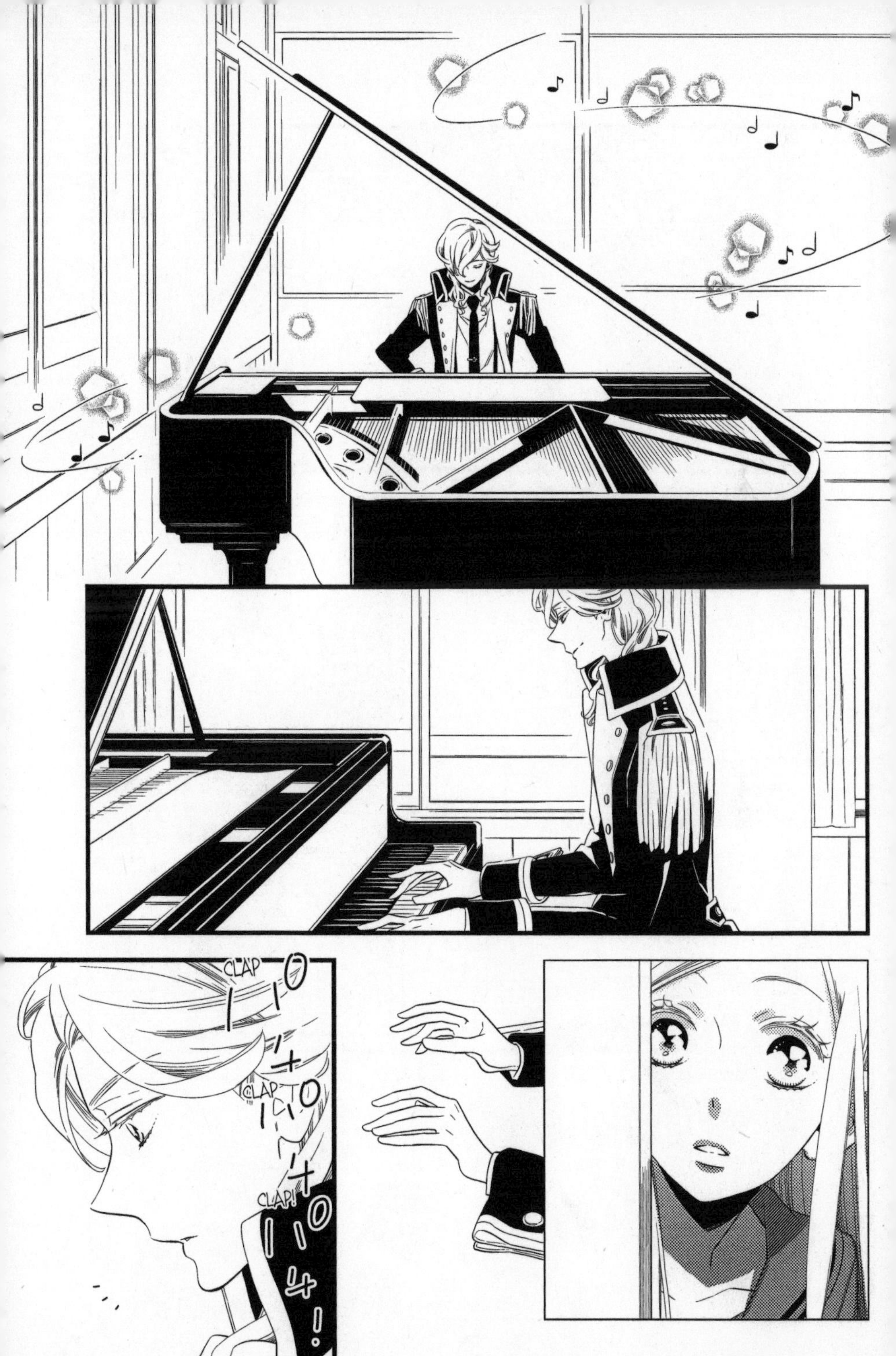
CLAP
CLAP
CLAP!

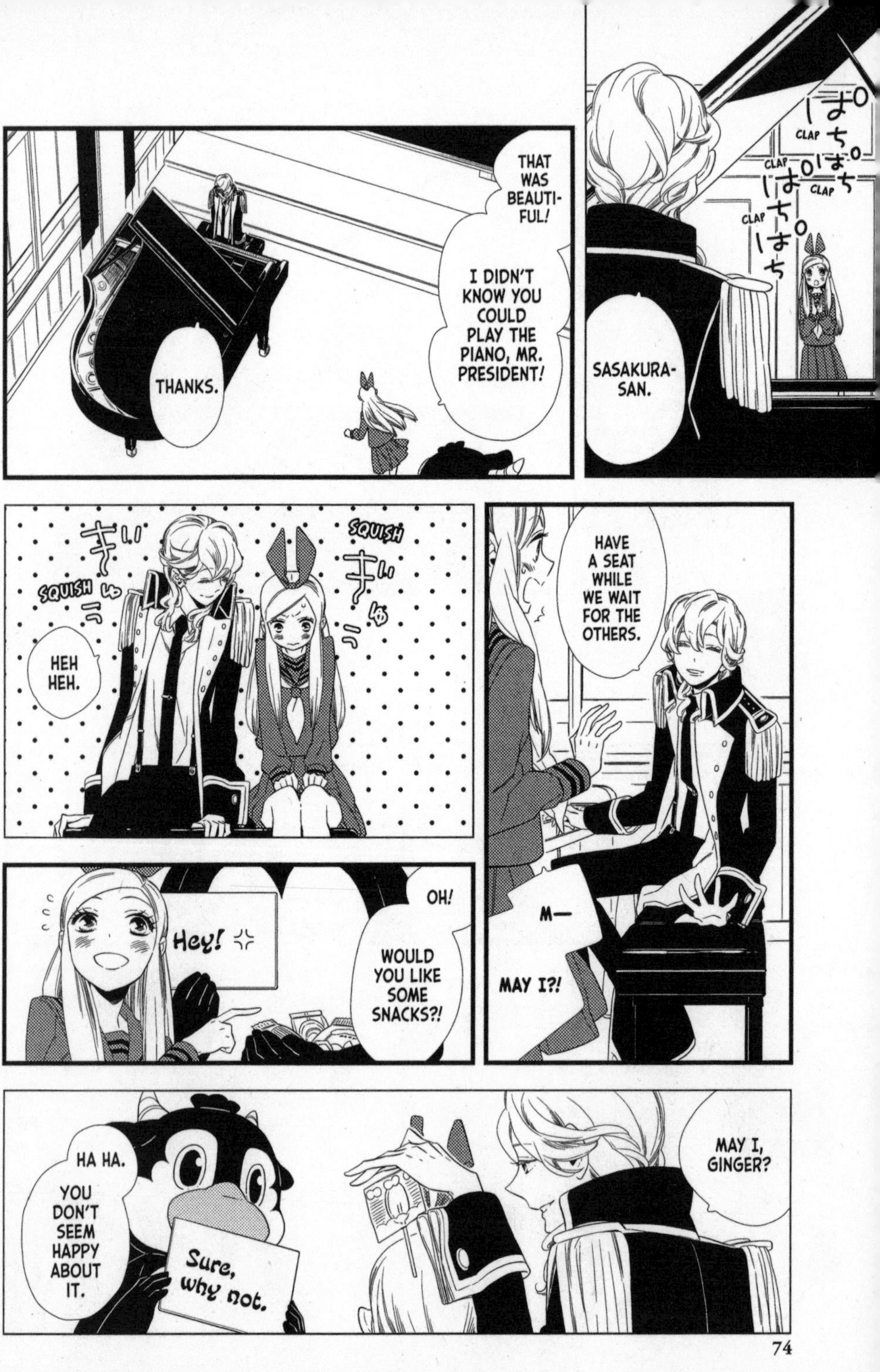
ぱち。ぱち。ぱち。ぱち。
CLAP CLAP CLAP CLAP
SASAKURA-SAN.
THAT WAS BEAUTI-FUL!
I DIDN'T KNOW YOU COULD PLAY THE PIANO, MR. PRESIDENT!
THANKS.
HAVE A SEAT WHILE WE WAIT FOR THE OTHERS.
M—
MAY I?!
ぎゅう
SQUISH
ぎゅう
SQUISH
HEH HEH.
OH!
WOULD YOU LIKE SOME SNACKS?!
Hey!
MAY I, GINGER?
HA HA.
YOU DON'T SEEM HAPPY ABOUT IT.
Sure, why not.

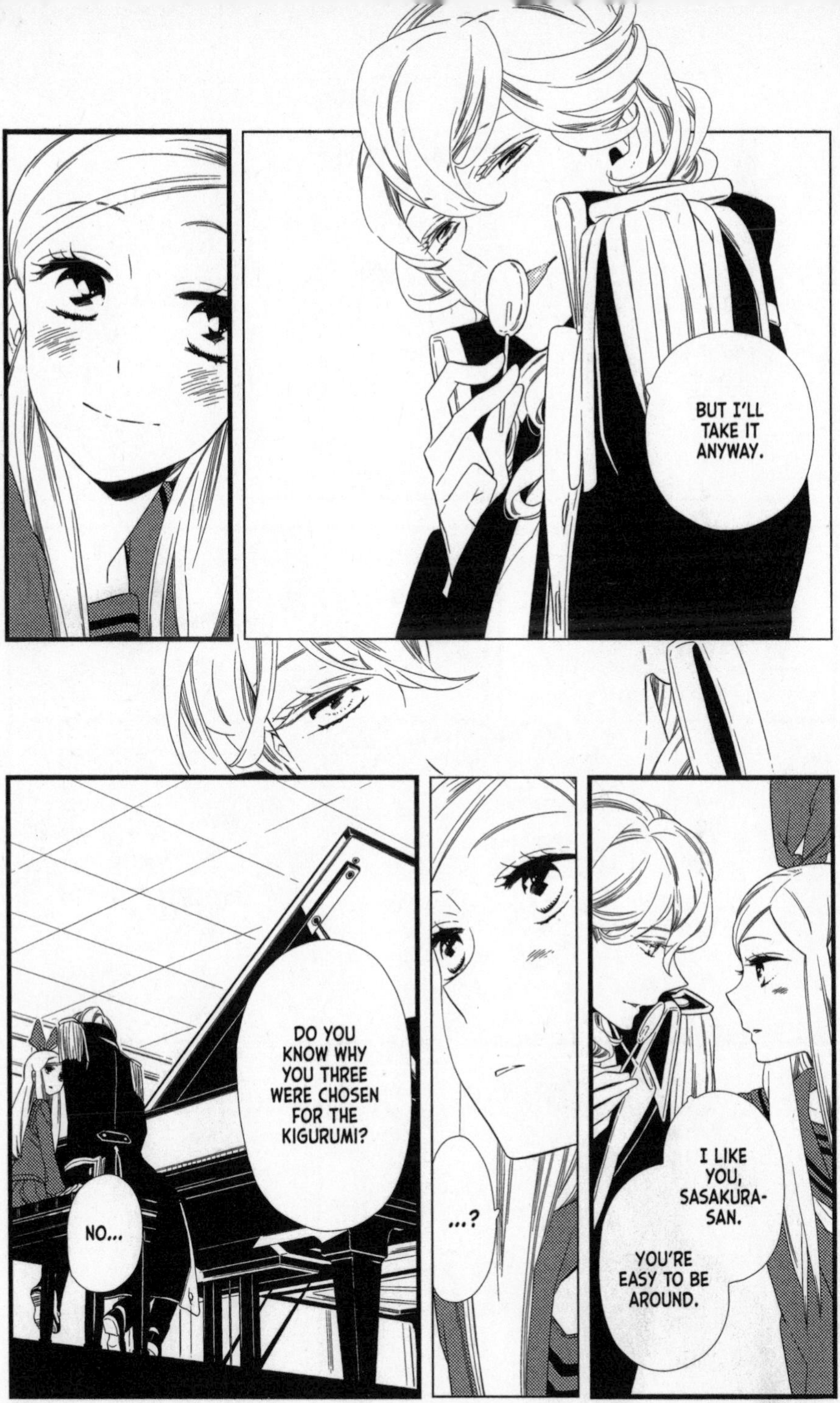
BUT I'LL TAKE IT ANYWAY.
I LIKE YOU, SASAKURA-SAN.
YOU'RE EASY TO BE AROUND.
...?
DO YOU KNOW WHY YOU THREE WERE CHOSEN FOR THE KIGURUMI?
NO...

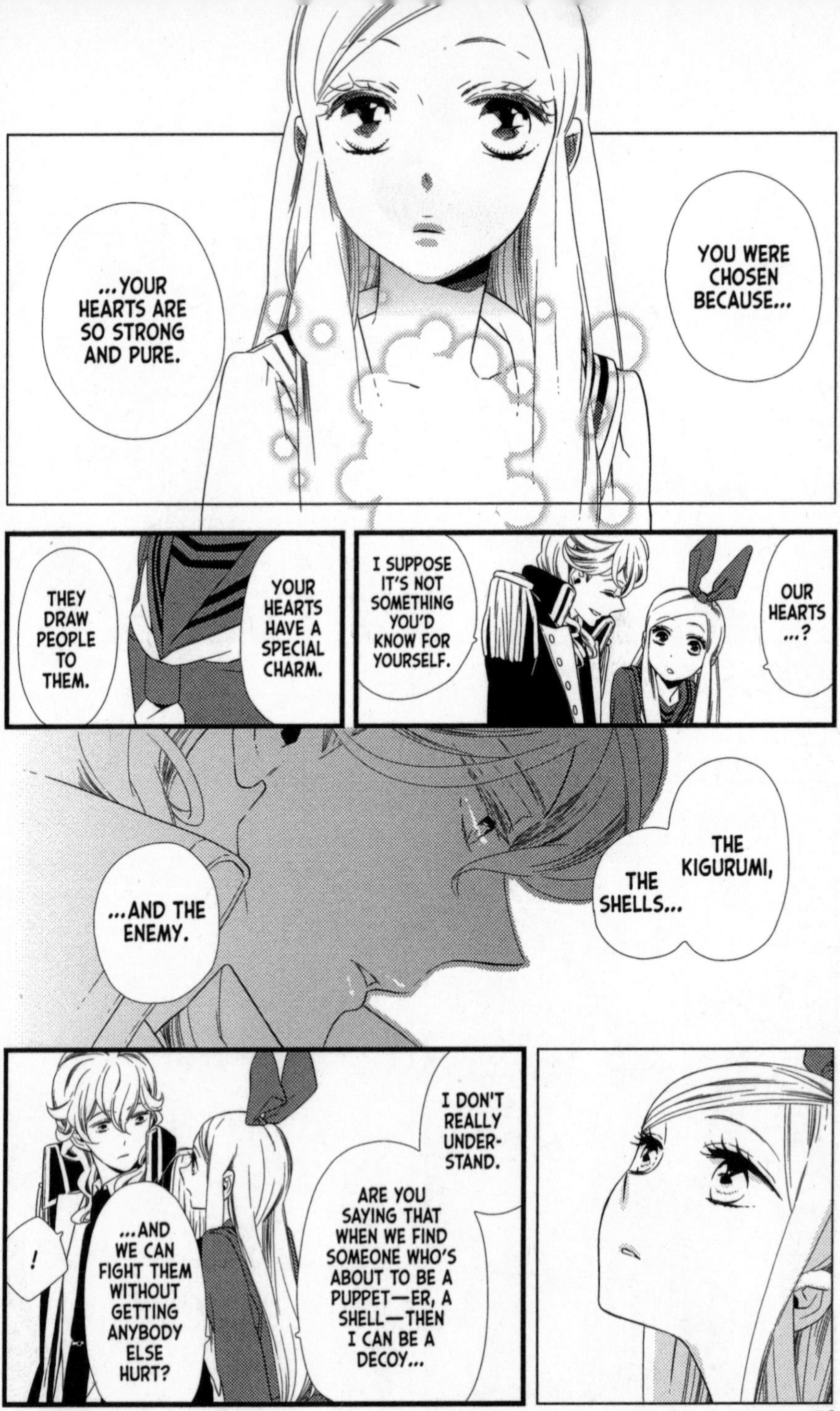
YOU WERE CHOSEN BECAUSE...
...YOUR HEARTS ARE SO STRONG AND PURE.
OUR HEARTS ...?
I SUPPOSE IT'S NOT SOMETHING YOU'D KNOW FOR YOURSELF.
YOUR HEARTS HAVE A SPECIAL CHARM.
THEY DRAW PEOPLE TO THEM.
THE KIGURUMI, THE SHELLS...
...AND THE ENEMY.
I DON'T REALLY UNDER-STAND.
ARE YOU SAYING THAT WHEN WE FIND SOMEONE WHO'S ABOUT TO BE A PUPPET—ER, A SHELL—THEN I CAN BE A DECOY...
...AND WE CAN FIGHT THEM WITHOUT GETTING ANYBODY ELSE HURT?
!

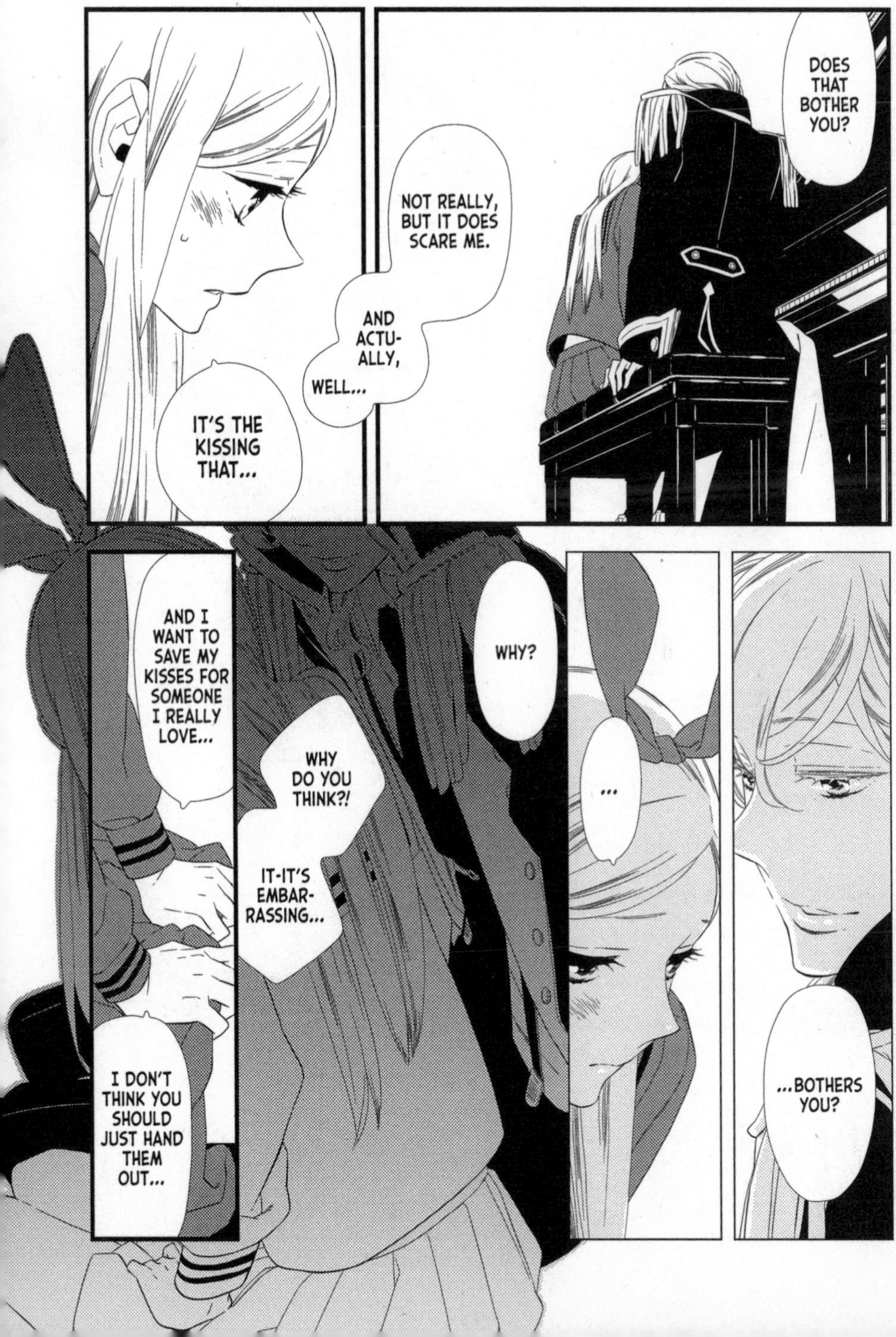
DOES THAT BOTHER YOU?
NOT REALLY, BUT IT DOES SCARE ME.
AND ACTU-ALLY, WELL...
IT'S THE KISSING THAT...
...BOTHERS YOU?
...
WHY?
WHY DO YOU THINK?!
IT-IT'S EMBAR-RASSING...
AND I WANT TO SAVE MY KISSES FOR SOMEONE I REALLY LOVE...
I DON'T THINK YOU SHOULD JUST HAND THEM OUT...

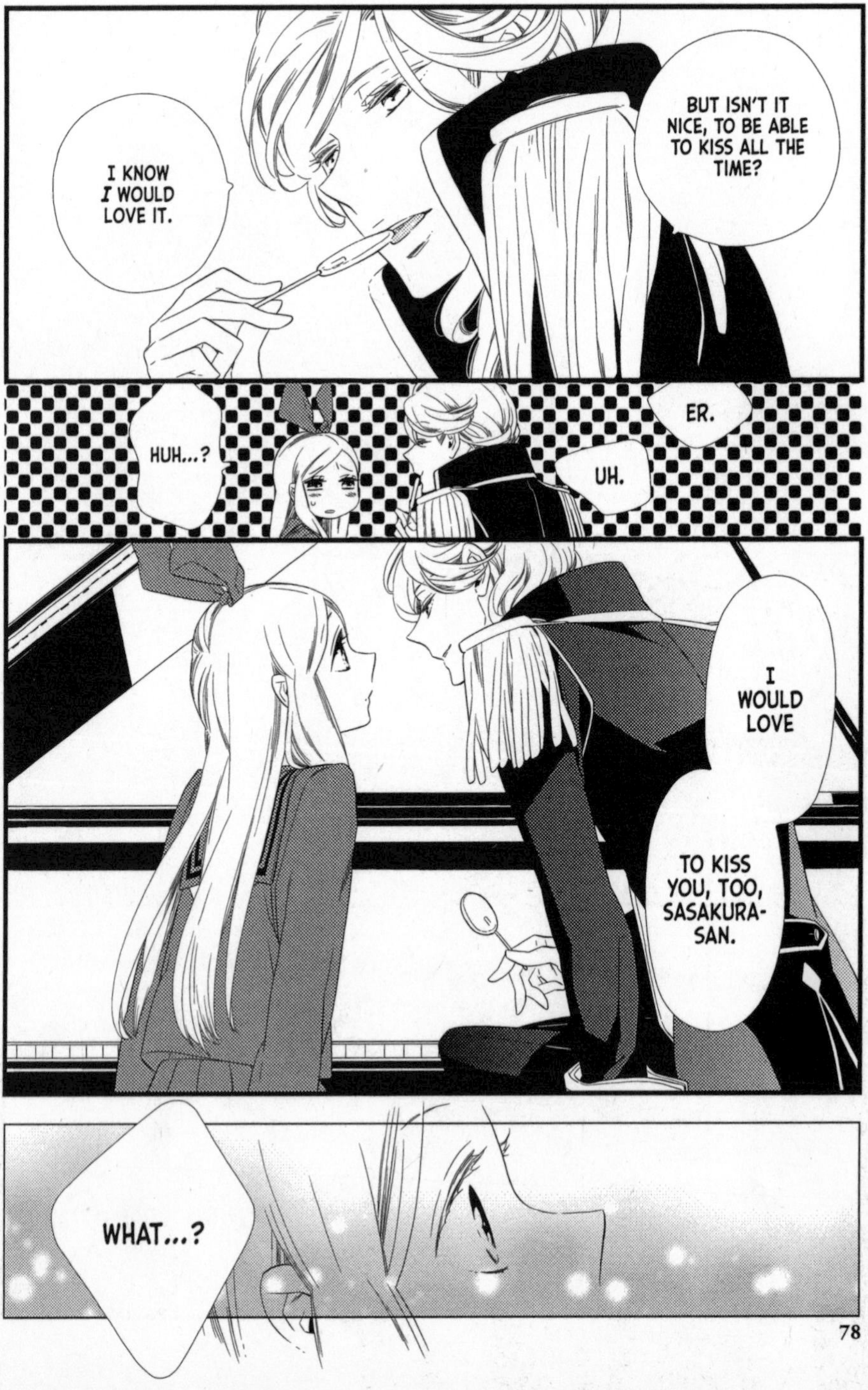
BUT ISN'T IT NICE, TO BE ABLE TO KISS ALL THE TIME?
I KNOW *I* WOULD LOVE IT.
ER.
UH.
HUH...?
I WOULD LOVE
TO KISS YOU, TOO, SASAKURA-SAN.
WHAT...?

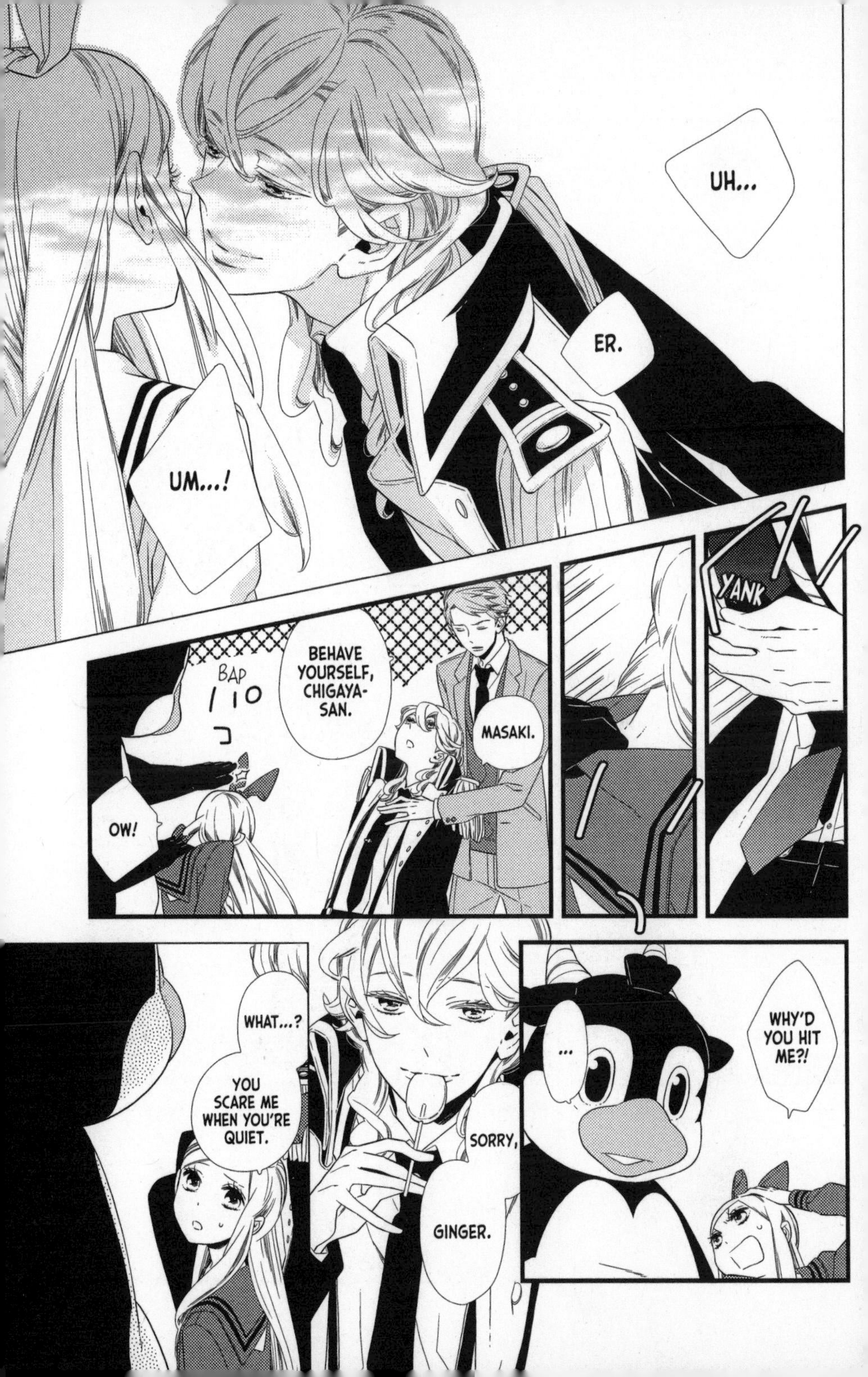
UH...
ER.
UM...!
YANK
BEHAVE YOURSELF, CHIGAYA-SAN.
MASAKI.
BAP
OW!
WHY'D YOU HIT ME?!
...
WHAT...?
YOU SCARE ME WHEN YOU'RE QUIET.
SORRY,
GINGER.

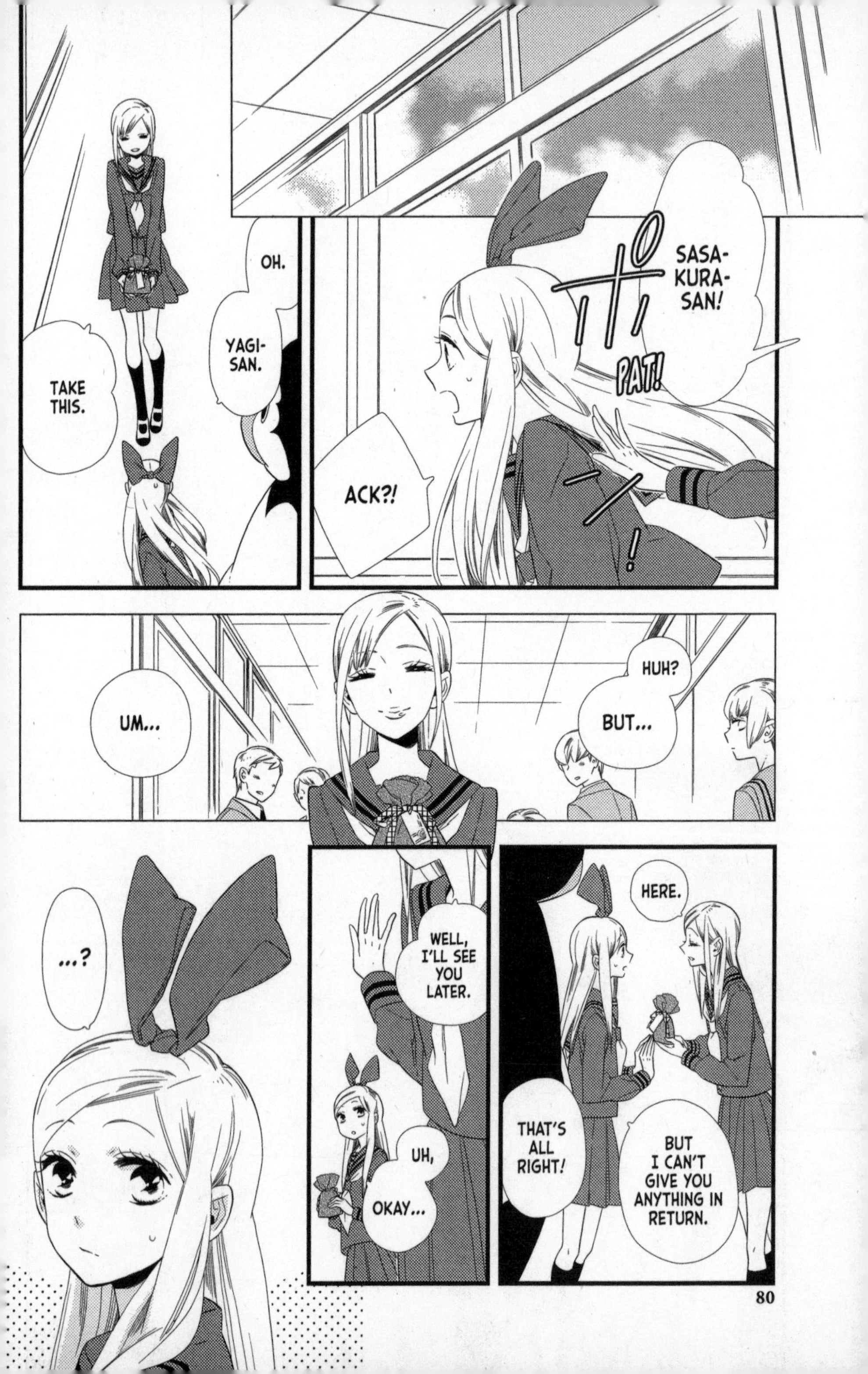
SASA-KURA-SAN!
PAT!
ACK?!
OH.
YAGI-SAN.
TAKE THIS.
HUH?
BUT...
UM...
HERE.
BUT I CAN'T GIVE YOU ANYTHING IN RETURN.
THAT'S ALL RIGHT!
WELL, I'LL SEE YOU LATER.
UH,
OKAY...
...?

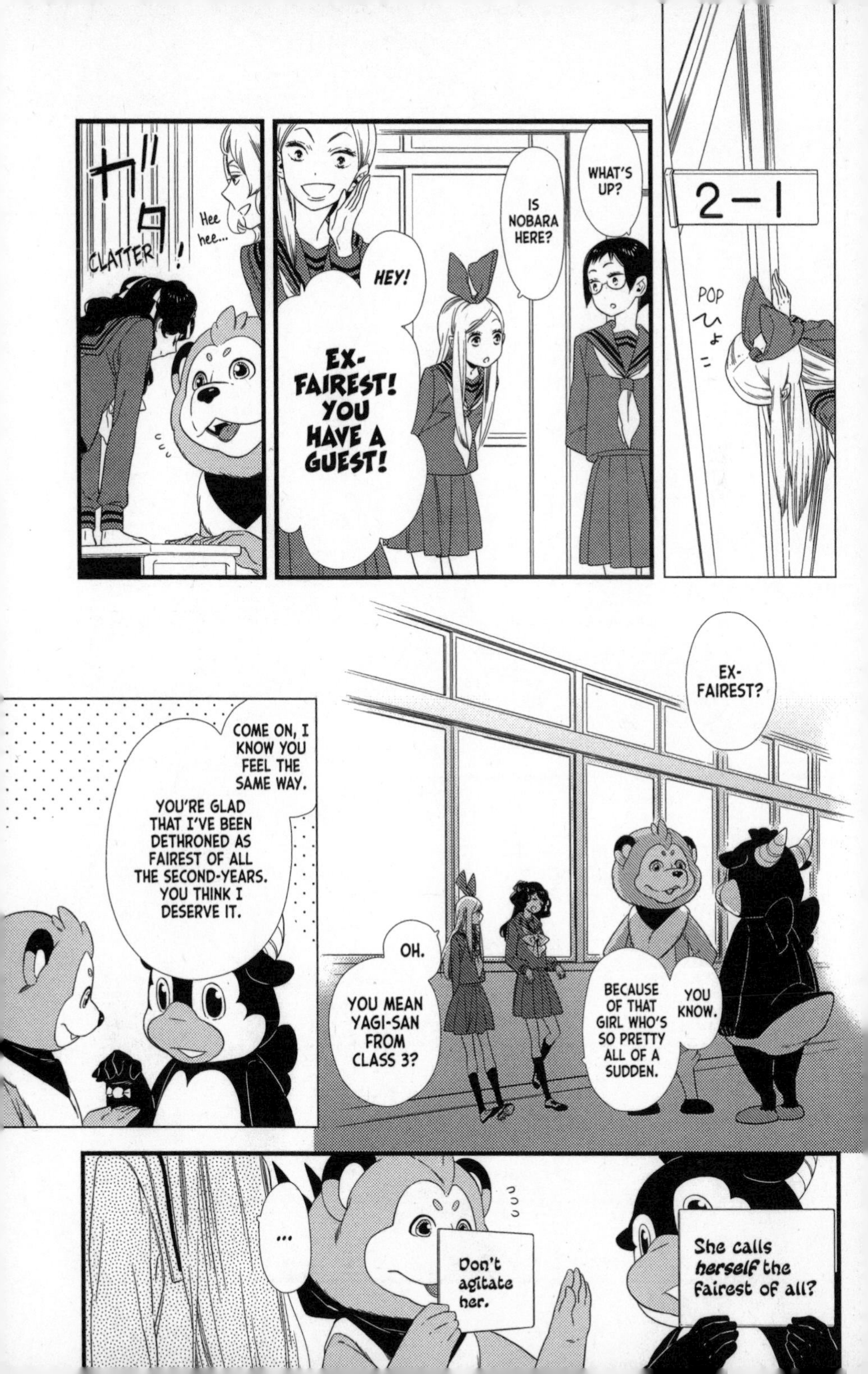
2-1
POP
ぴょ
WHAT'S UP?
IS NOBARA HERE?
HEY!
EX-FAIREST! YOU HAVE A GUEST!
ガタ
CLATTER
Hee hee...
EX-FAIREST?
YOU KNOW.
BECAUSE OF THAT GIRL WHO'S SO PRETTY ALL OF A SUDDEN.
OH.
YOU MEAN YAGI-SAN FROM CLASS 3?
COME ON, I KNOW YOU FEEL THE SAME WAY.
YOU'RE GLAD THAT I'VE BEEN DETHRONED AS FAIREST OF ALL THE SECOND-YEARS. YOU THINK I DESERVE IT.
She calls herself the fairest of all?
Don't agitate her.
...

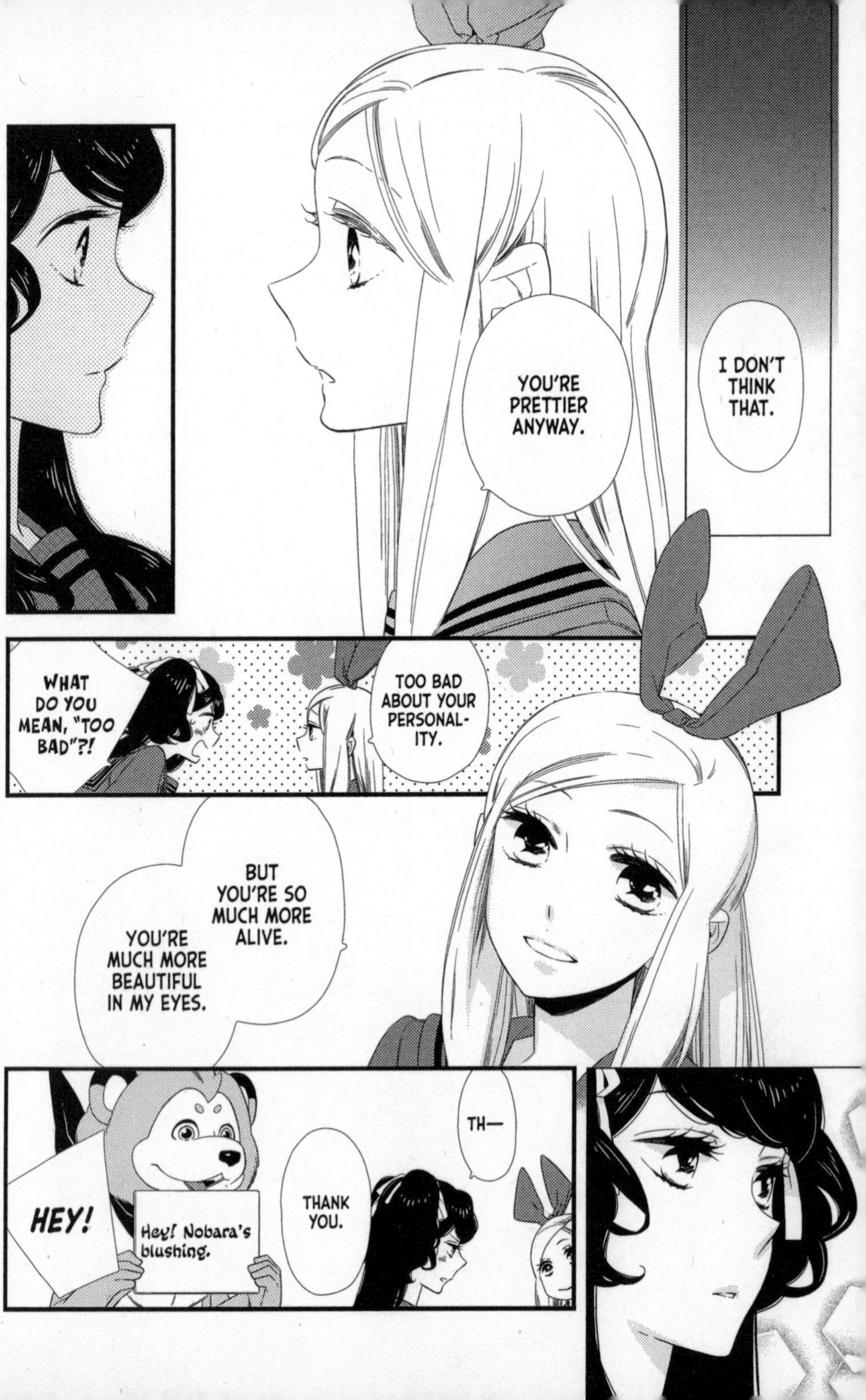
I DON'T THINK THAT.
YOU'RE PRETTIER ANYWAY.
TOO BAD ABOUT YOUR PERSONAL-ITY.
WHAT DO YOU MEAN, "TOO BAD"?!
BUT YOU'RE SO MUCH MORE ALIVE.
YOU'RE MUCH MORE BEAUTIFUL IN MY EYES.
TH—
THANK YOU.
HEY!
Hey! Nobara's blushing.

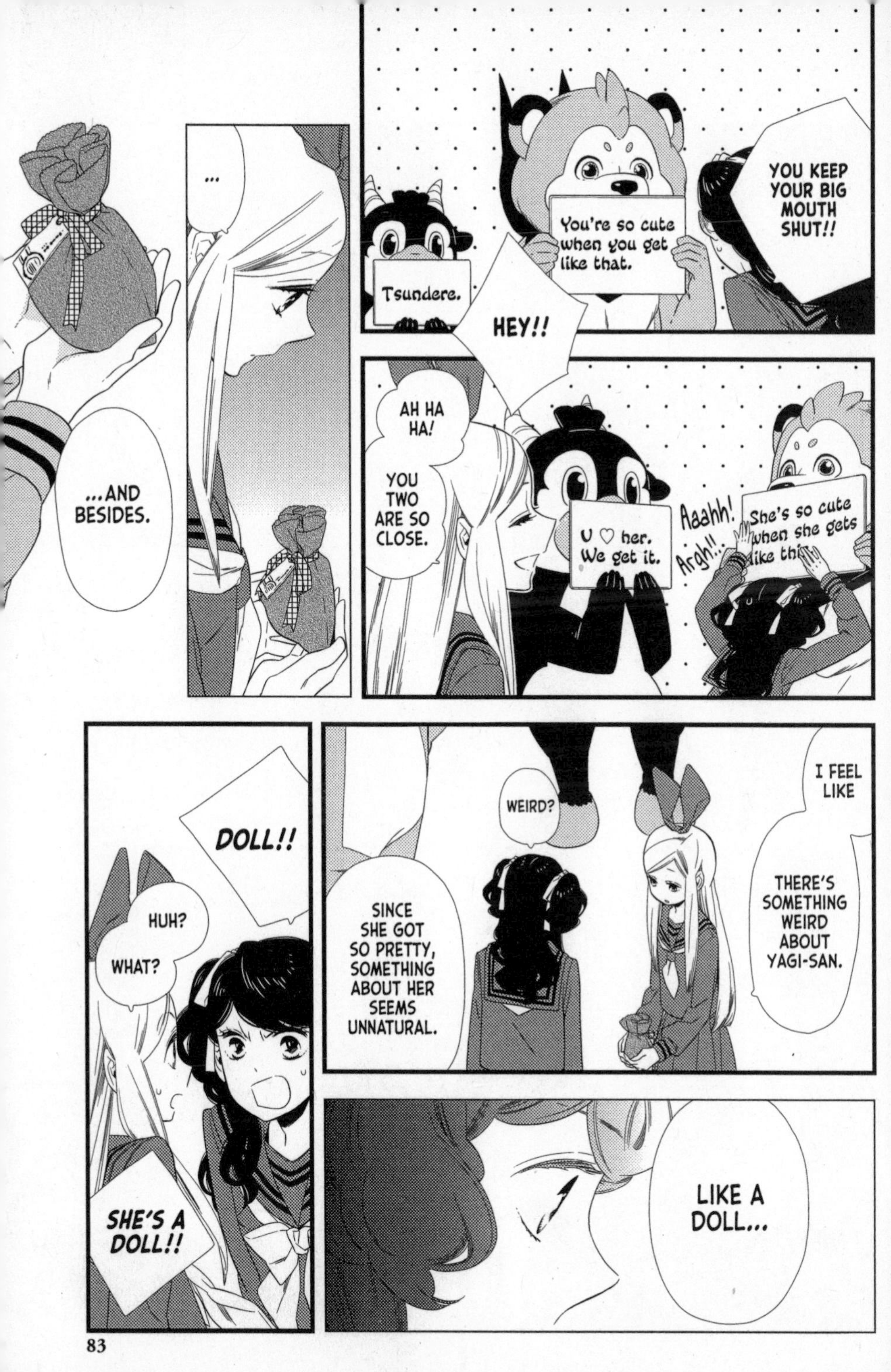
YOU KEEP YOUR BIG MOUTH SHUT!!
You're so cute when you get like that.
Tsundere.
HEY!!
Aaahh!
Argh!!
She's so cute when she gets like thi
U ♡ her. We get it.
AH HA HA!
YOU TWO ARE SO CLOSE.
...
...AND BESIDES.
I FEEL LIKE
THERE'S SOMETHING WEIRD ABOUT YAGI-SAN.
WEIRD?
SINCE SHE GOT SO PRETTY, SOMETHING ABOUT HER SEEMS UNNATURAL.
LIKE A DOLL...
DOLL!!
HUH?
WHAT?
SHE'S A DOLL!!

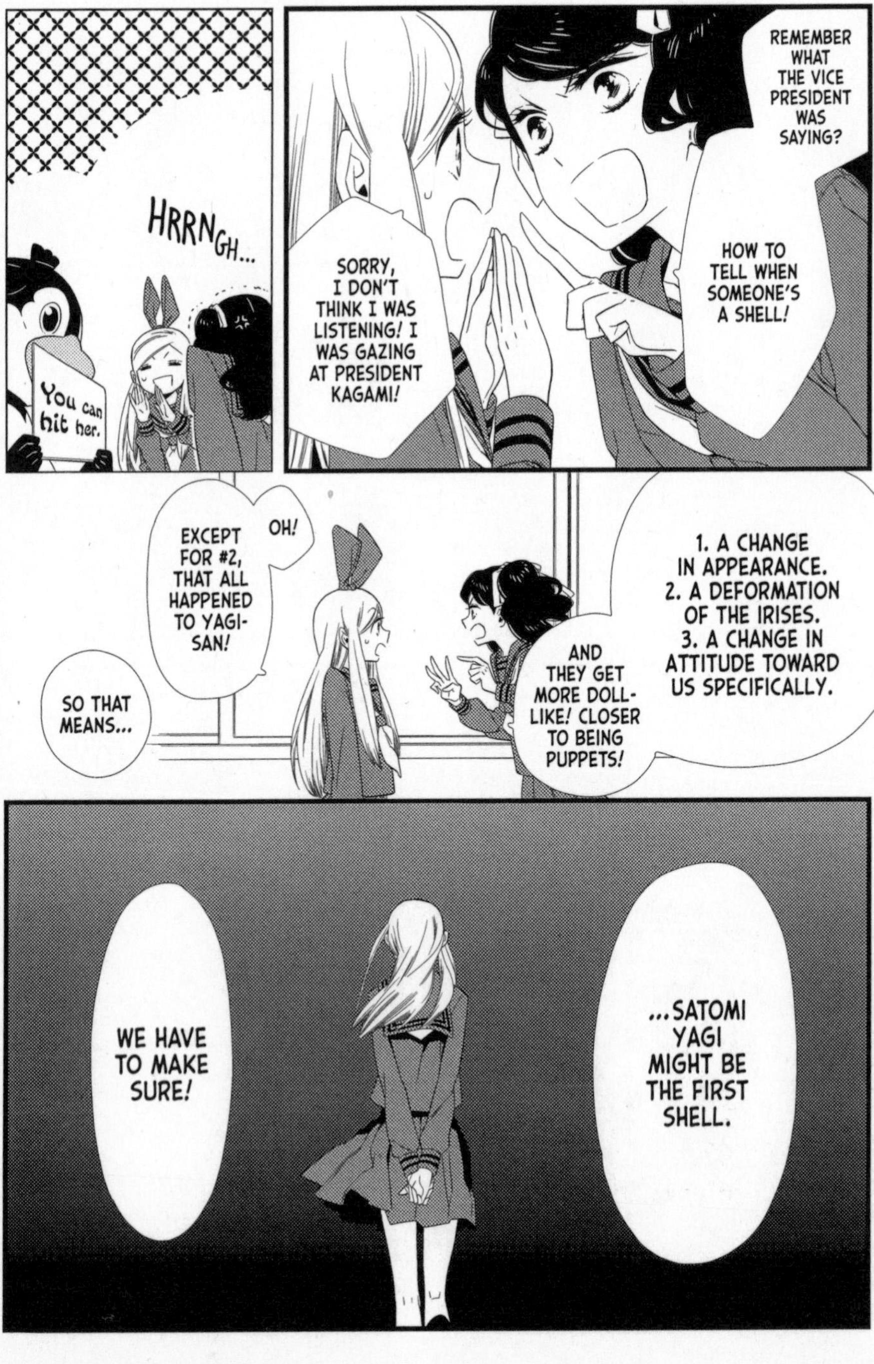
REMEMBER WHAT THE VICE PRESIDENT WAS SAYING?
HOW TO TELL WHEN SOMEONE'S A SHELL!
SORRY, I DON'T THINK I WAS LISTENING! I WAS GAZING AT PRESIDENT KAGAMI!
HRRNGH...
You can hit her.
1. A CHANGE IN APPEARANCE. 2. A DEFORMATION OF THE IRISES. 3. A CHANGE IN ATTITUDE TOWARD US SPECIFICALLY.
AND THEY GET MORE DOLL-LIKE! CLOSER TO BEING PUPPETS!
OH!
EXCEPT FOR #2, THAT ALL HAPPENED TO YAGI-SAN!
SO THAT MEANS...
...SATOMI YAGI MIGHT BE THE FIRST SHELL.
WE HAVE TO MAKE SURE!

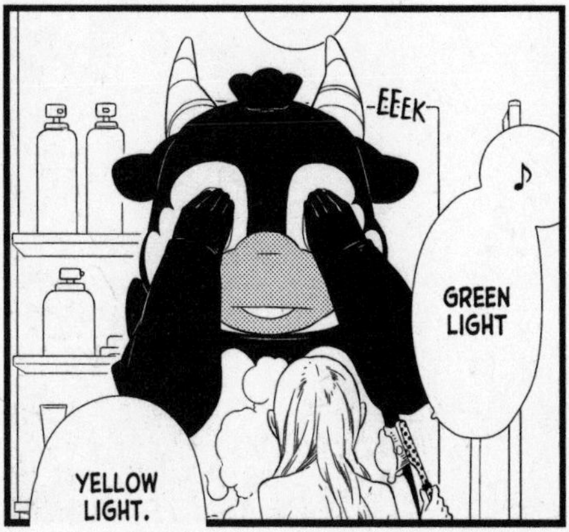
-EEEK-
♪
GREEN LIGHT
YELLOW LIGHT.

Kigurumi GUARDIANS

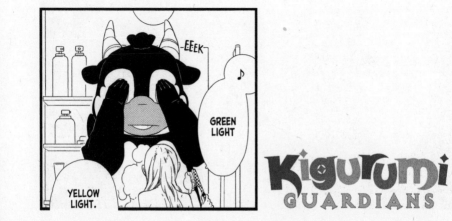

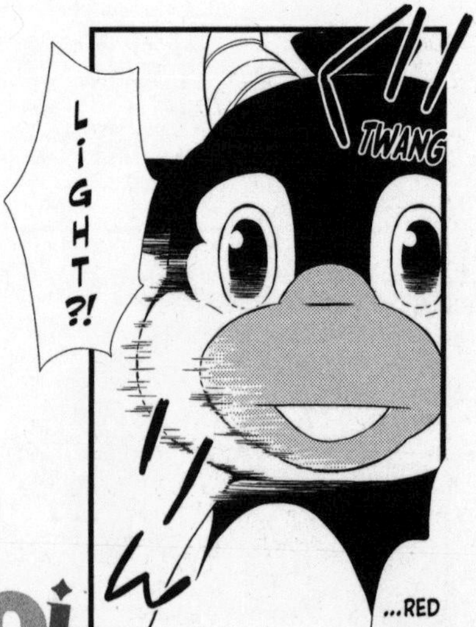
TWANG
LIGHT?!
...RED

Kigurumi
GUARDIANS

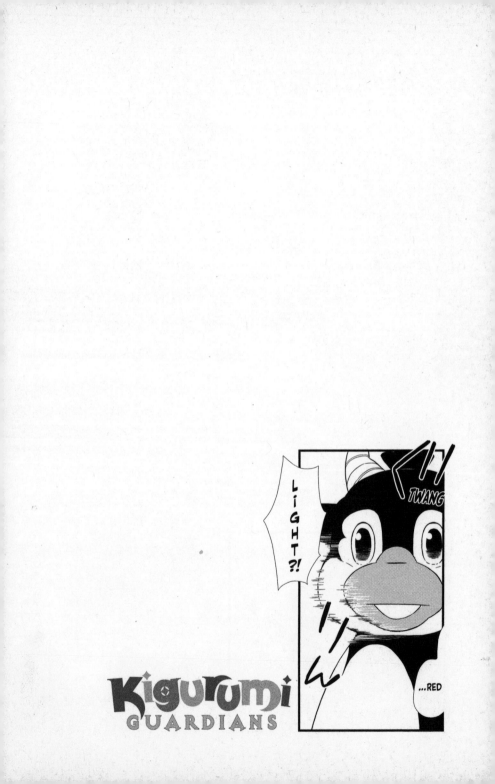

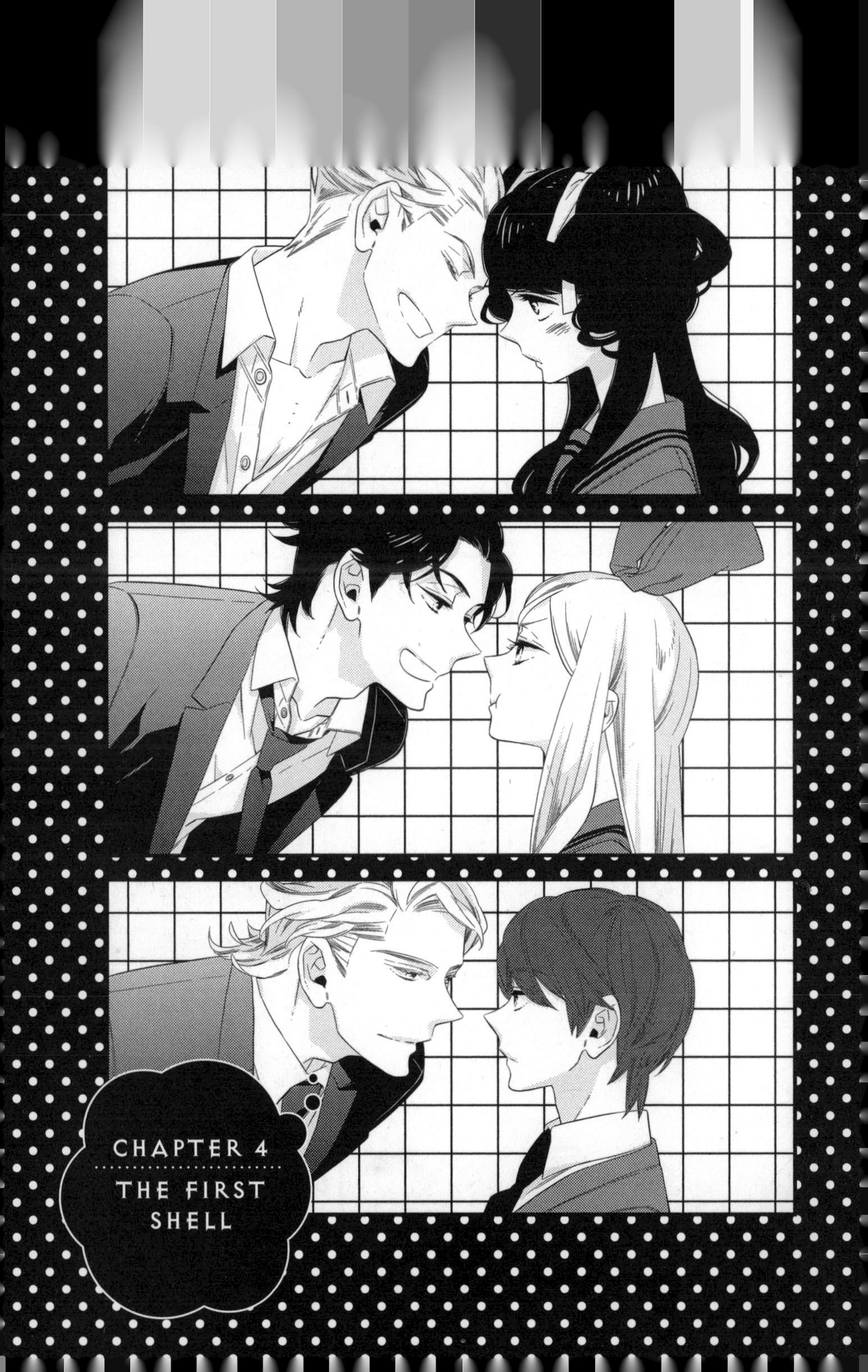
CHAPTER 4
THE FIRST SHELL

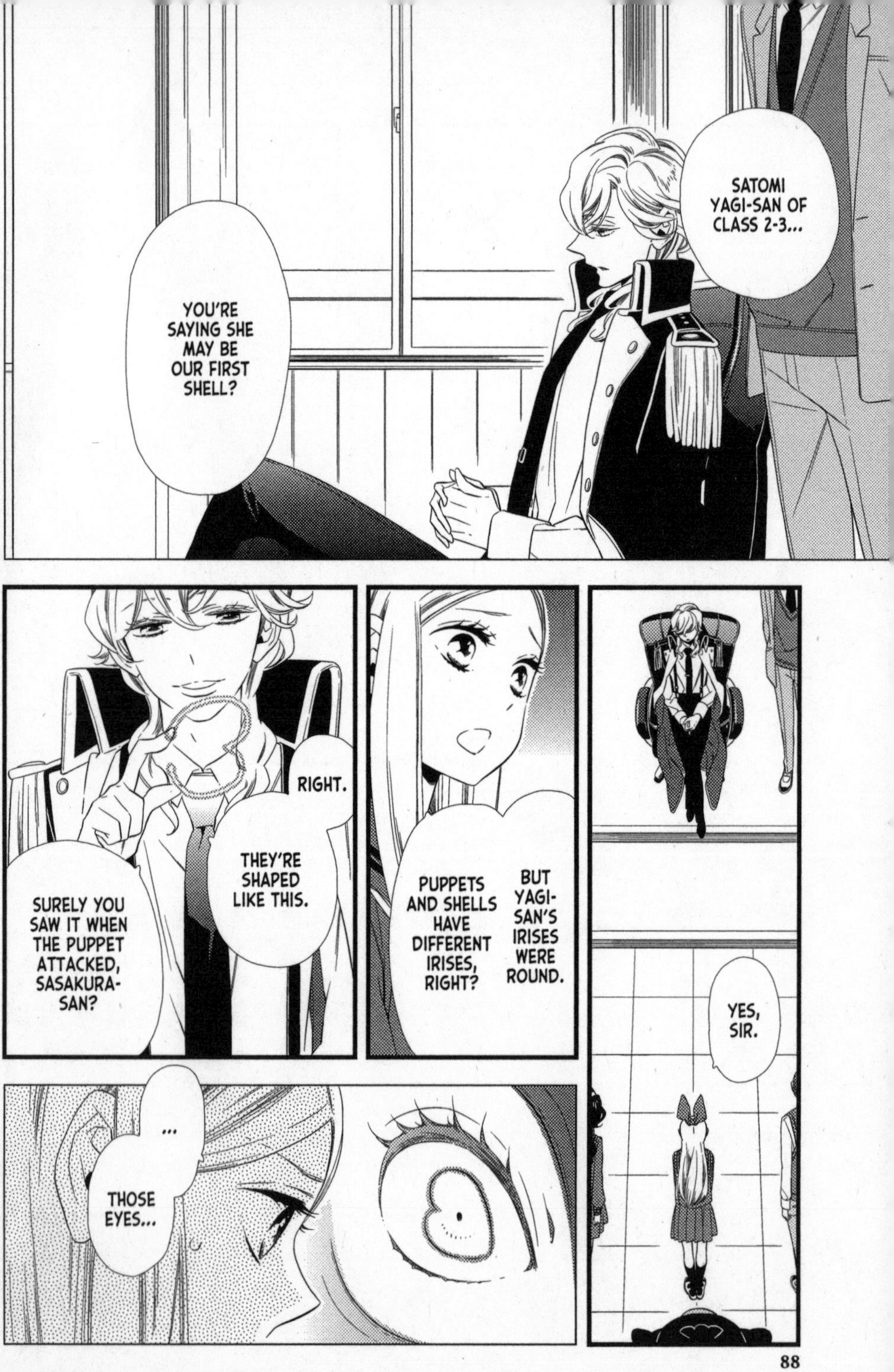
SATOMI YAGI-SAN OF CLASS 2-3...
YOU'RE SAYING SHE MAY BE OUR FIRST SHELL?
YES, SIR.
BUT YAGI-SAN'S IRISES WERE ROUND.
PUPPETS AND SHELLS HAVE DIFFERENT IRISES, RIGHT?
RIGHT.
THEY'RE SHAPED LIKE THIS.
SURELY YOU SAW IT WHEN THE PUPPET ATTACKED, SASAKURA-SAN?
...
THOSE EYES...

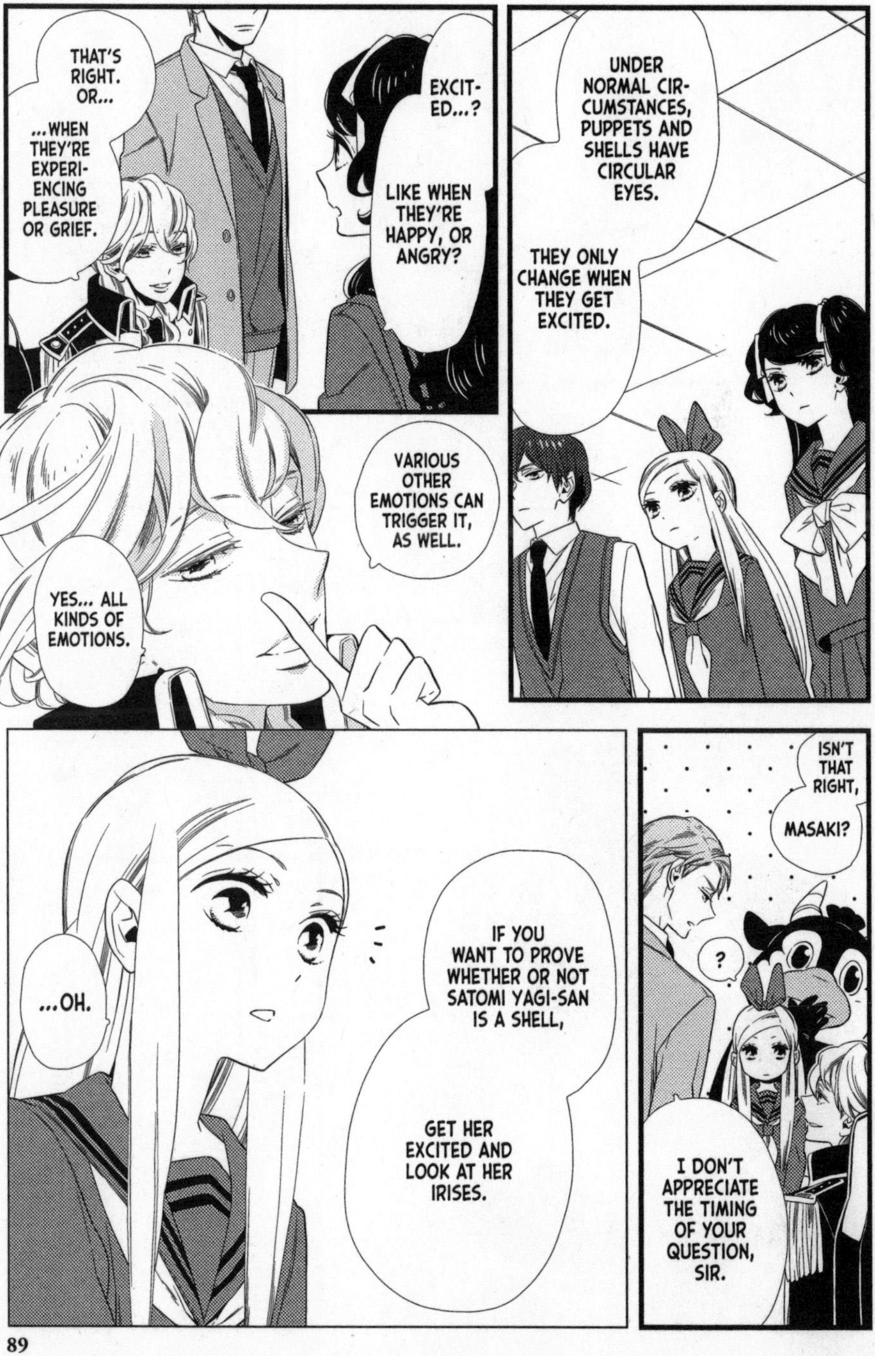
UNDER NORMAL CIRCUMSTANCES, PUPPETS AND SHELLS HAVE CIRCULAR EYES.
THEY ONLY CHANGE WHEN THEY GET EXCITED.
EXCITED...?
LIKE WHEN THEY'RE HAPPY, OR ANGRY?
THAT'S RIGHT. OR...
...WHEN THEY'RE EXPERIENCING PLEASURE OR GRIEF.
VARIOUS OTHER EMOTIONS CAN TRIGGER IT, AS WELL.
YES... ALL KINDS OF EMOTIONS.
ISN'T THAT RIGHT,
MASAKI?
?
I DON'T APPRECIATE THE TIMING OF YOUR QUESTION, SIR.
IF YOU WANT TO PROVE WHETHER OR NOT SATOMI YAGI-SAN IS A SHELL,
GET HER EXCITED AND LOOK AT HER IRISES.
...OH.

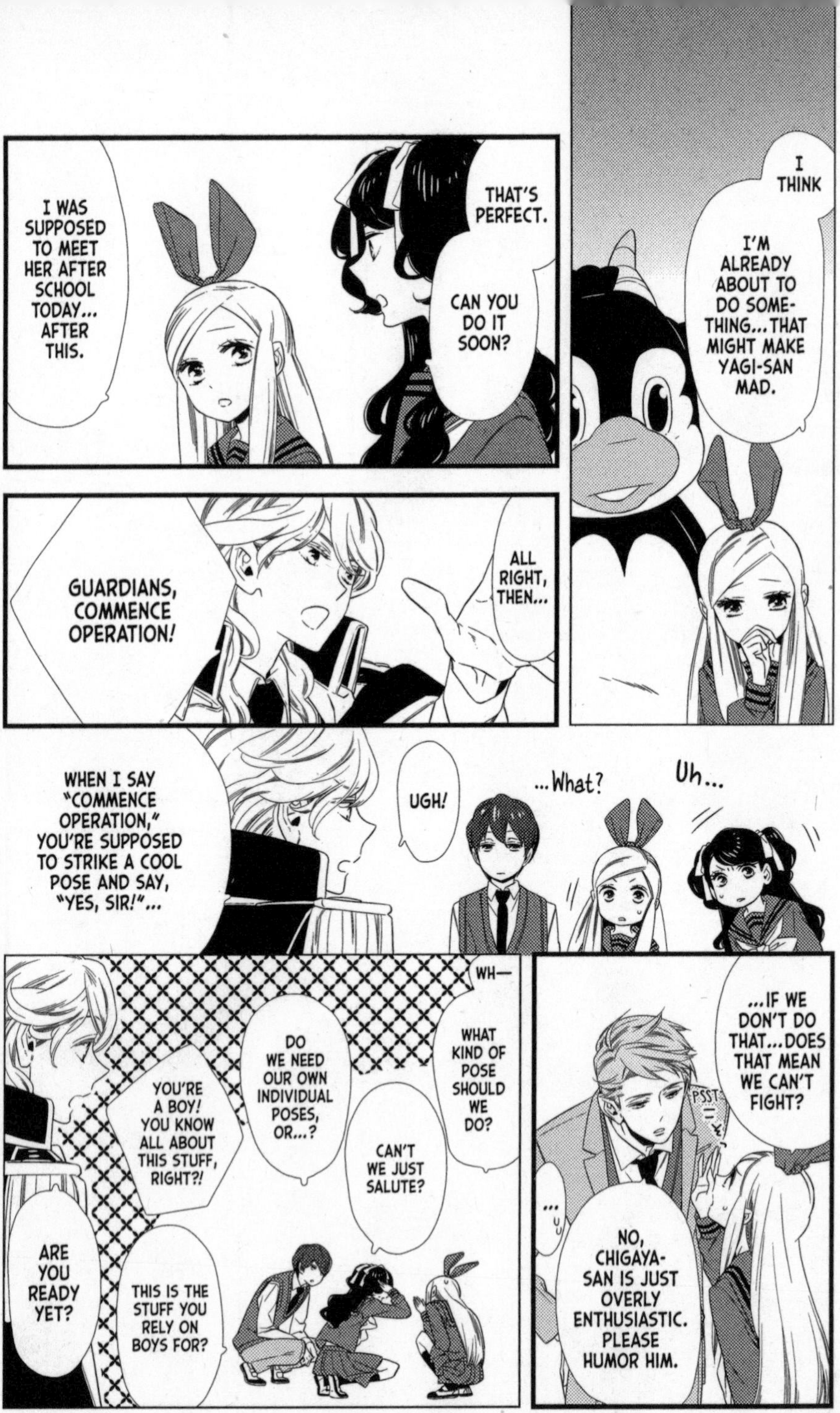
I THINK
I'M ALREADY ABOUT TO DO SOME-THING...THAT MIGHT MAKE YAGI-SAN MAD.
THAT'S PERFECT.
CAN YOU DO IT SOON?
I WAS SUPPOSED TO MEET HER AFTER SCHOOL TODAY... AFTER THIS.
ALL RIGHT, THEN...
GUARDIANS, COMMENCE OPERATION!
Uh...
...What?
UGH!
WHEN I SAY "COMMENCE OPERATION," YOU'RE SUPPOSED TO STRIKE A COOL POSE AND SAY, "YES, SIR!"...
...IF WE DON'T DO THAT...DOES THAT MEAN WE CAN'T FIGHT?
PSST
...
NO, CHIGAYA-SAN IS JUST OVERLY ENTHUSIASTIC. PLEASE HUMOR HIM.
WH—
WHAT KIND OF POSE SHOULD WE DO?
DO WE NEED OUR OWN INDIVIDUAL POSES, OR...?
CAN'T WE JUST SALUTE?
YOU'RE A BOY! YOU KNOW ALL ABOUT THIS STUFF, RIGHT?!
THIS IS THE STUFF YOU RELY ON BOYS FOR?
ARE YOU READY YET?

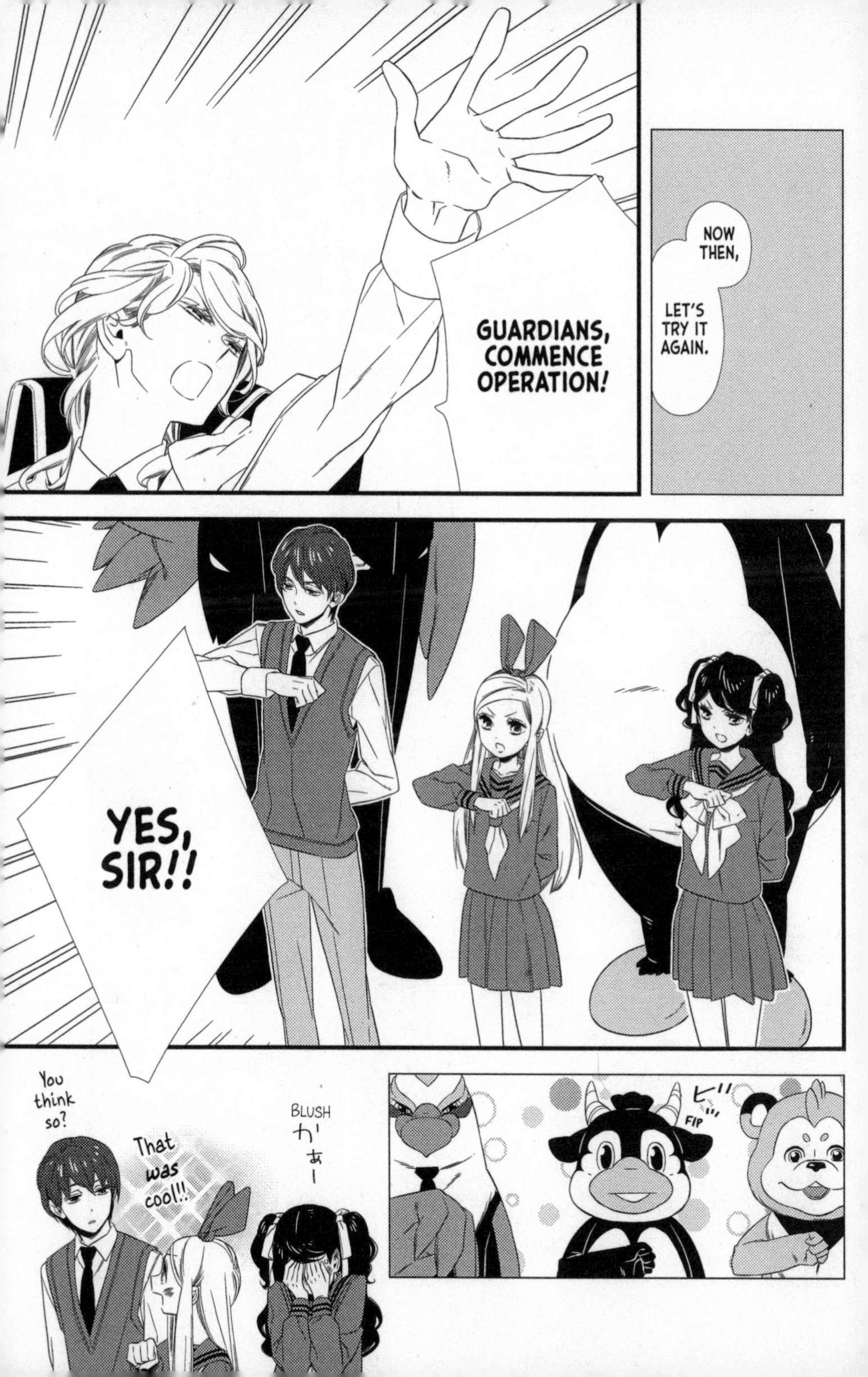
NOW THEN,
LET'S TRY IT AGAIN.
GUARDIANS, COMMENCE OPERATION!
YES, SIR!!
ビッ
FIP
BLUSH
かぁー
That was cool!!
You think so?

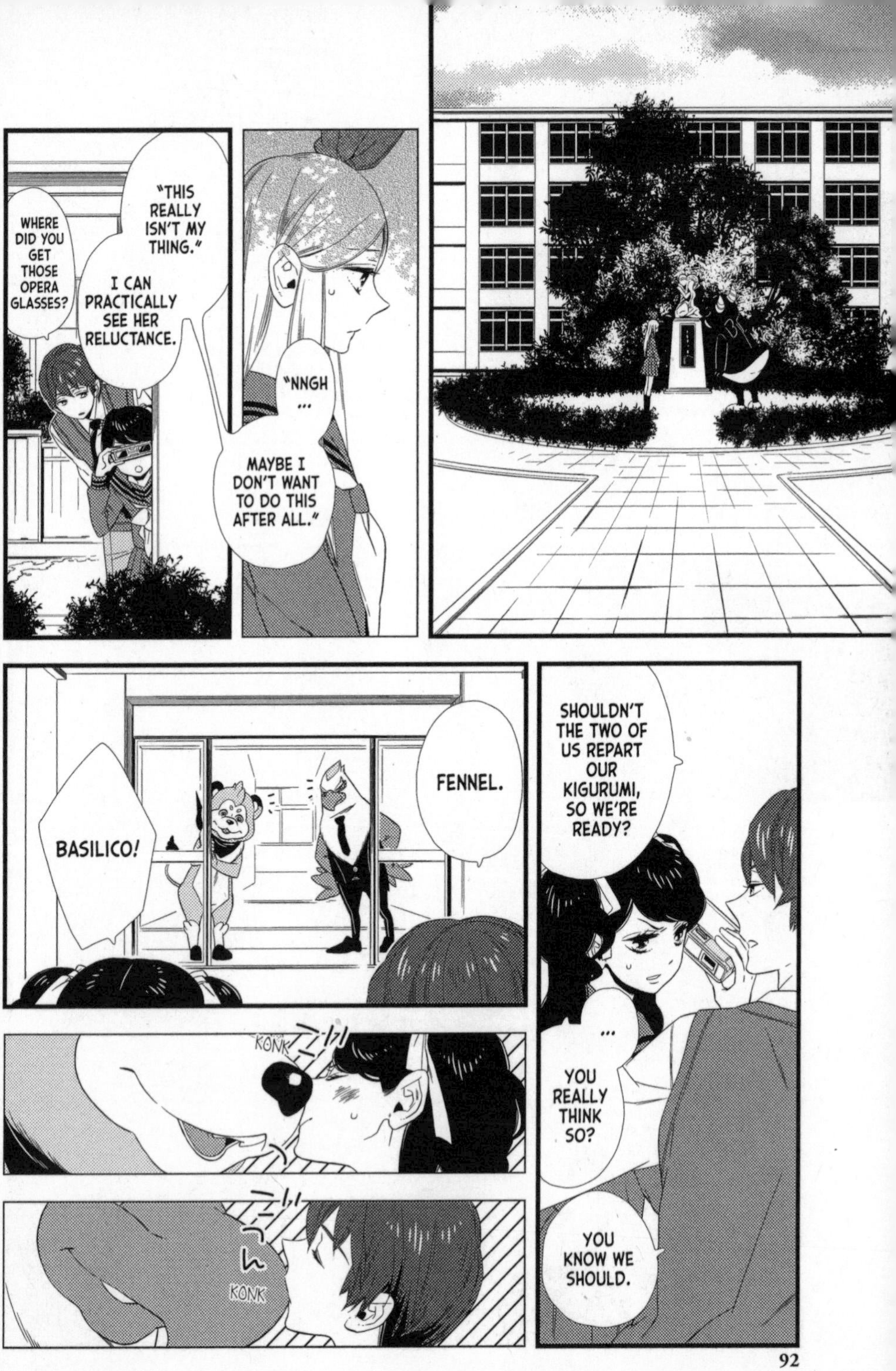
"NNGH ...
MAYBE I DON'T WANT TO DO THIS AFTER ALL."
"THIS REALLY ISN'T MY THING."
I CAN PRACTICALLY SEE HER RELUCTANCE.
WHERE DID YOU GET THOSE OPERA GLASSES?
SHOULDN'T THE TWO OF US REPART OUR KIGURUMI, SO WE'RE READY?
...
YOU REALLY THINK SO?
YOU KNOW WE SHOULD.
FENNEL.
BASILICO!
KONK
KONK

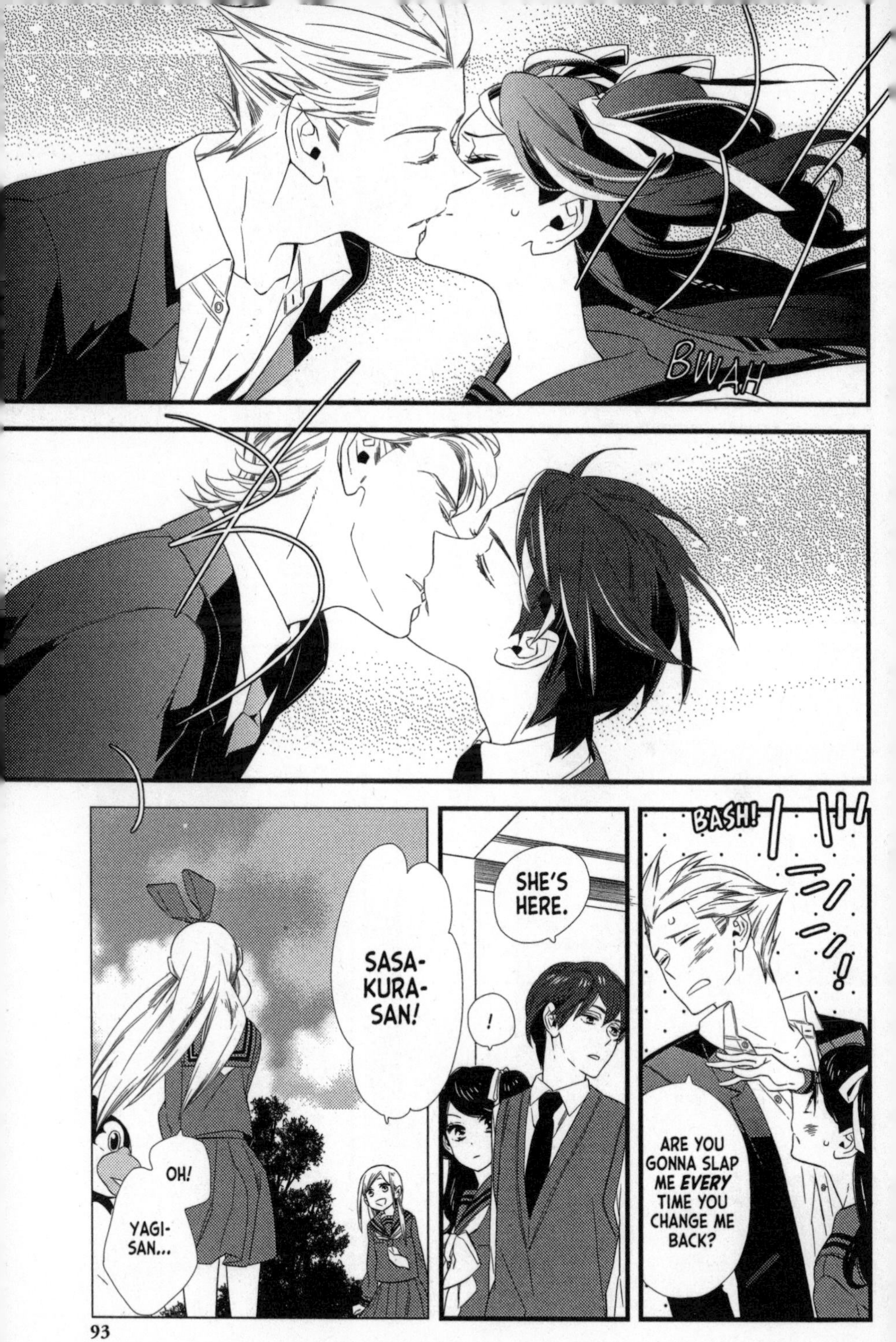
BWAH
BASH!
ARE YOU GONNA SLAP ME *EVERY* TIME YOU CHANGE ME BACK?
SHE'S HERE.
!
SASA-KURA-SAN!
OH!
YAGI-SAN...

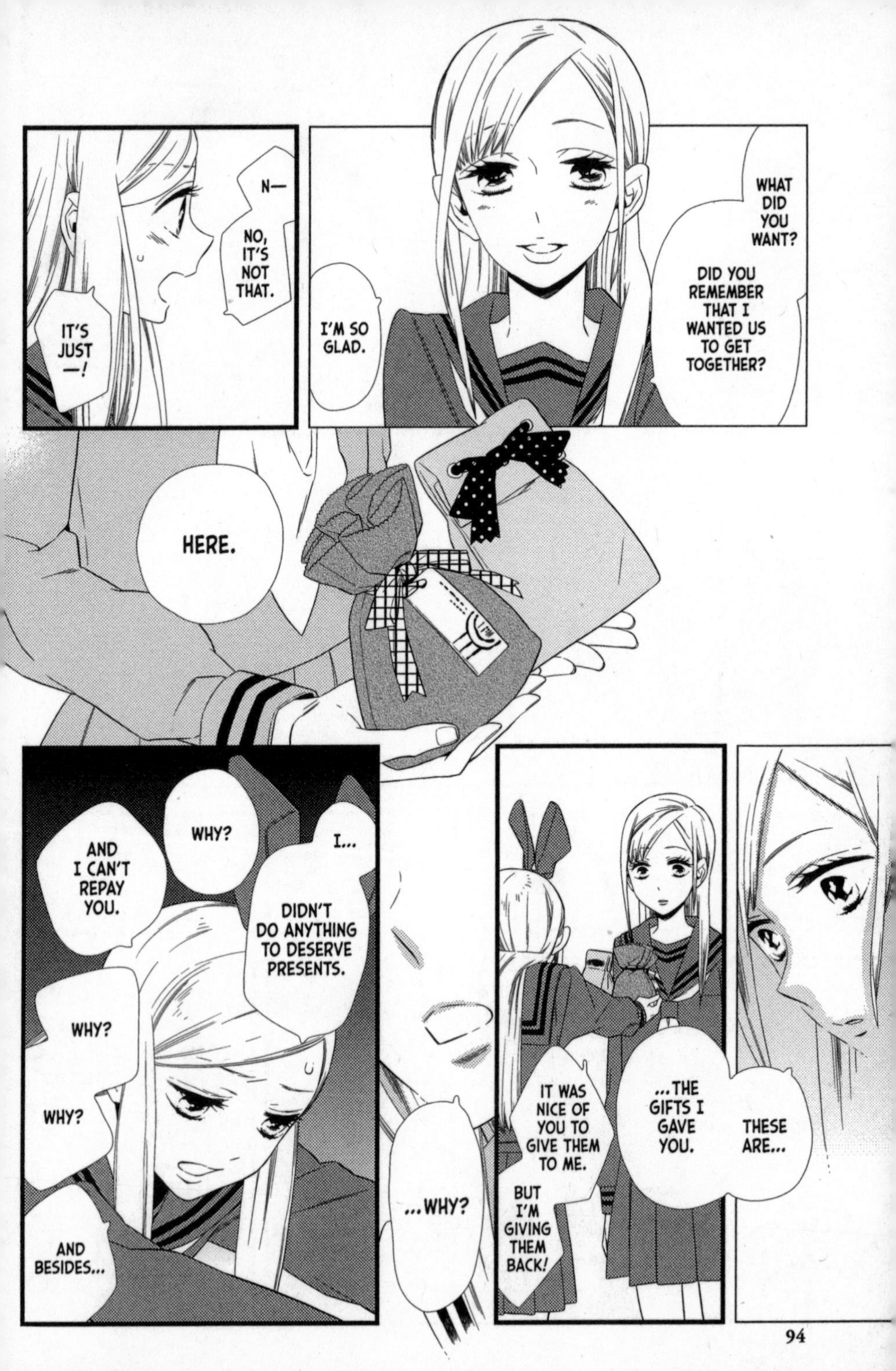
WHAT DID YOU WANT?
DID YOU REMEMBER THAT I WANTED US TO GET TOGETHER?
I'M SO GLAD.
N—
NO, IT'S NOT THAT.
IT'S JUST —!
HERE.
THESE ARE...
...THE GIFTS I GAVE YOU.
IT WAS NICE OF YOU TO GIVE THEM TO ME.
BUT I'M GIVING THEM BACK!
...WHY?
I...
DIDN'T DO ANYTHING TO DESERVE PRESENTS.
WHY?
AND I CAN'T REPAY YOU.
WHY?
WHY?
AND BESIDES...

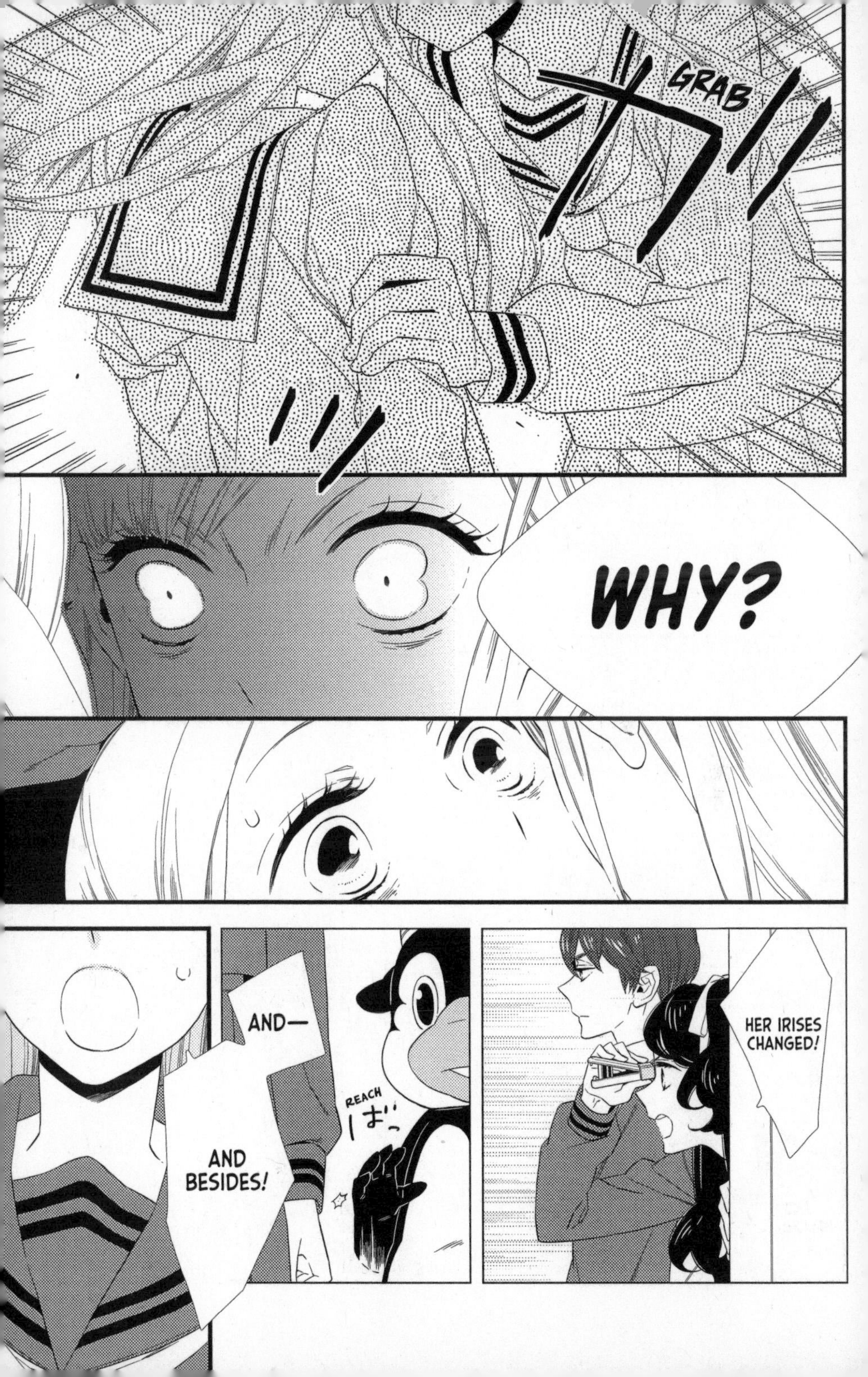
GRAB
WHY?
HER IRISES CHANGED!
AND—
REACH
AND BESIDES!

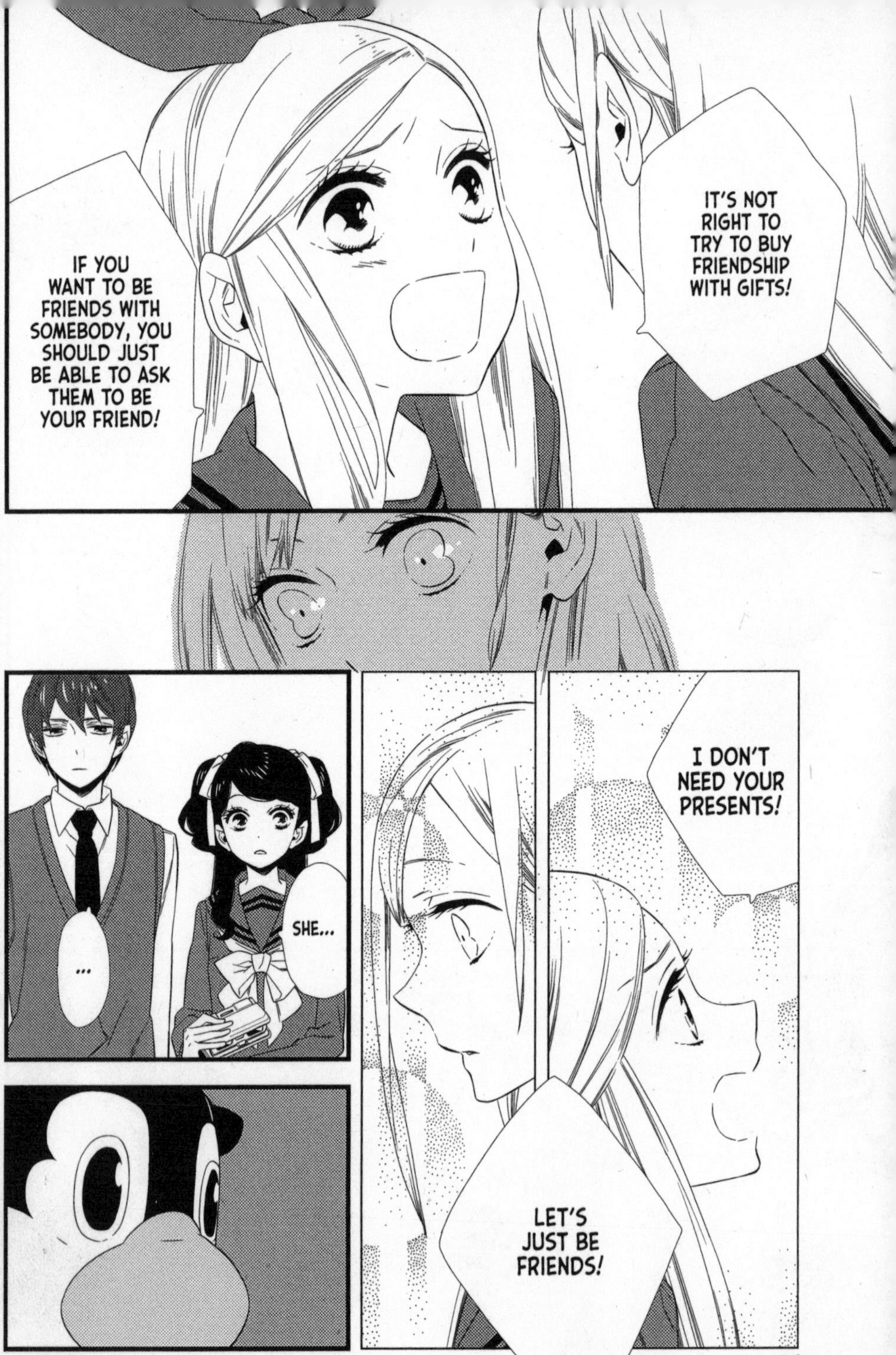
IT'S NOT RIGHT TO TRY TO BUY FRIENDSHIP WITH GIFTS!
IF YOU WANT TO BE FRIENDS WITH SOMEBODY, YOU SHOULD JUST BE ABLE TO ASK THEM TO BE YOUR FRIEND!
I DON'T NEED YOUR PRESENTS!
LET'S JUST BE FRIENDS!
SHE...
...

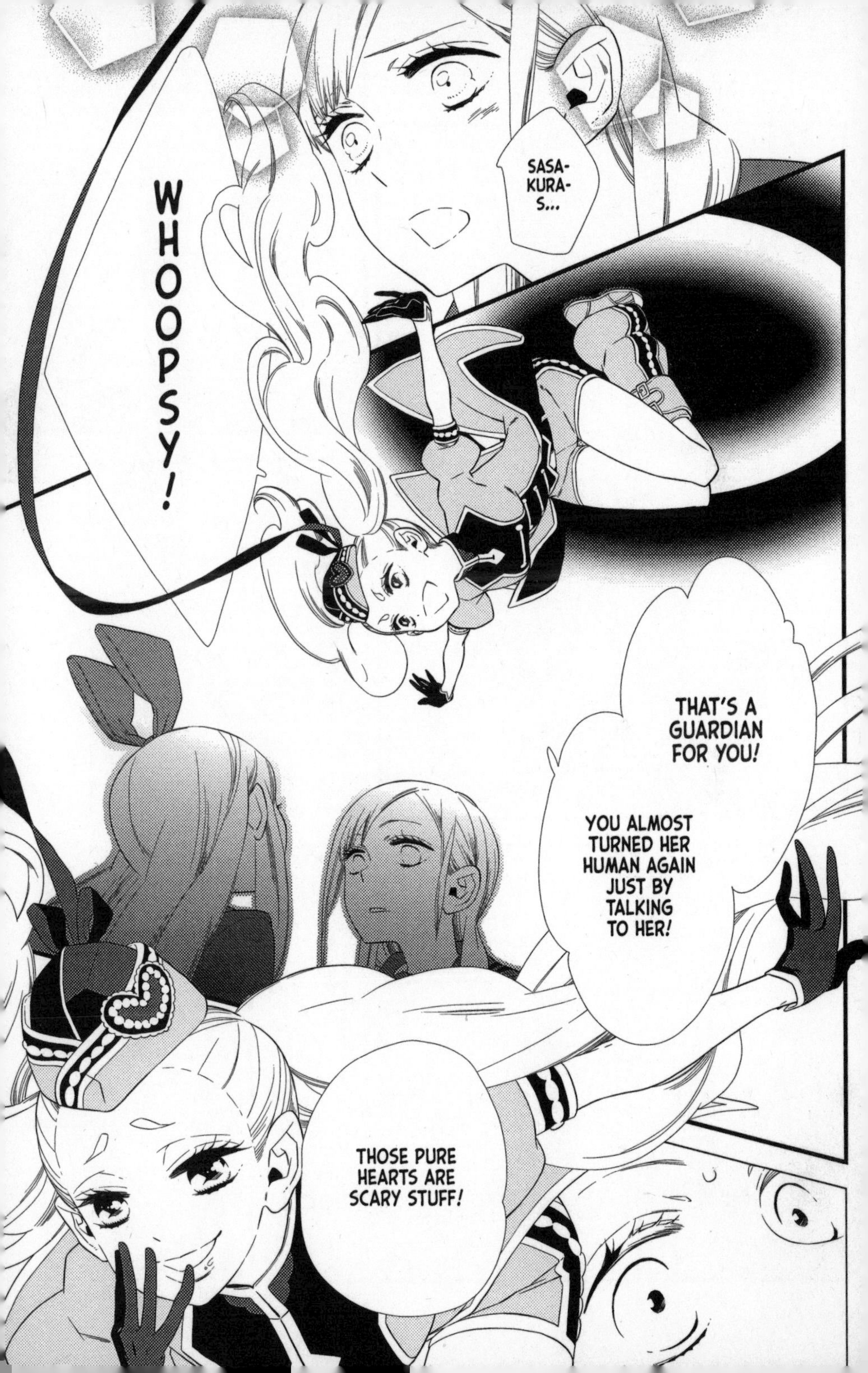
SASA-KURA-S...
WHOOPSY!
THAT'S A GUARDIAN FOR YOU!
YOU ALMOST TURNED HER HUMAN AGAIN JUST BY TALKING TO HER!
THOSE PURE HEARTS ARE SCARY STUFF!

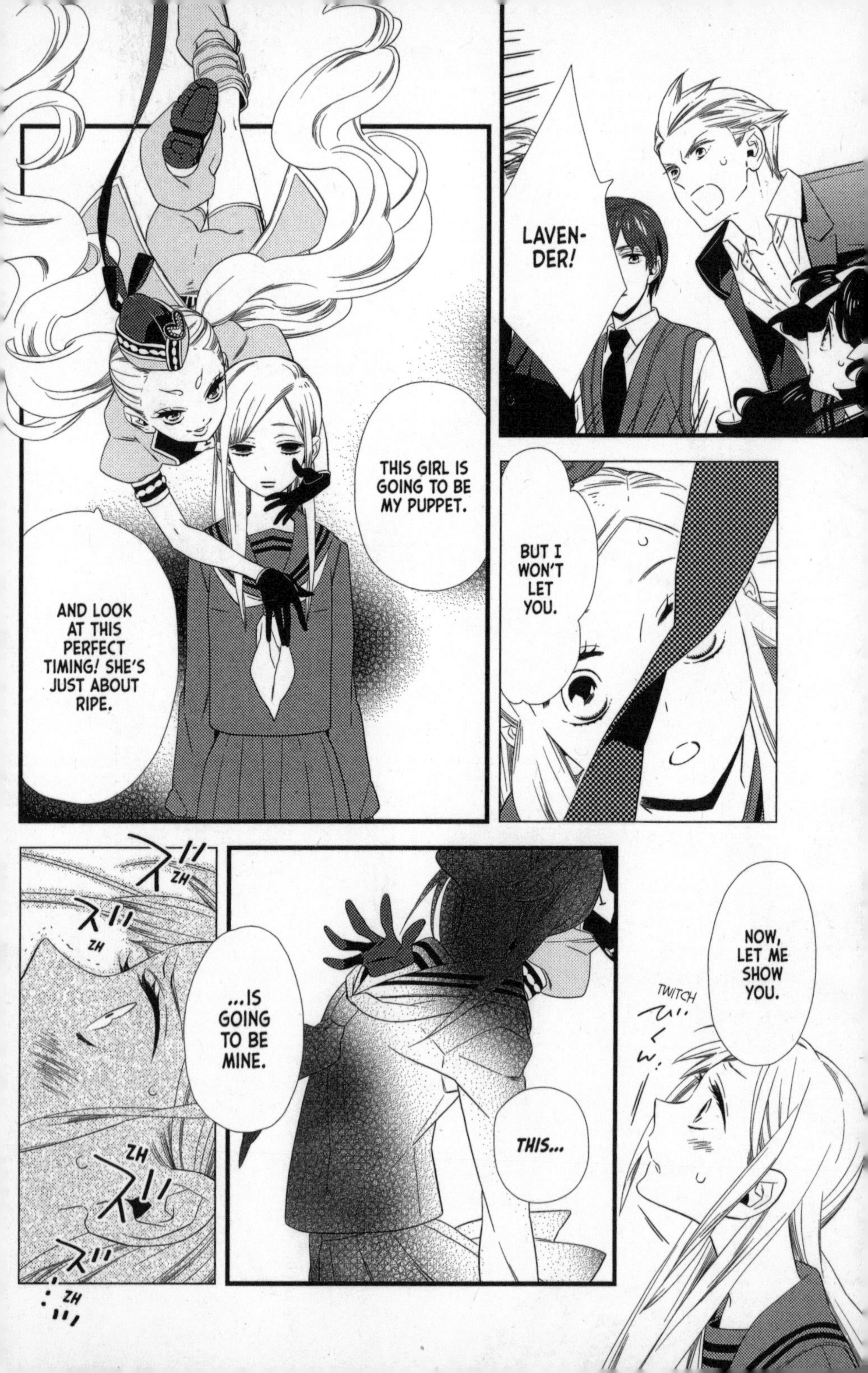
LAVENDER!
BUT I WON'T LET YOU.
THIS GIRL IS GOING TO BE MY PUPPET.
AND LOOK AT THIS PERFECT TIMING! SHE'S JUST ABOUT RIPE.
NOW, LET ME SHOW YOU.
TWITCH
THIS...
...IS GOING TO BE MINE.
ZH
ZH
ZH
ZH

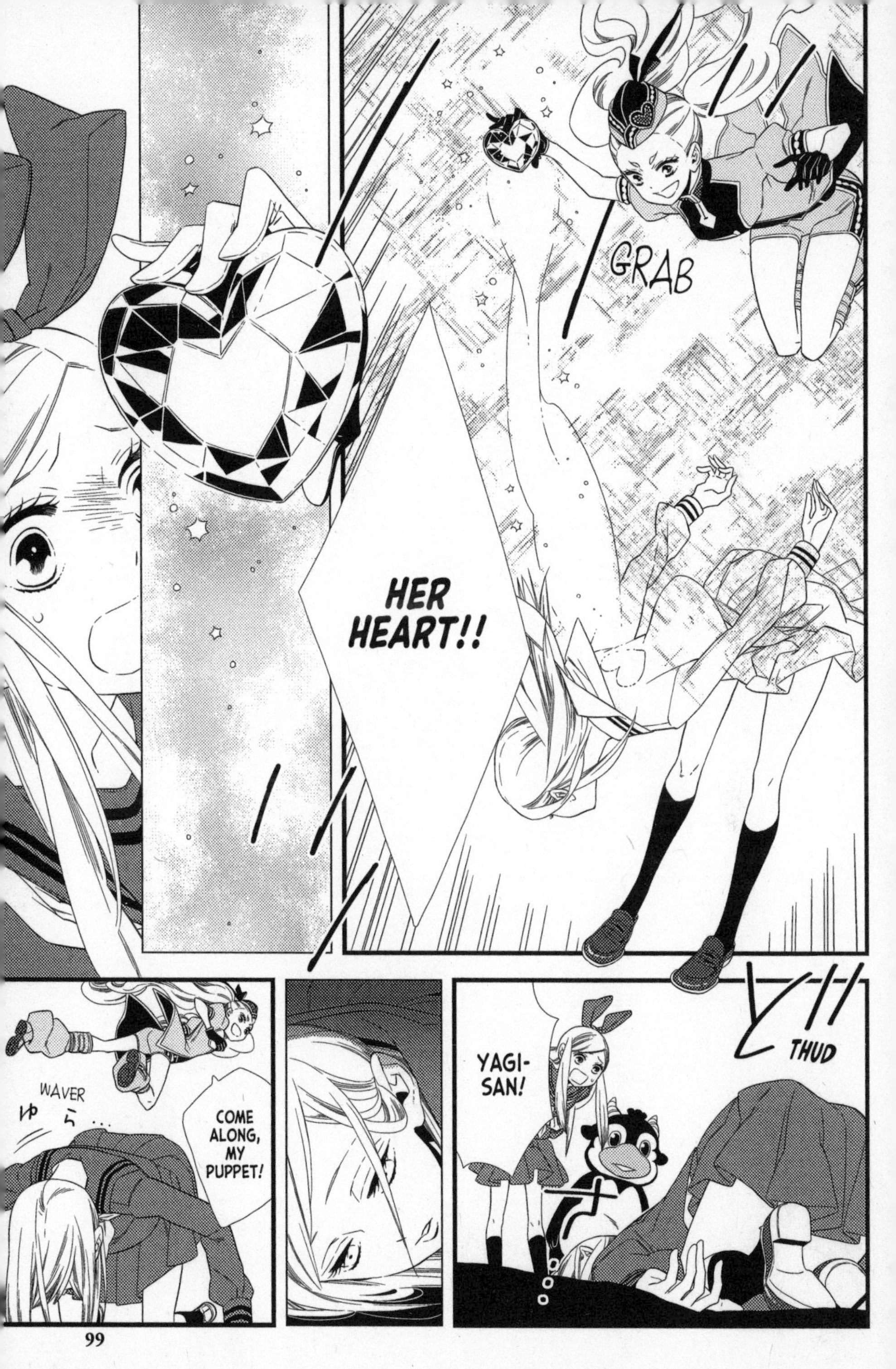
GRAB
HER HEART!!
THUD
YAGI-SAN!
WAVER
ゆら...
COME ALONG, MY PUPPET!

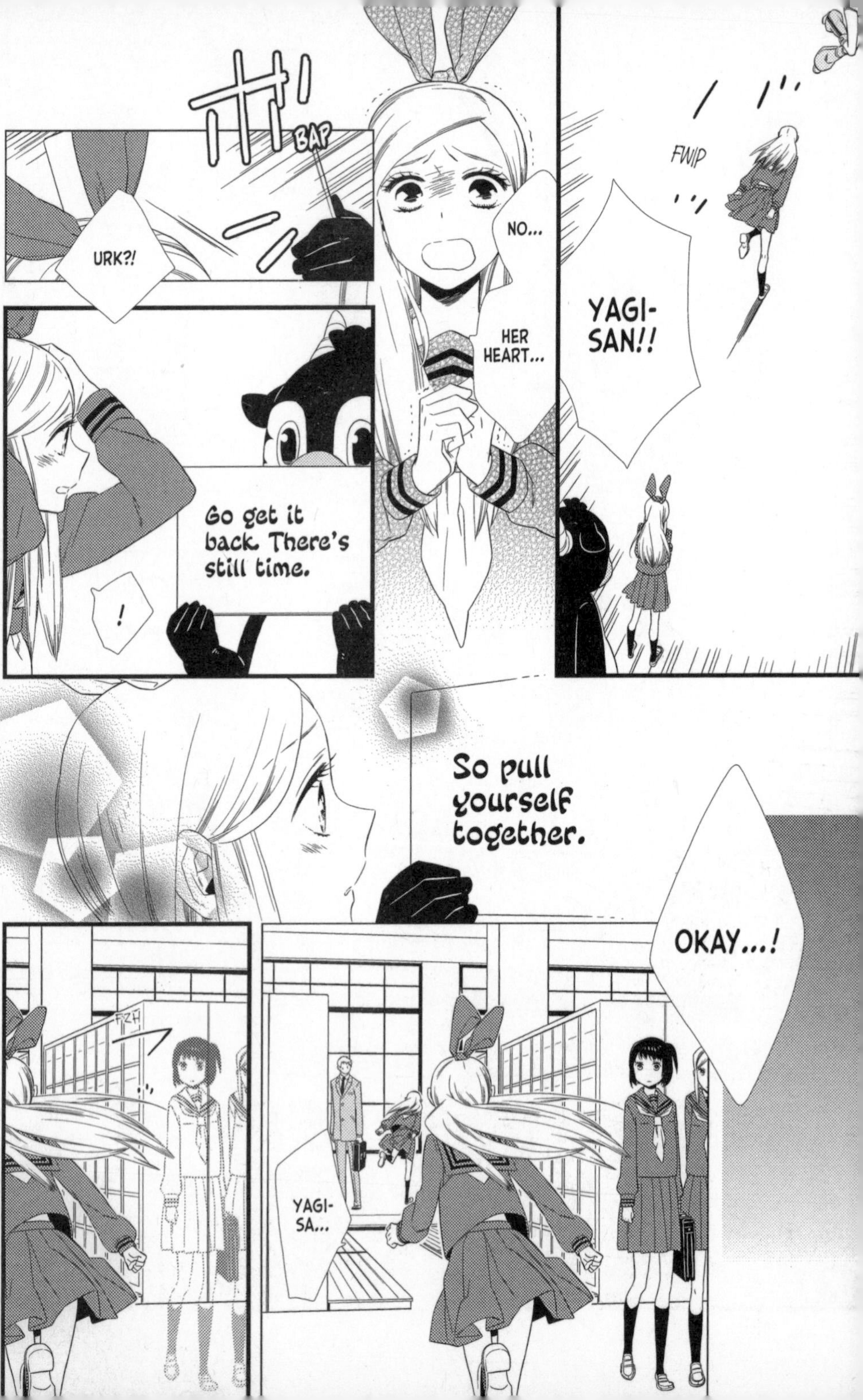
FWIP
YAGI-SAN!!
NO...
HER HEART...
BAP
URK?!
Go get it back. There's still time.
!
So pull yourself together.
OKAY...!
YAGI-SA...

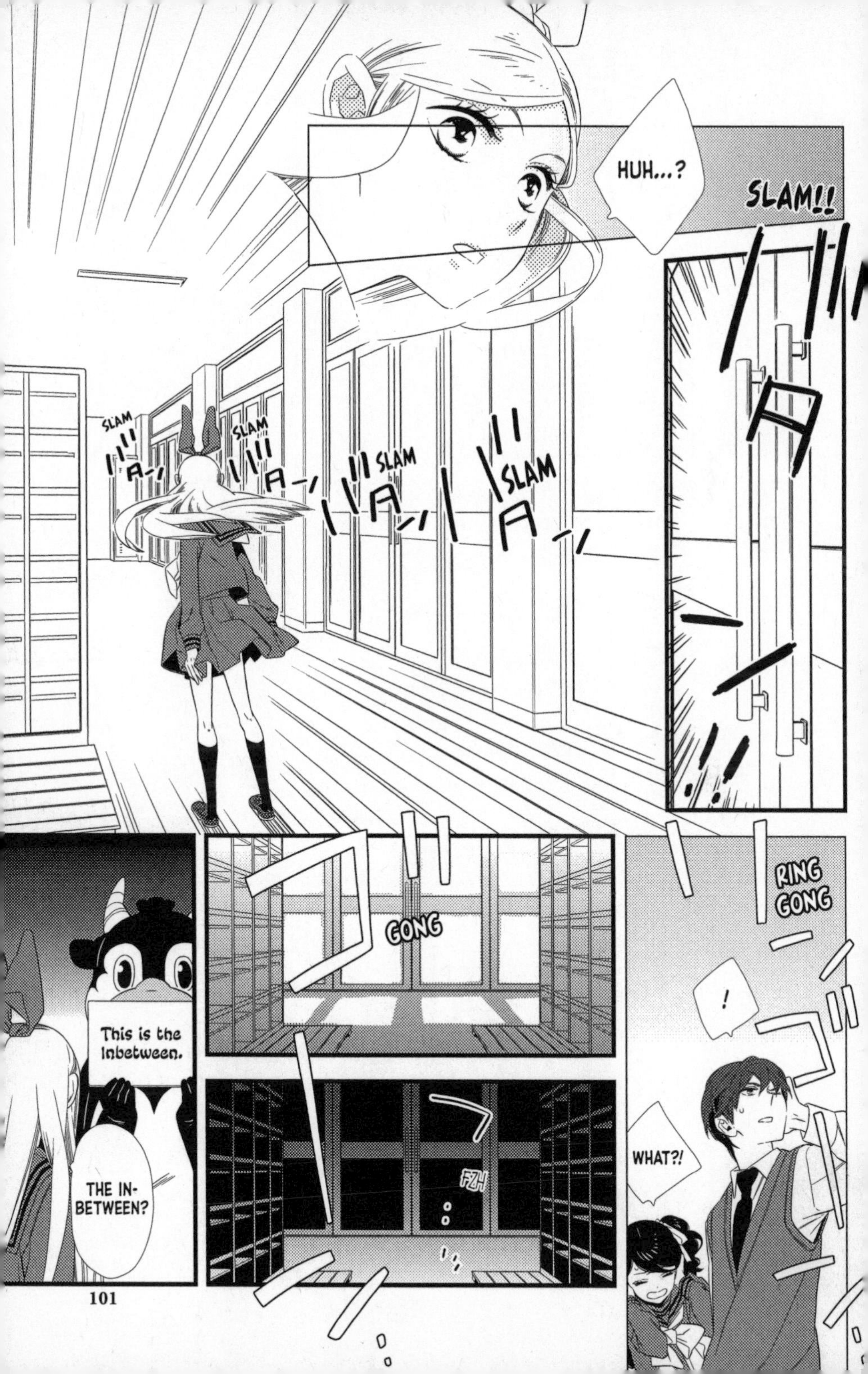
SLAM!!
HUH...?
SLAM
SLAM
SLAM
SLAM
RING GONG
!
WHAT?!
GONG
FZH
This is the Inbetween.
THE IN-BETWEEN?

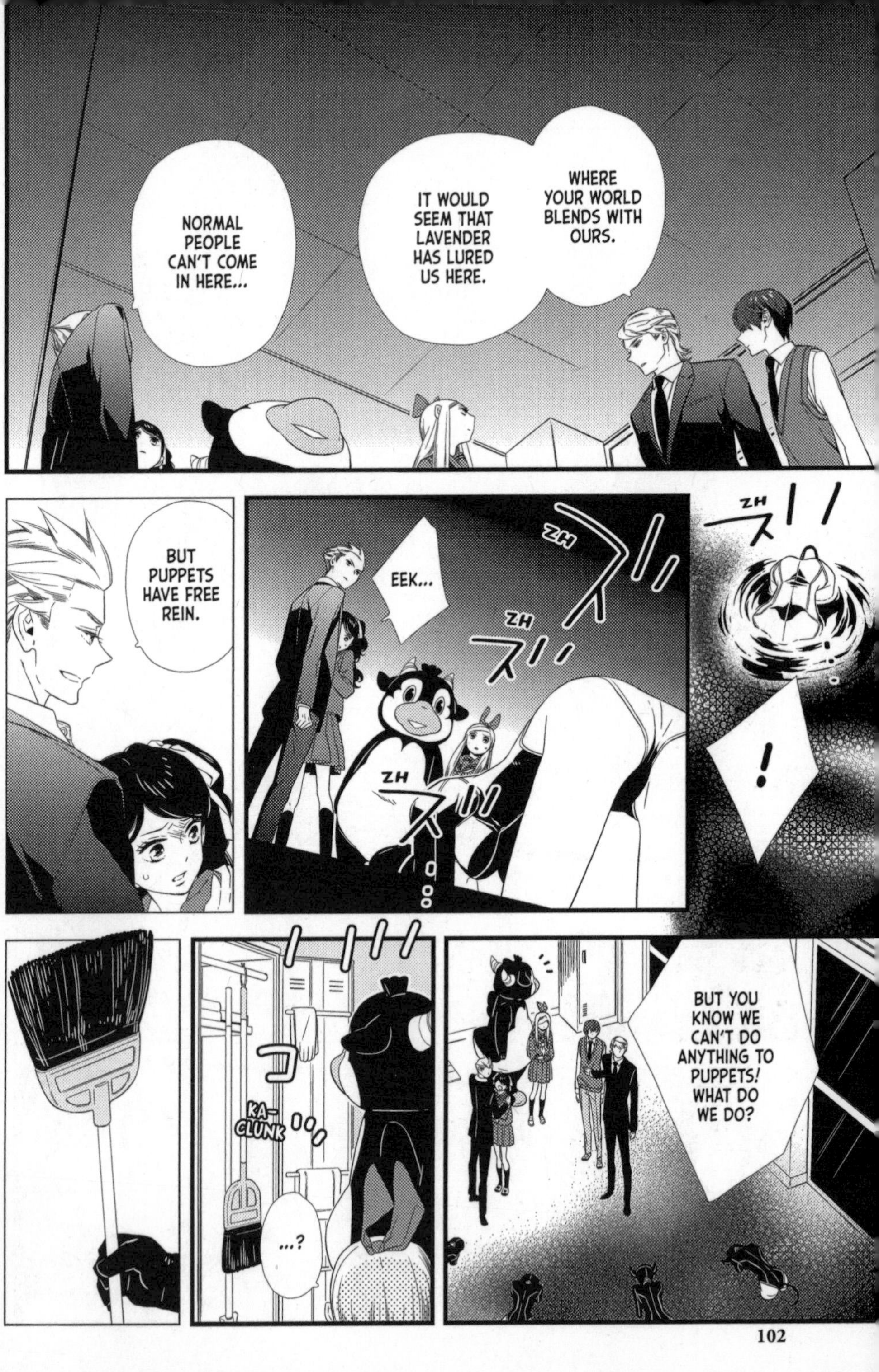
WHERE YOUR WORLD BLENDS WITH OURS.
IT WOULD SEEM THAT LAVENDER HAS LURED US HERE.
NORMAL PEOPLE CAN'T COME IN HERE...
ZH
!
ZH
EEK...
ZH
ZH
BUT PUPPETS HAVE FREE REIN.
BUT YOU KNOW WE CAN'T DO ANYTHING TO PUPPETS! WHAT DO WE DO?
KA-CLUNK
...?

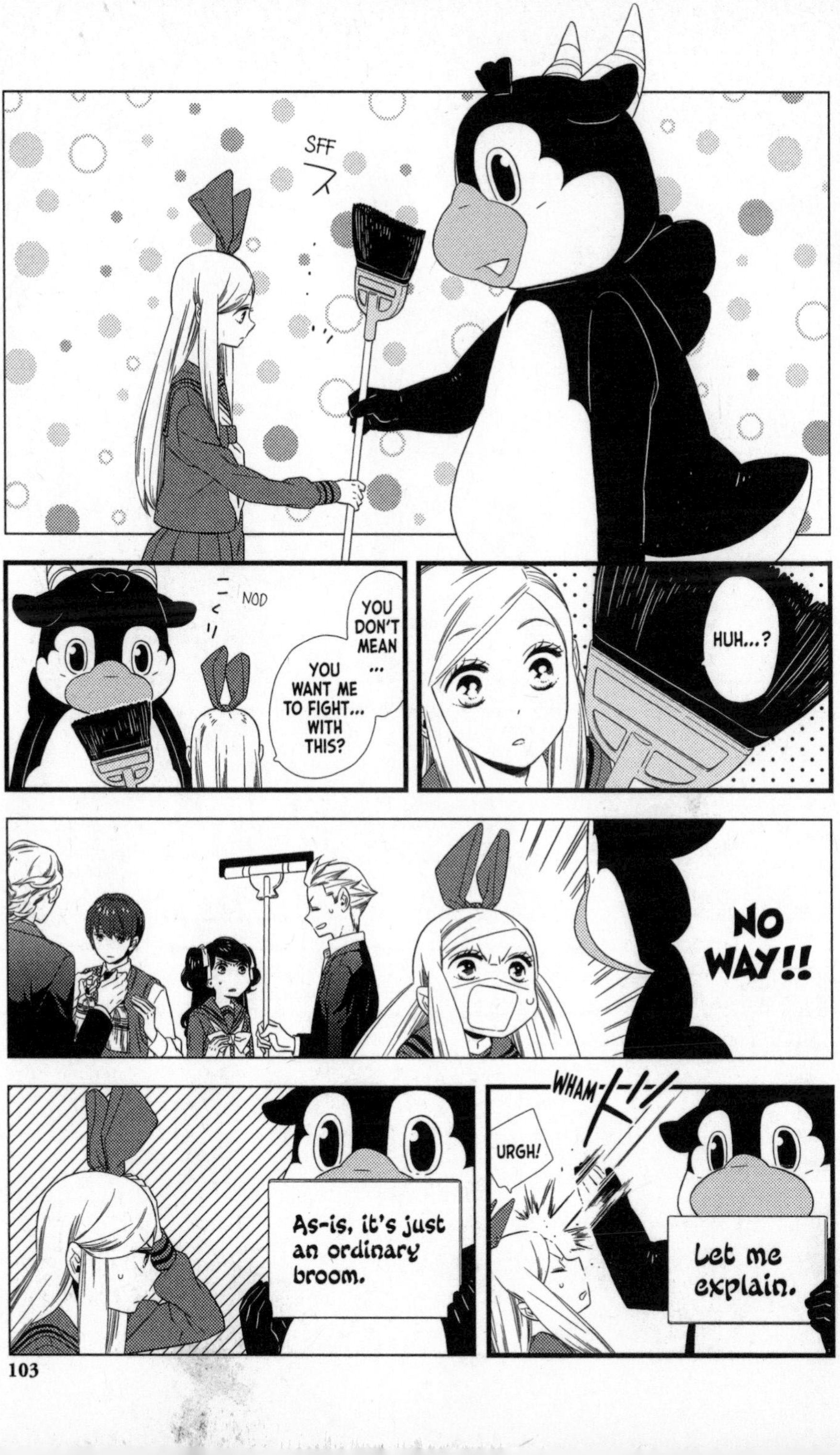
SFF
ス
HUH...?
YOU DON'T MEAN ... YOU WANT ME TO FIGHT... WITH THIS?
NOD
NO WAY!!
WHAM
URGH!
Let me explain.
As-is, it's just an ordinary broom.

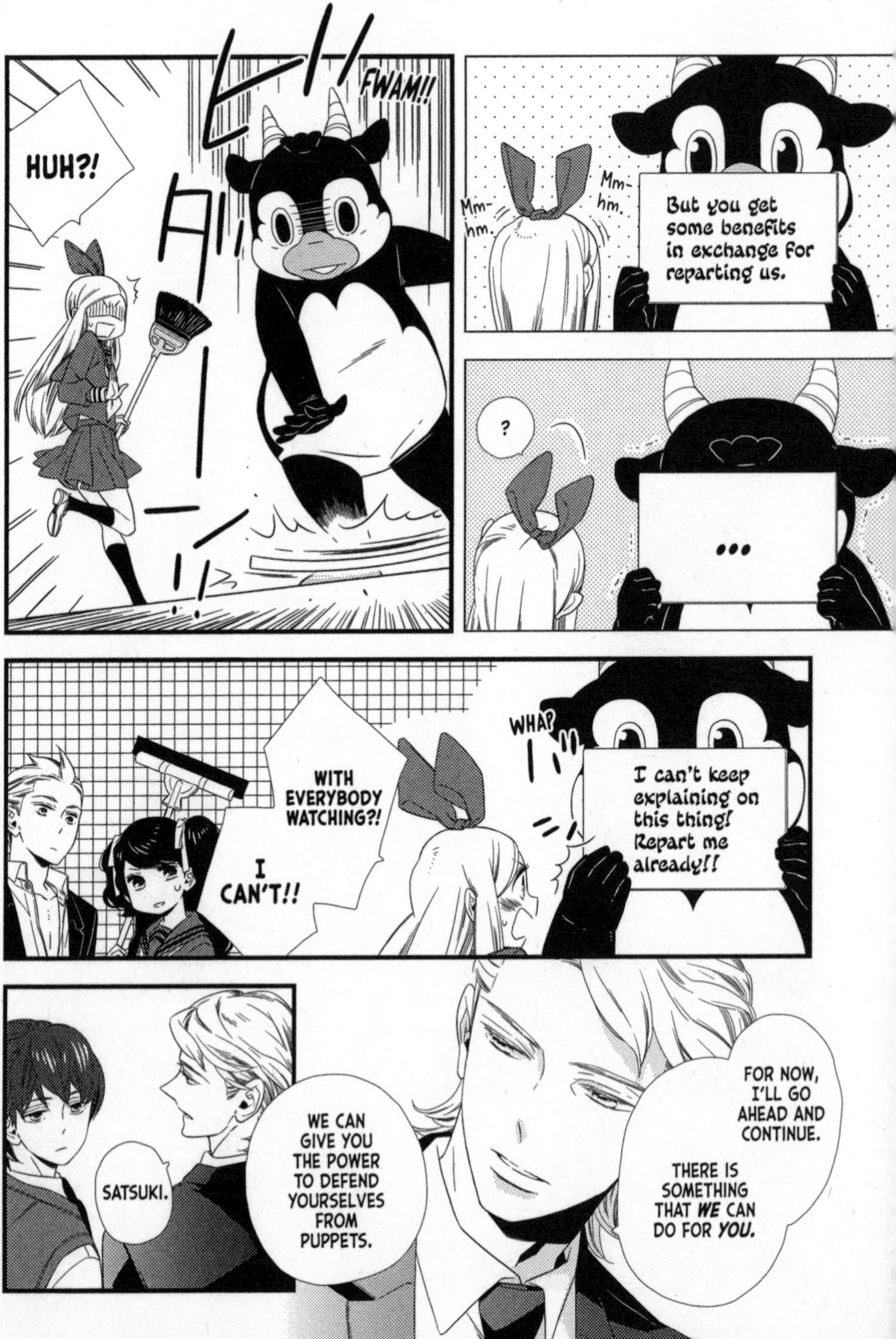
But you get some benefits in exchange for reparting us.
Mm-hm.
Mm-hm.
?
...
FWAM!!
HUH?!
I can't keep explaining on this thing! Repart me already!!
WHAP
WITH EVERYBODY WATCHING?!
I CAN'T!!
FOR NOW, I'LL GO AHEAD AND CONTINUE.
THERE IS SOMETHING THAT *WE* CAN DO FOR *YOU.*
WE CAN GIVE YOU THE POWER TO DEFEND YOURSELVES FROM PUPPETS.
SATSUKI.

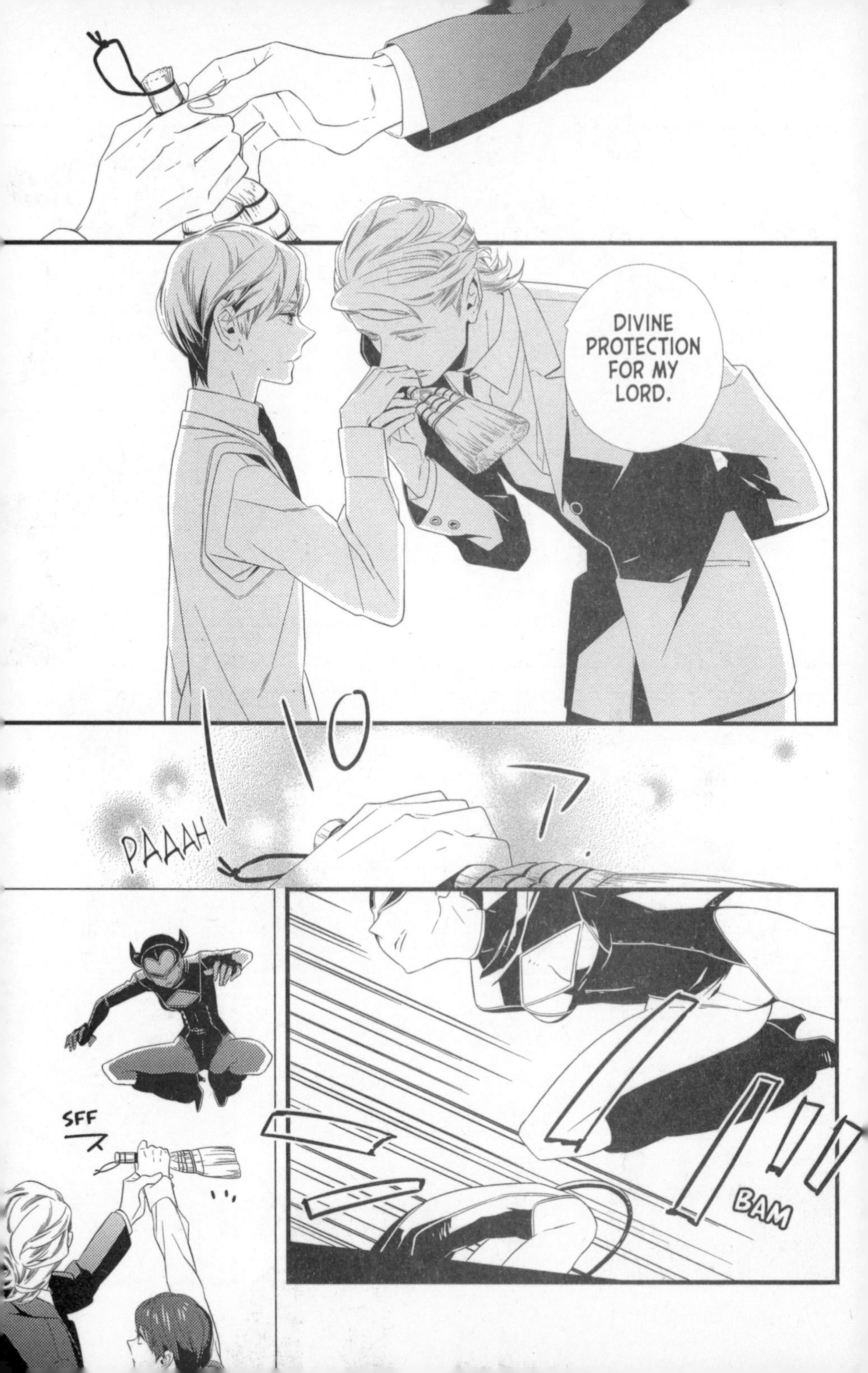
DIVINE PROTECTION FOR MY LORD.
PAAAH
BAM
SFF

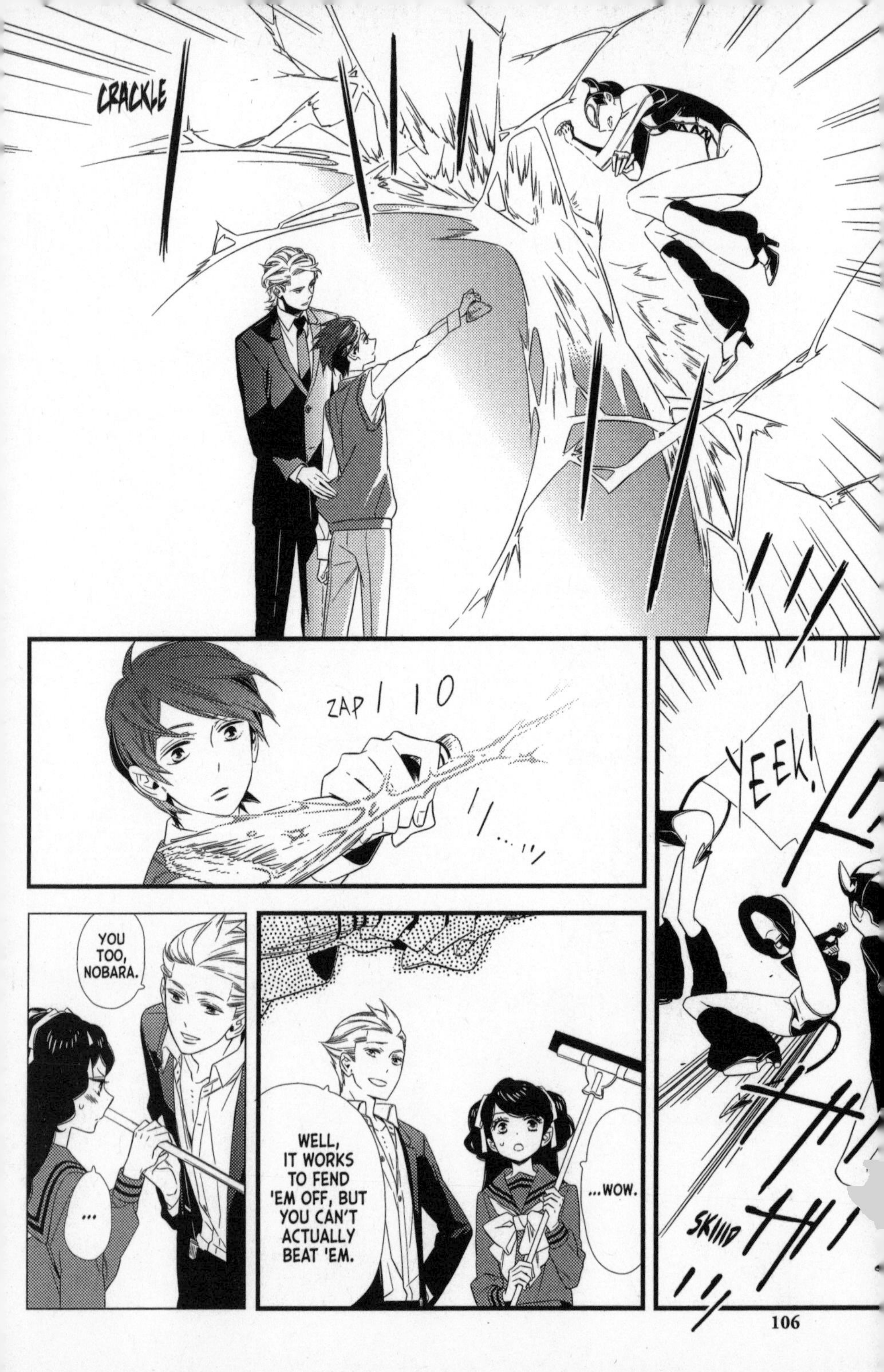
CRACKLE
YEEK!
SKIIID
ZAP
...!!
...WOW.
WELL, IT WORKS TO FEND 'EM OFF, BUT YOU CAN'T ACTUALLY BEAT 'EM.
YOU TOO, NOBARA.
...

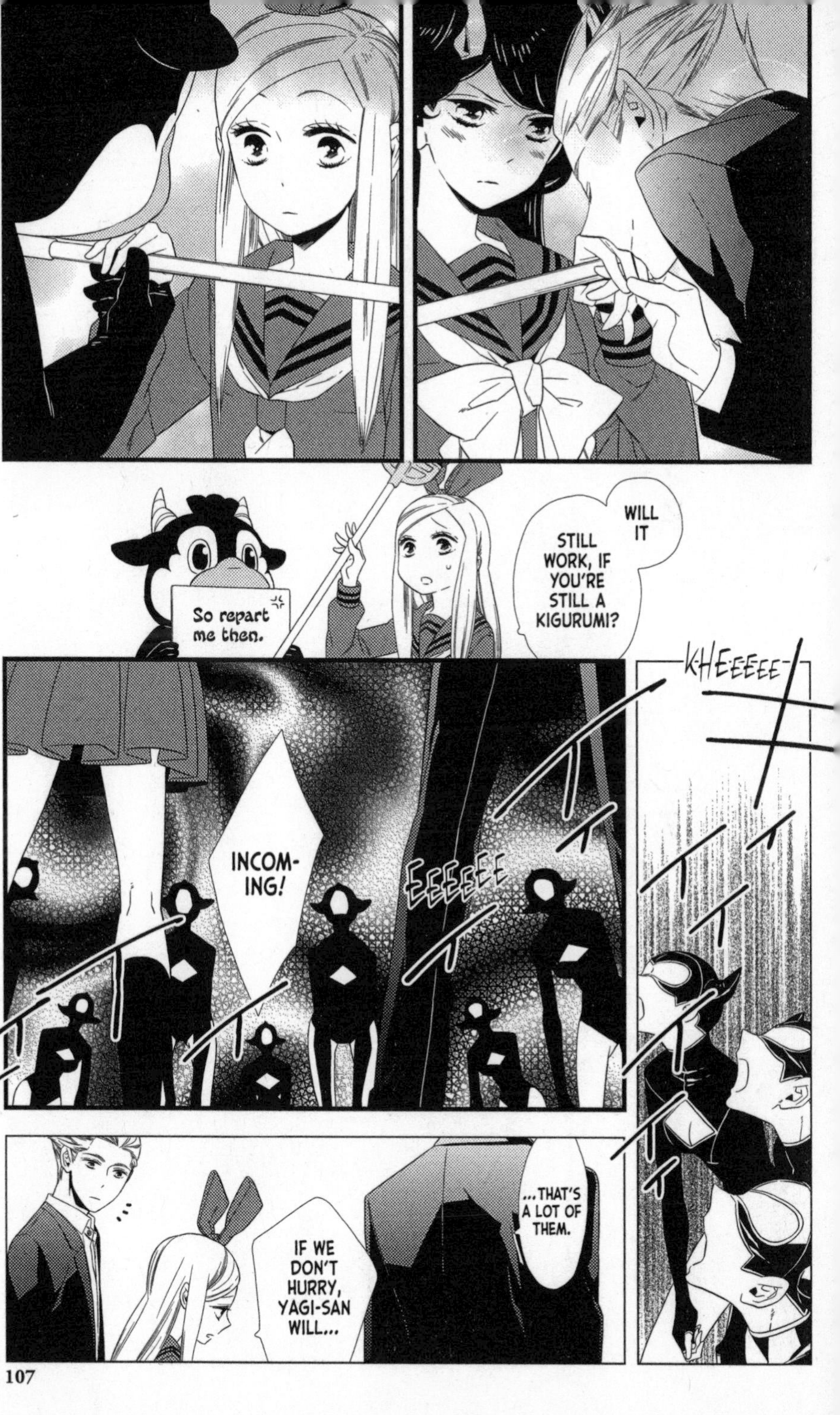
WILL IT STILL WORK, IF YOU'RE STILL A KIGURUMI?
So repart me then.
K-HE-EEEEE
INCOM-ING!
EEEEEE
...THAT'S A LOT OF THEM.
IF WE DON'T HURRY, YAGI-SAN WILL...

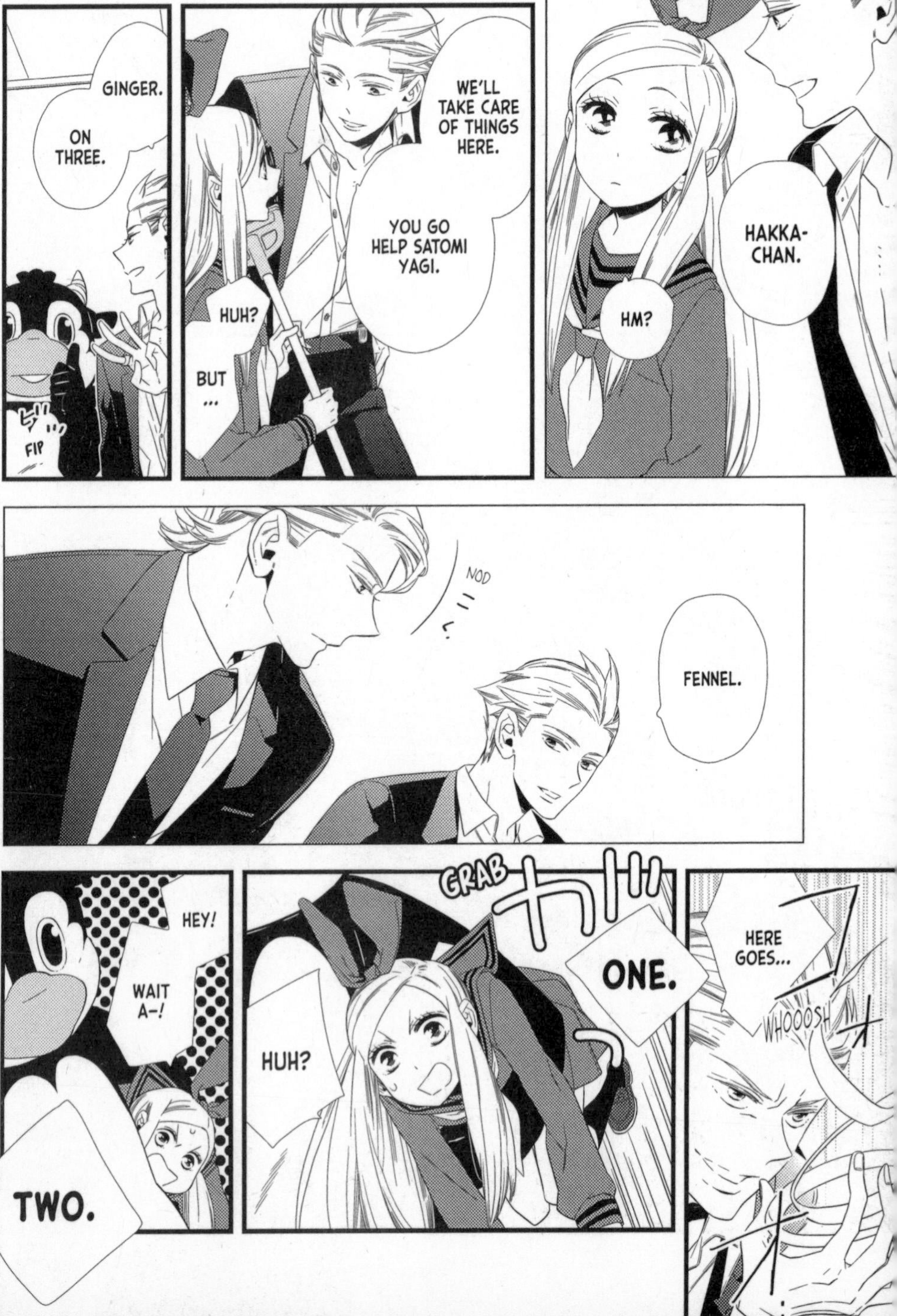
HAKKA-CHAN.
HM?
WE'LL TAKE CARE OF THINGS HERE.
YOU GO HELP SATOMI YAGI.
HUH?
BUT ...
GINGER.
ON THREE.
FIP
FENNEL.
NOD
HERE GOES...
ONE.
WHOOOSH
GRAB
HUH?
HEY!
WAIT A-!
TWO.

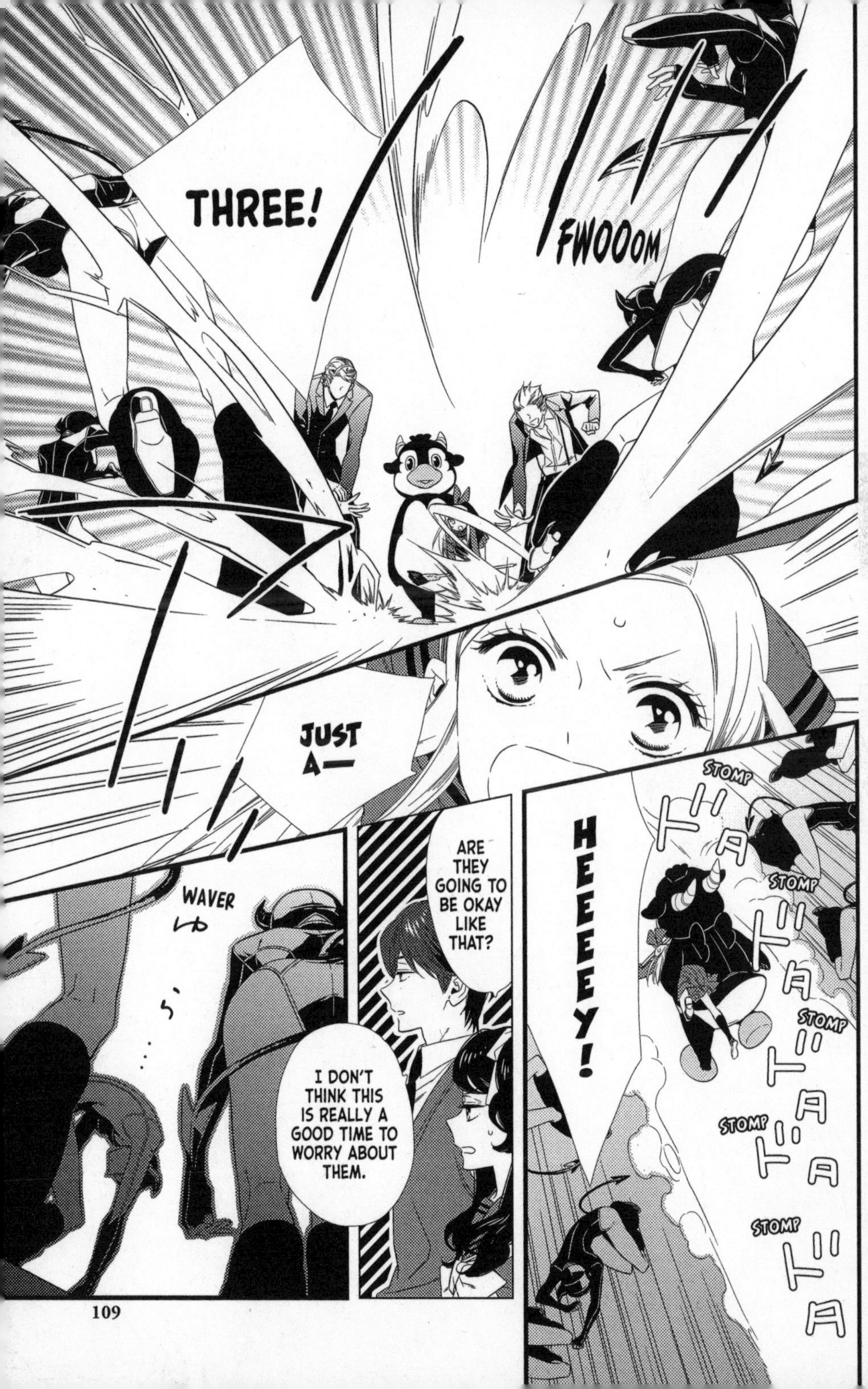
THREE!
FWOOOM
JUST A—
HEEEEEY!
STOMP
STOMP
STOMP
STOMP
STOMP
ARE THEY GOING TO BE OKAY LIKE THAT?
I DON'T THINK THIS IS REALLY A GOOD TIME TO WORRY ABOUT THEM.
WAVER
...

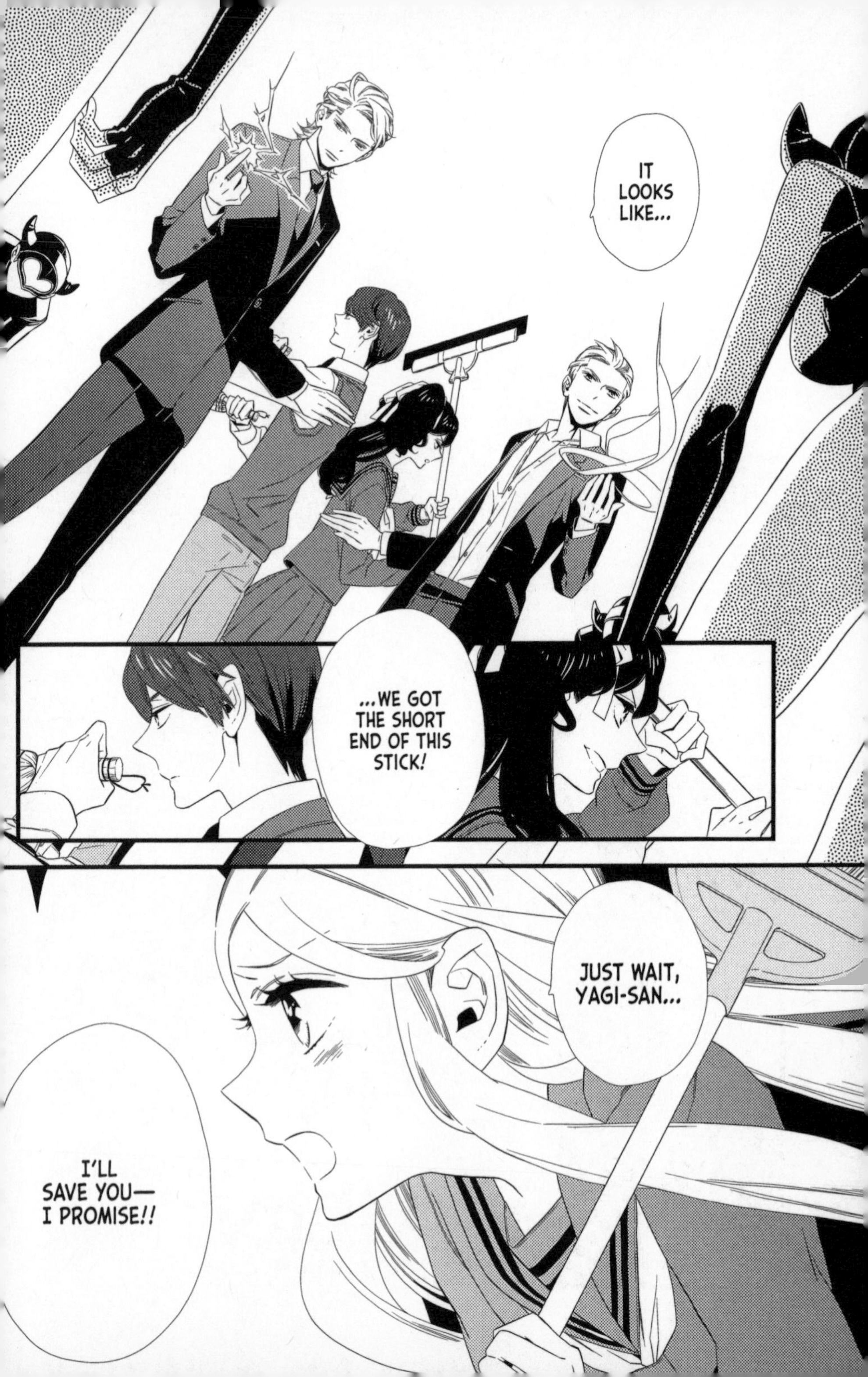
IT LOOKS LIKE...
...WE GOT THE SHORT END OF THIS STICK!
JUST WAIT, YAGI-SAN...
I'LL SAVE YOU— I PROMISE!!

KONK

Kigurumi
GUARDIANS

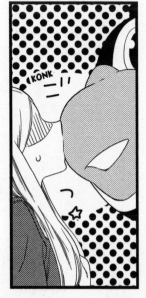

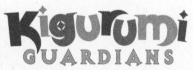

BWAH
ぶ
わ
っ

Kigurumi GUARDIANS

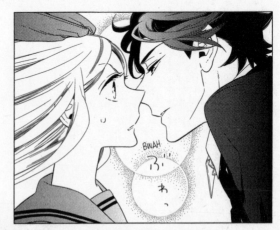

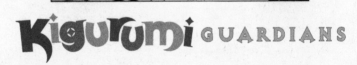

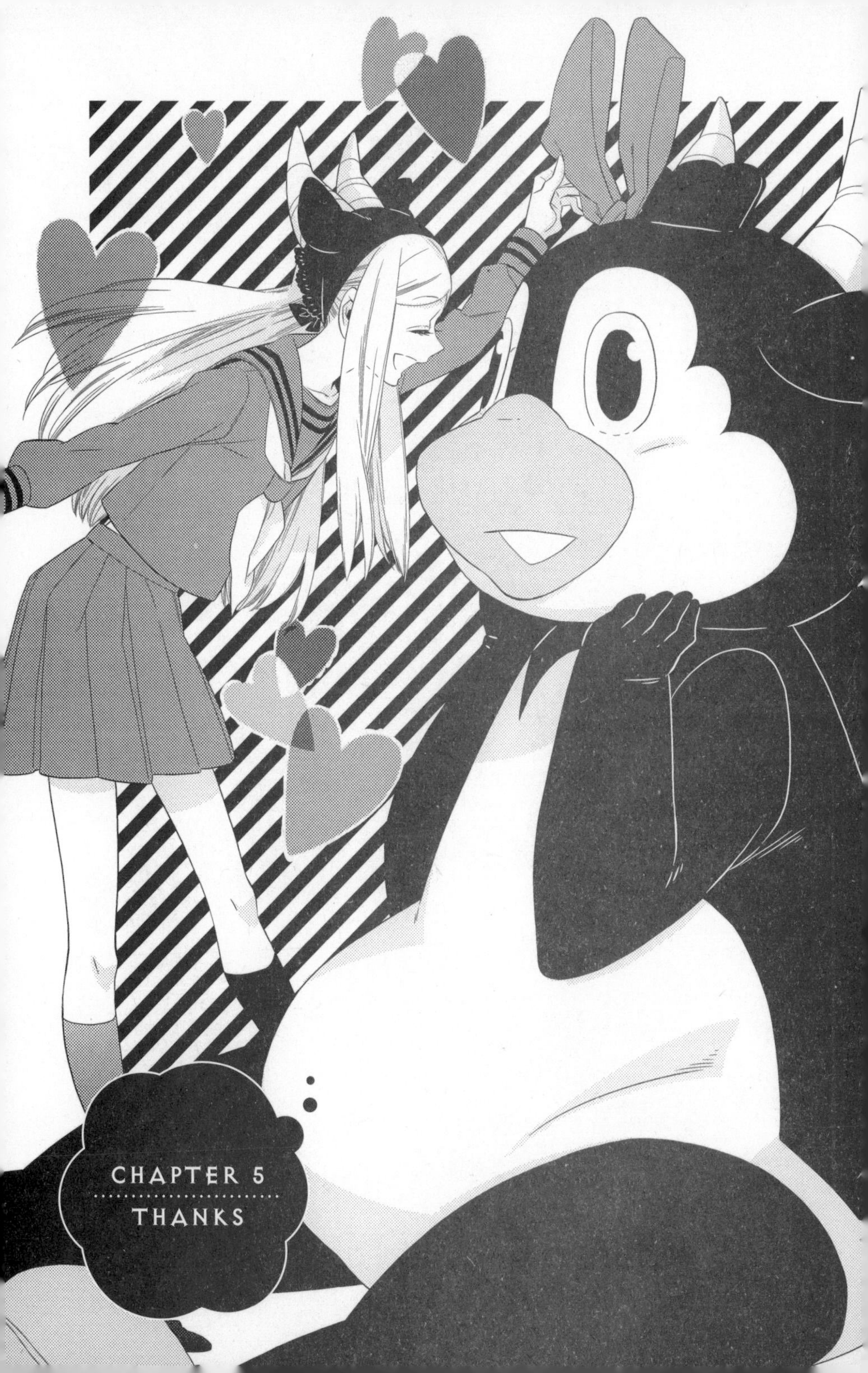
CHAPTER 5
THANKS

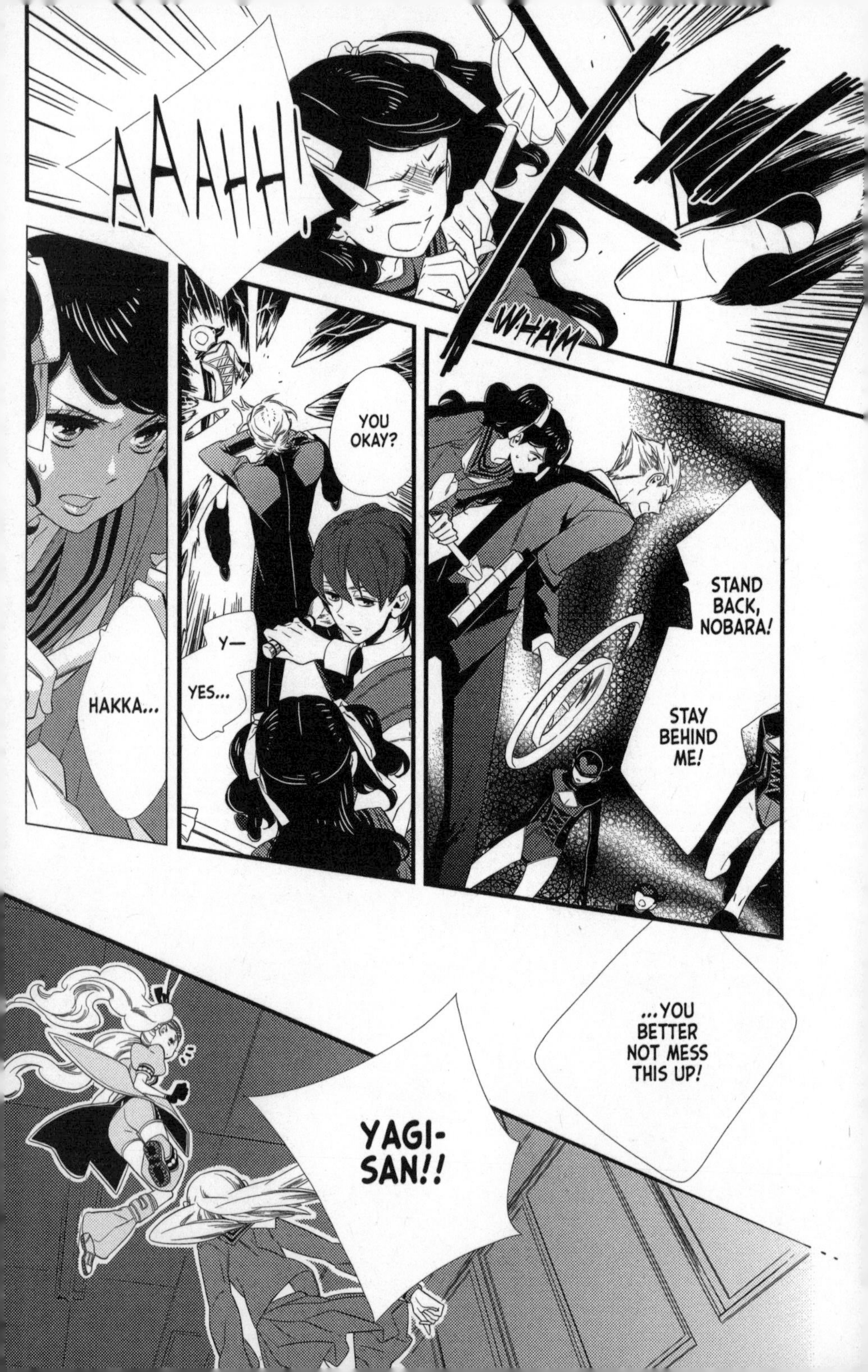
AAAHH!
WHAM
STAND BACK, NOBARA!
STAY BEHIND ME!
YOU OKAY?
Y—
YES...
HAKKA...
...YOU BETTER NOT MESS THIS UP!
YAGI-SAN!!

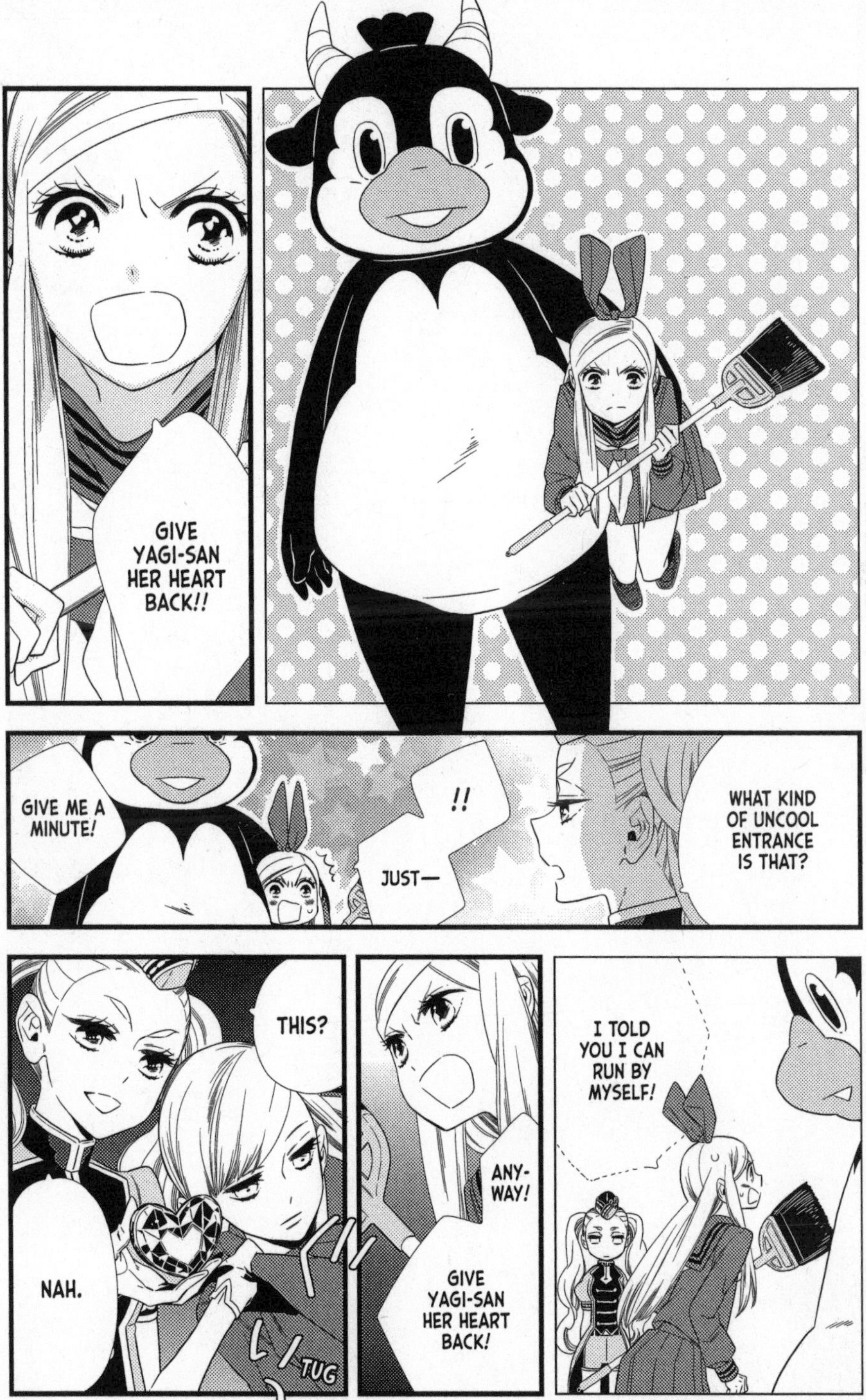
GIVE YAGI-SAN HER HEART BACK!!
WHAT KIND OF UNCOOL ENTRANCE IS THAT?
!!
JUST—
GIVE ME A MINUTE!
I TOLD YOU I CAN RUN BY MYSELF!
ANY-WAY!
GIVE YAGI-SAN HER HEART BACK!
THIS?
NAH.
TUG

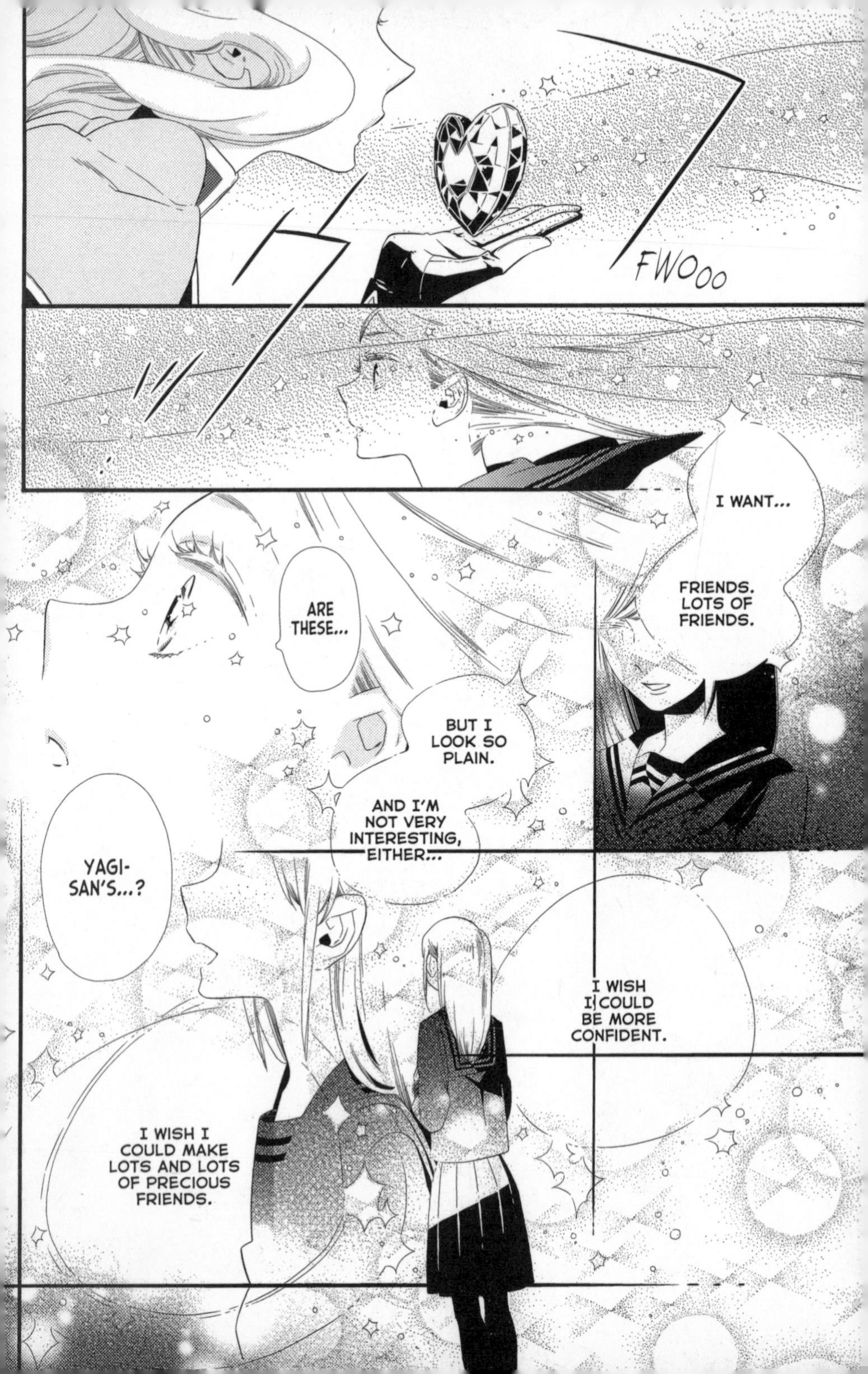
FWOoo
I WANT...
FRIENDS. LOTS OF FRIENDS.
ARE THESE...
BUT I LOOK SO PLAIN.
AND I'M NOT VERY INTERESTING, EITHER...
YAGI-SAN'S...?
I WISH I COULD BE MORE CONFIDENT.
I WISH I COULD MAKE LOTS AND LOTS OF PRECIOUS FRIENDS.

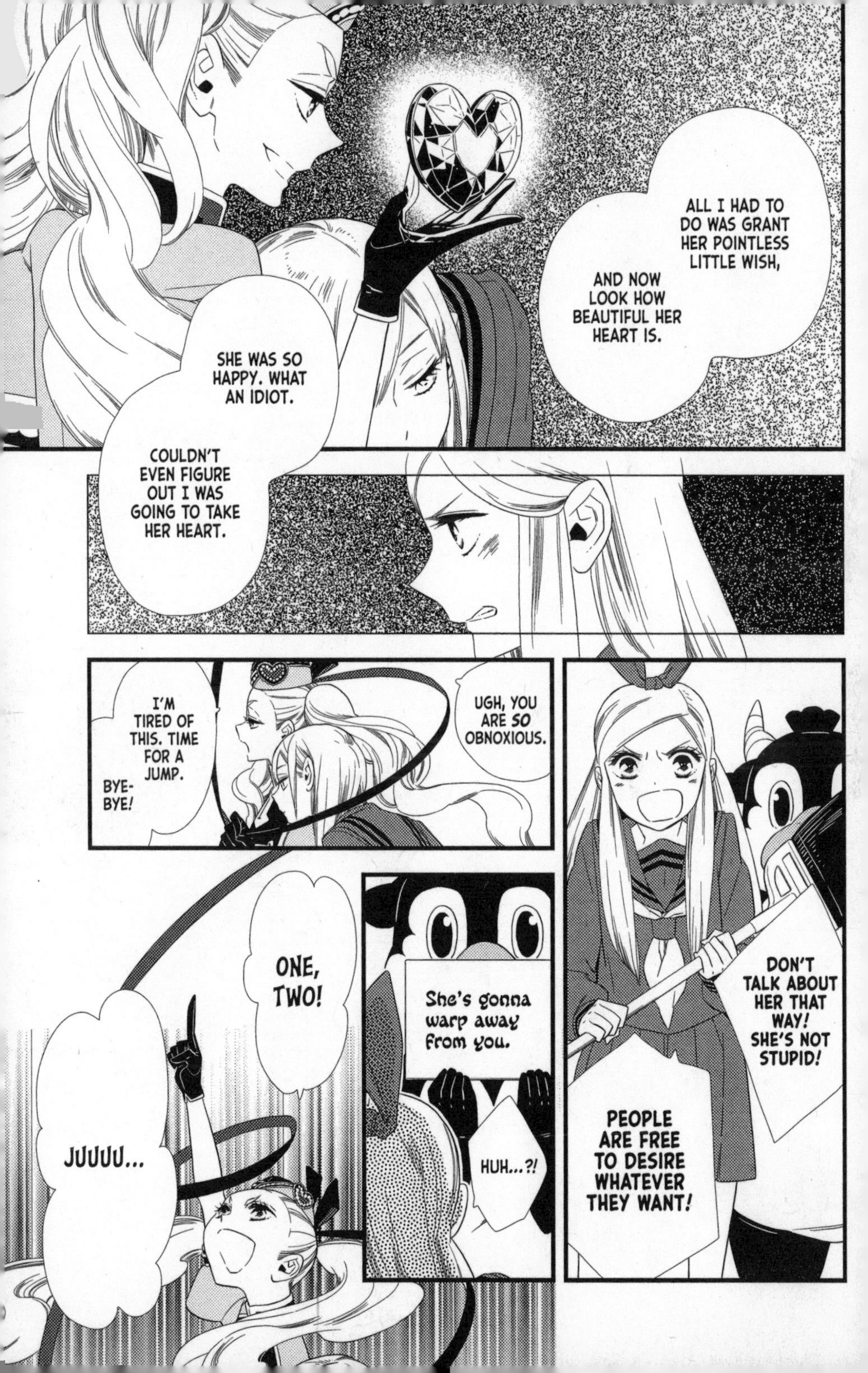
ALL I HAD TO DO WAS GRANT HER POINTLESS LITTLE WISH,
AND NOW LOOK HOW BEAUTIFUL HER HEART IS.
SHE WAS SO HAPPY. WHAT AN IDIOT.
COULDN'T EVEN FIGURE OUT I WAS GOING TO TAKE HER HEART.
DON'T TALK ABOUT HER THAT WAY! SHE'S NOT STUPID!
PEOPLE ARE FREE TO DESIRE WHATEVER THEY WANT!
UGH, YOU ARE *SO* OBNOXIOUS.
I'M TIRED OF THIS. TIME FOR A JUMP.
BYE-BYE!
She's gonna warp away from you.
HUH...?!
ONE, TWO!
JUUUU...

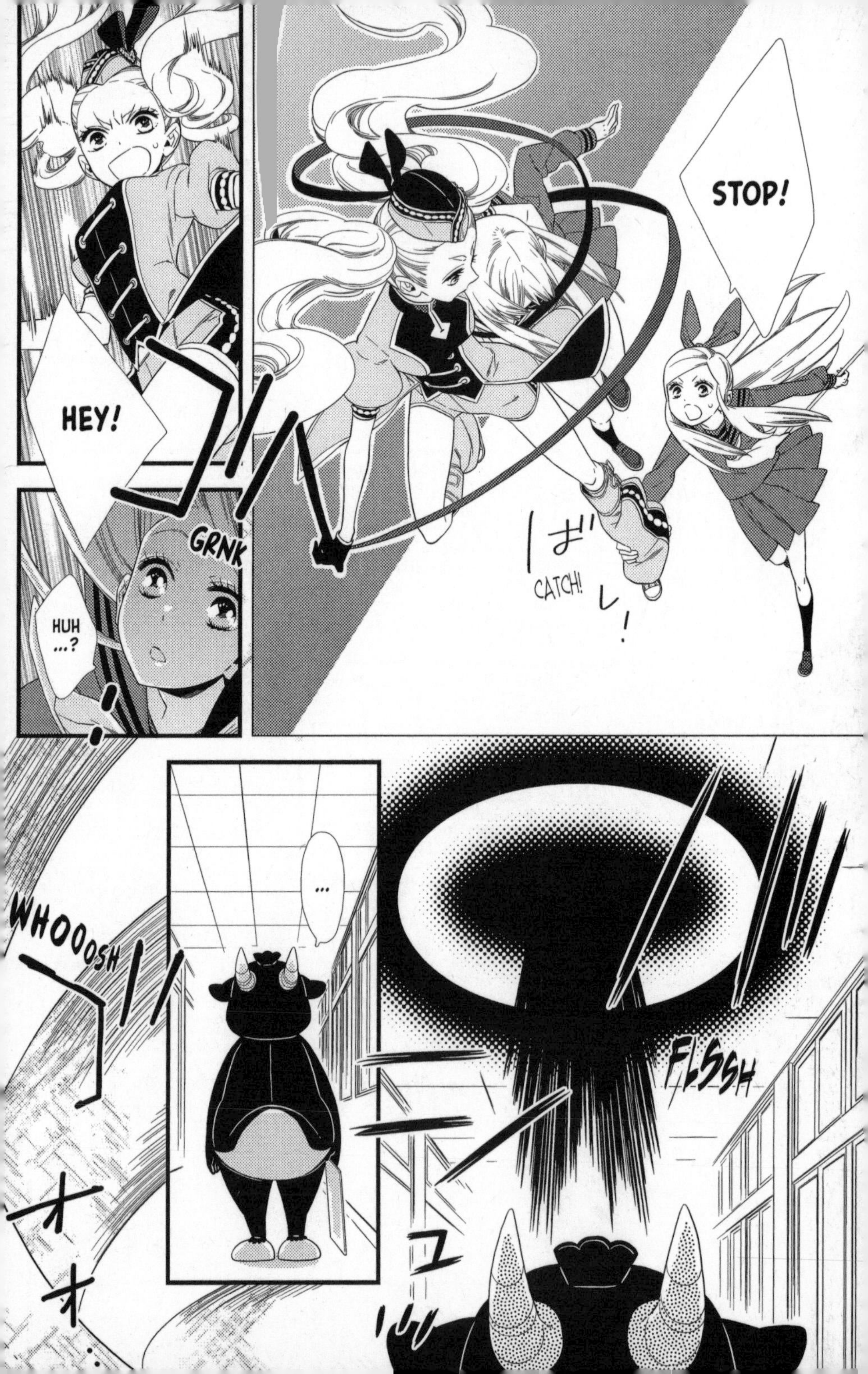
STOP!
CATCH!
HEY!
GRNK
HUH ...?
FLSSH
...
WHOOOSH

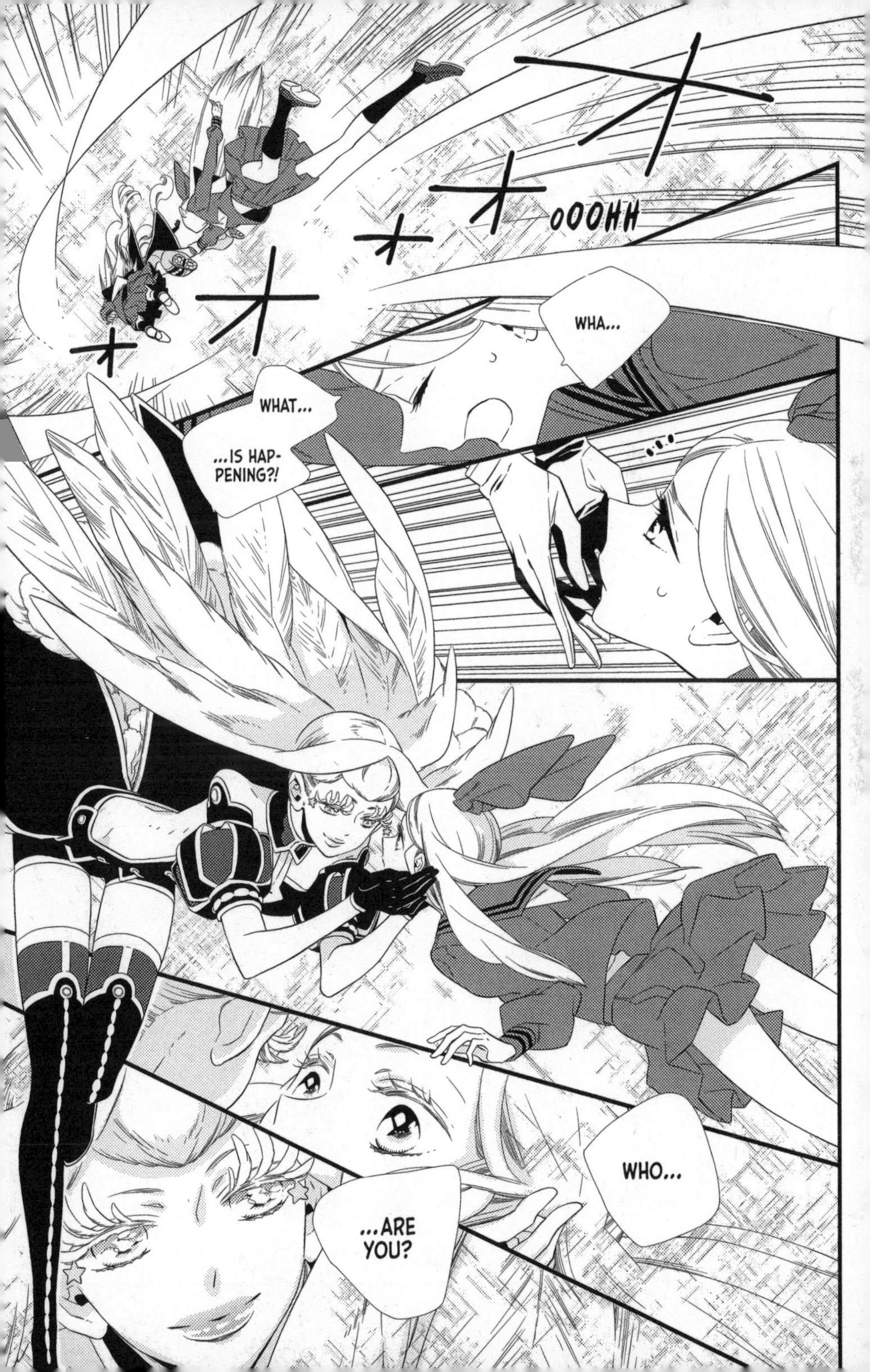
OOOHH
WHA...
WHAT...
...IS HAP-PENING?!
...
WHO...
...ARE YOU?

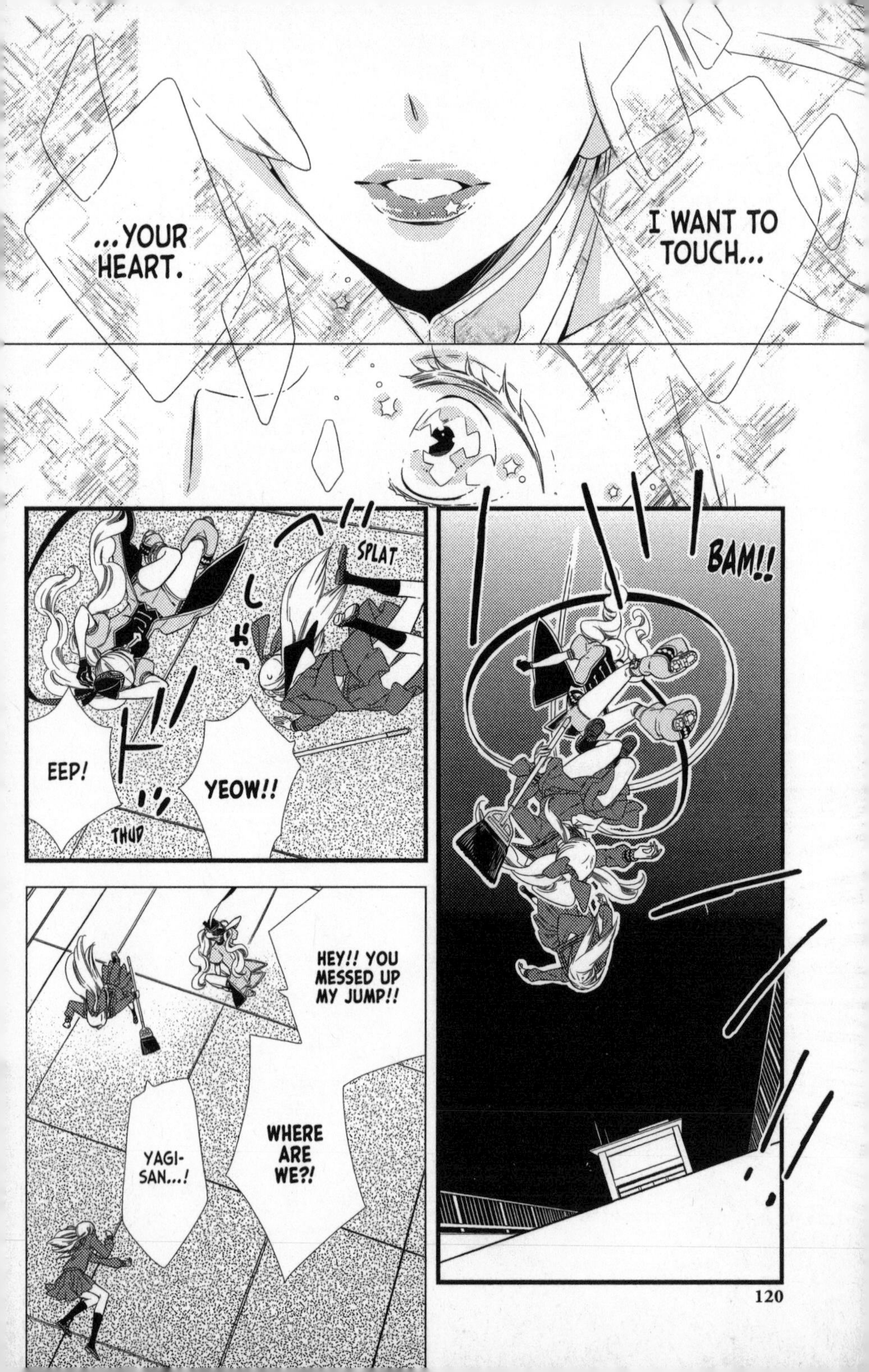
I WANT TO TOUCH...
...YOUR HEART.
BAM!!
SPLAT
YEOW!!
EEP!
THUD
HEY!! YOU MESSED UP MY JUMP!!
WHERE ARE WE?!
YAGI-SAN...!

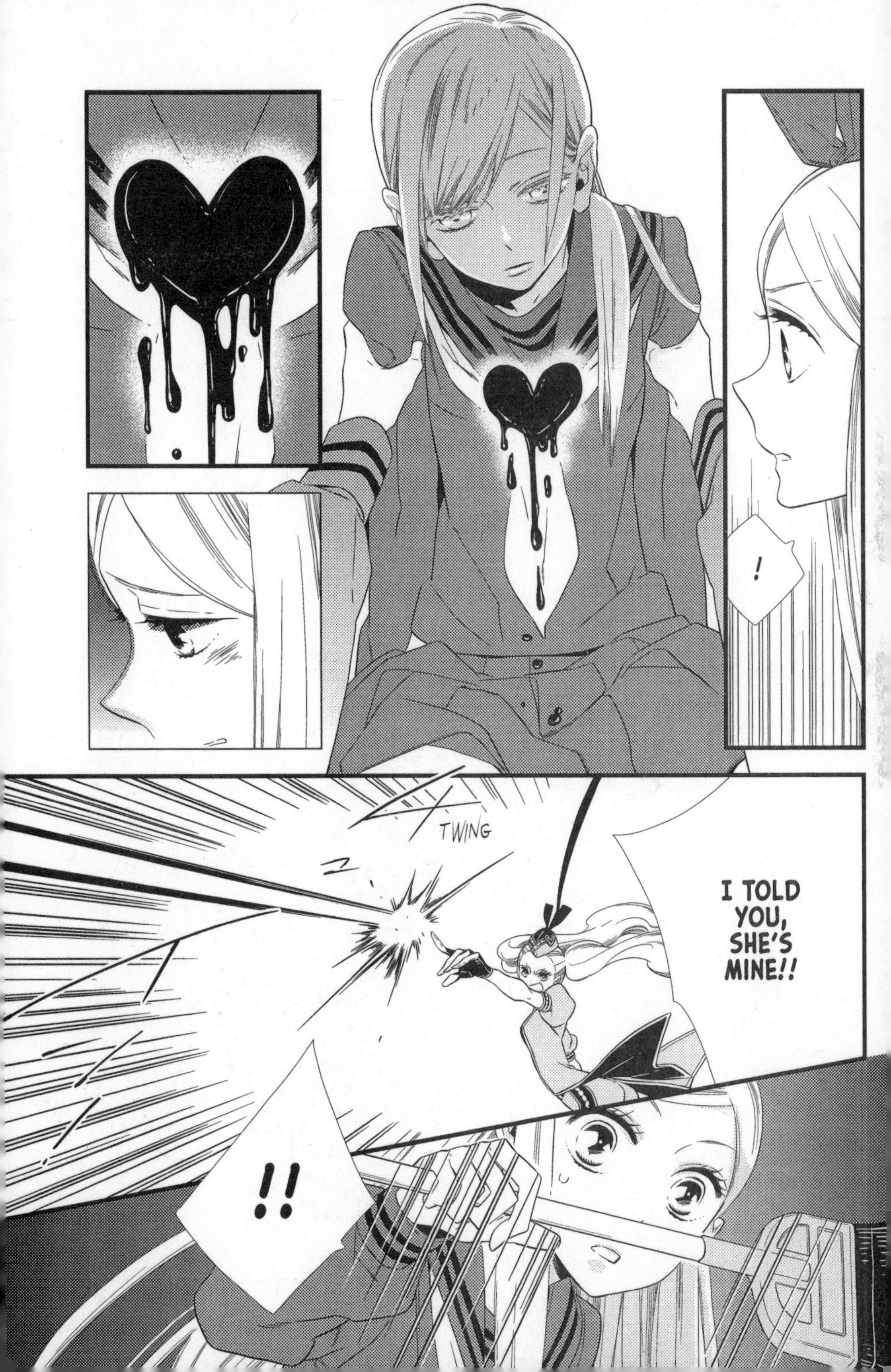
!
TWING
I TOLD YOU, SHE'S MINE!!
!!

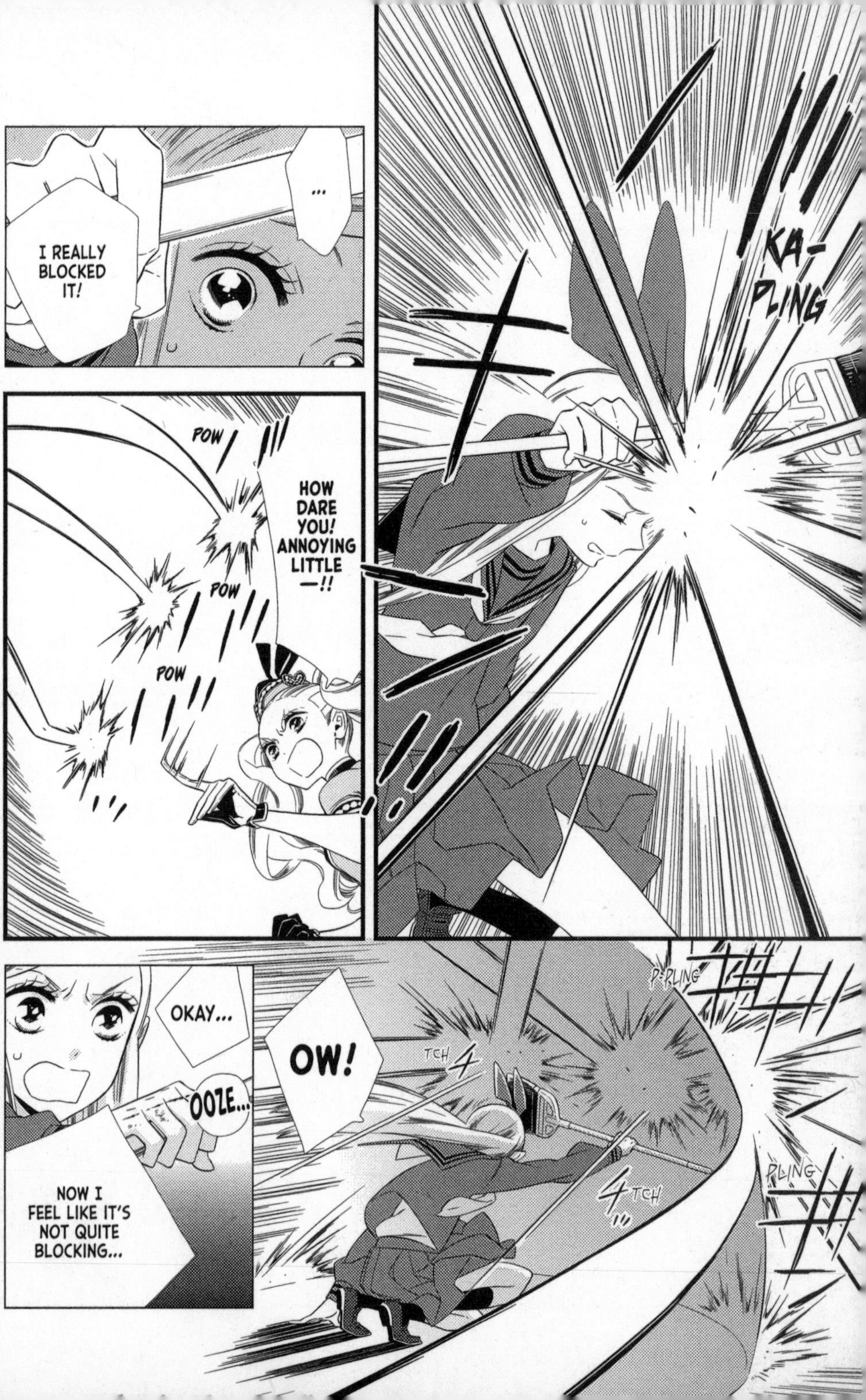
KA-PLING
...
I REALLY BLOCKED IT!
POW
HOW DARE YOU! ANNOYING LITTLE —!!
POW
POW
P-PLING
TCH
OW!
PLING
TCH
OKAY...
OOZE...
NOW I FEEL LIKE IT'S NOT QUITE BLOCKING...

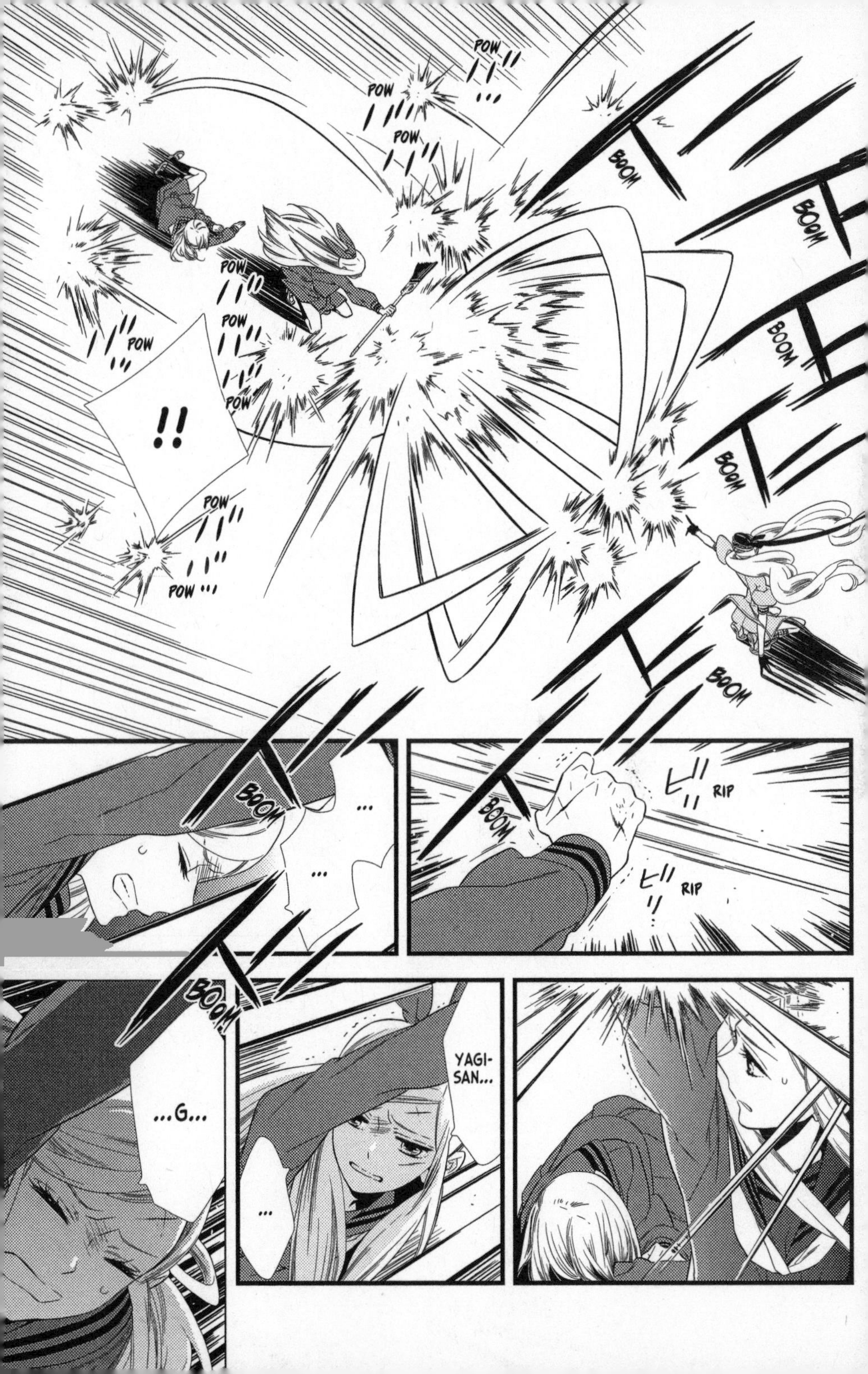
POW!!
POW!!!...
POW!!!
BOOM
BOOM
BOOM
BOOM
POW!!
POW!!!
POW!!!
POW
!!
POW!!!
POW...
BOOM
RIP
RIP
BOOM
BOOM
...
...
YAGI-SAN...
...
BOOM
...G...

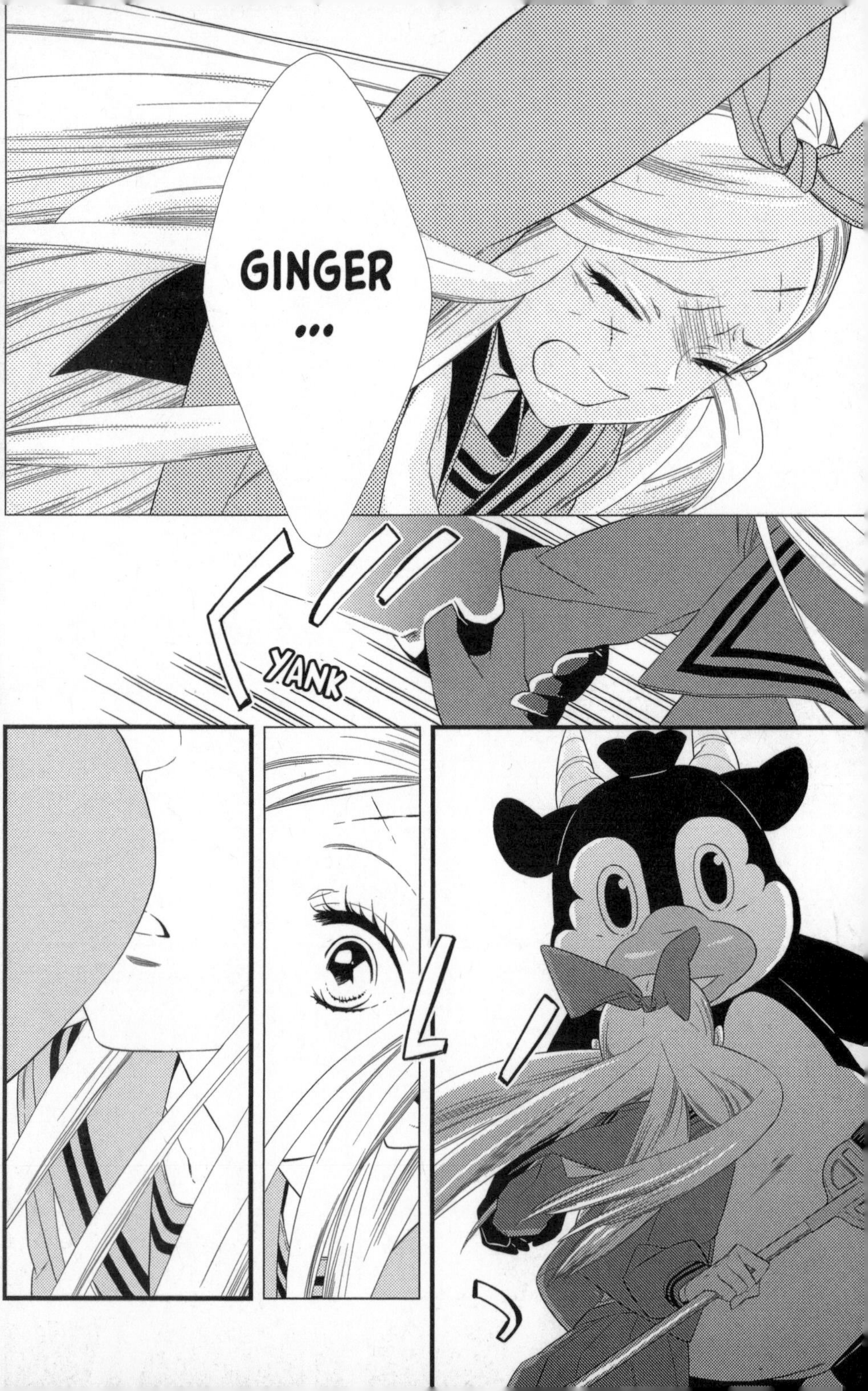
GINGER
...
YANK

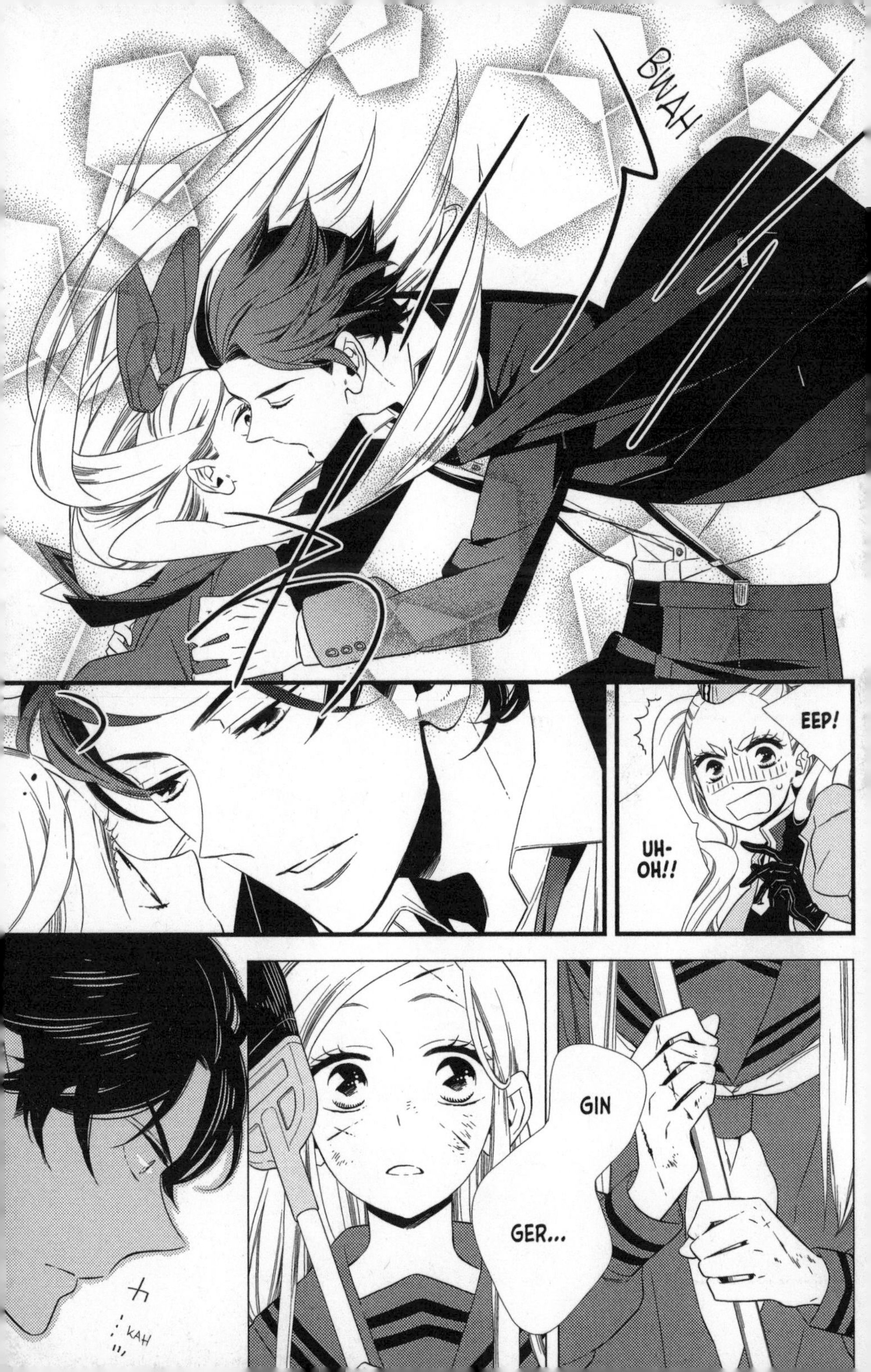
BWAH
EEP!
UH-OH!!
GIN
GER...
KAH

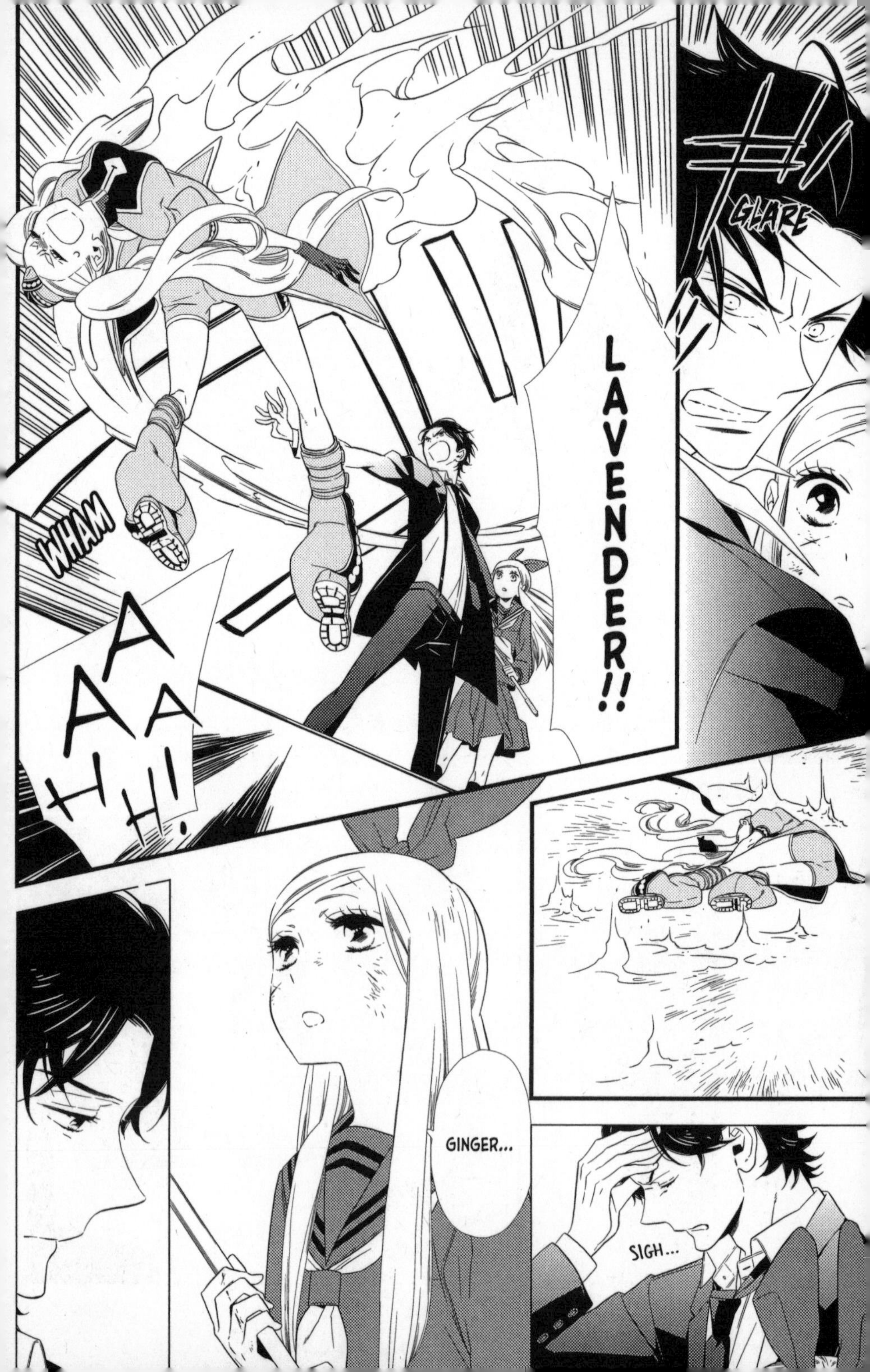
GLARE
LAVENDER!!
WHAM
AAAHH!
SIGH...
GINGER...

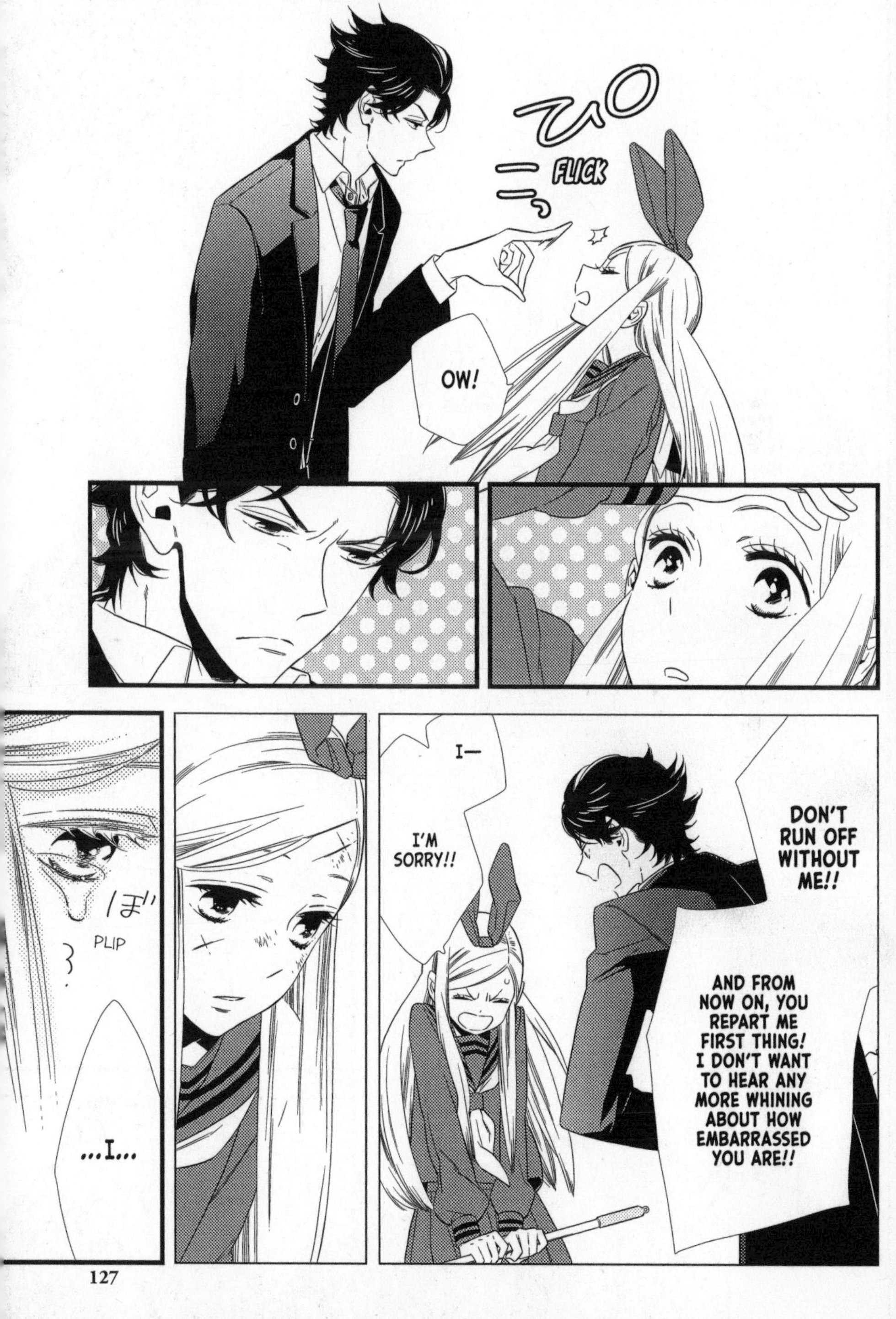
FLICK
OW!
DON'T RUN OFF WITHOUT ME!!
AND FROM NOW ON, YOU REPART ME FIRST THING! I DON'T WANT TO HEAR ANY MORE WHINING ABOUT HOW EMBARRASSED YOU ARE!!
I—
I'M SORRY!!
PLIP
...I...

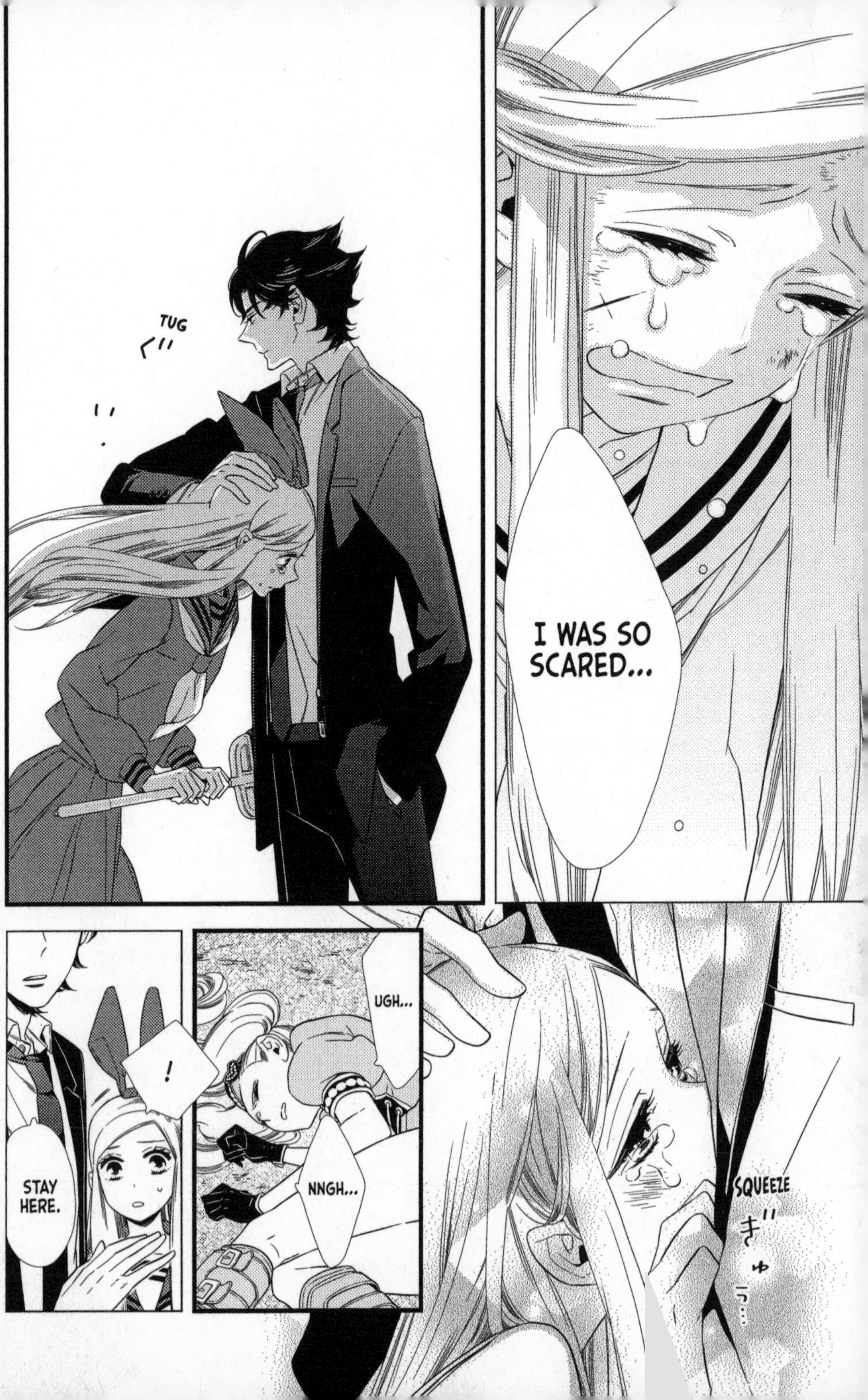
I WAS SO SCARED...
TUG
SQUEEZE
UGH...
NNGH...
!
STAY HERE.

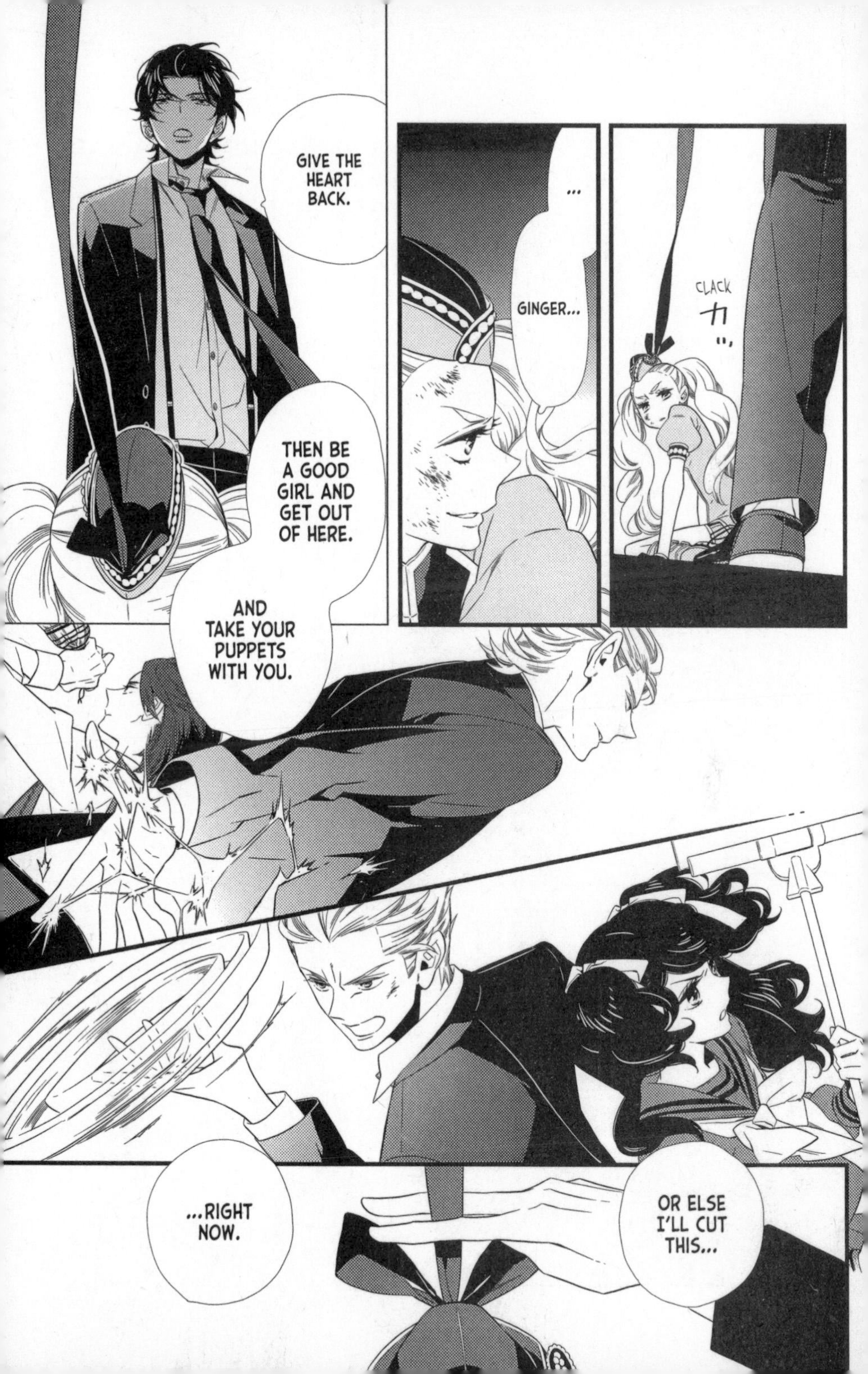
CLACK
カッ
...
GINGER...
GIVE THE HEART BACK.
THEN BE A GOOD GIRL AND GET OUT OF HERE.
AND TAKE YOUR PUPPETS WITH YOU.
OR ELSE I'LL CUT THIS...
...RIGHT NOW.

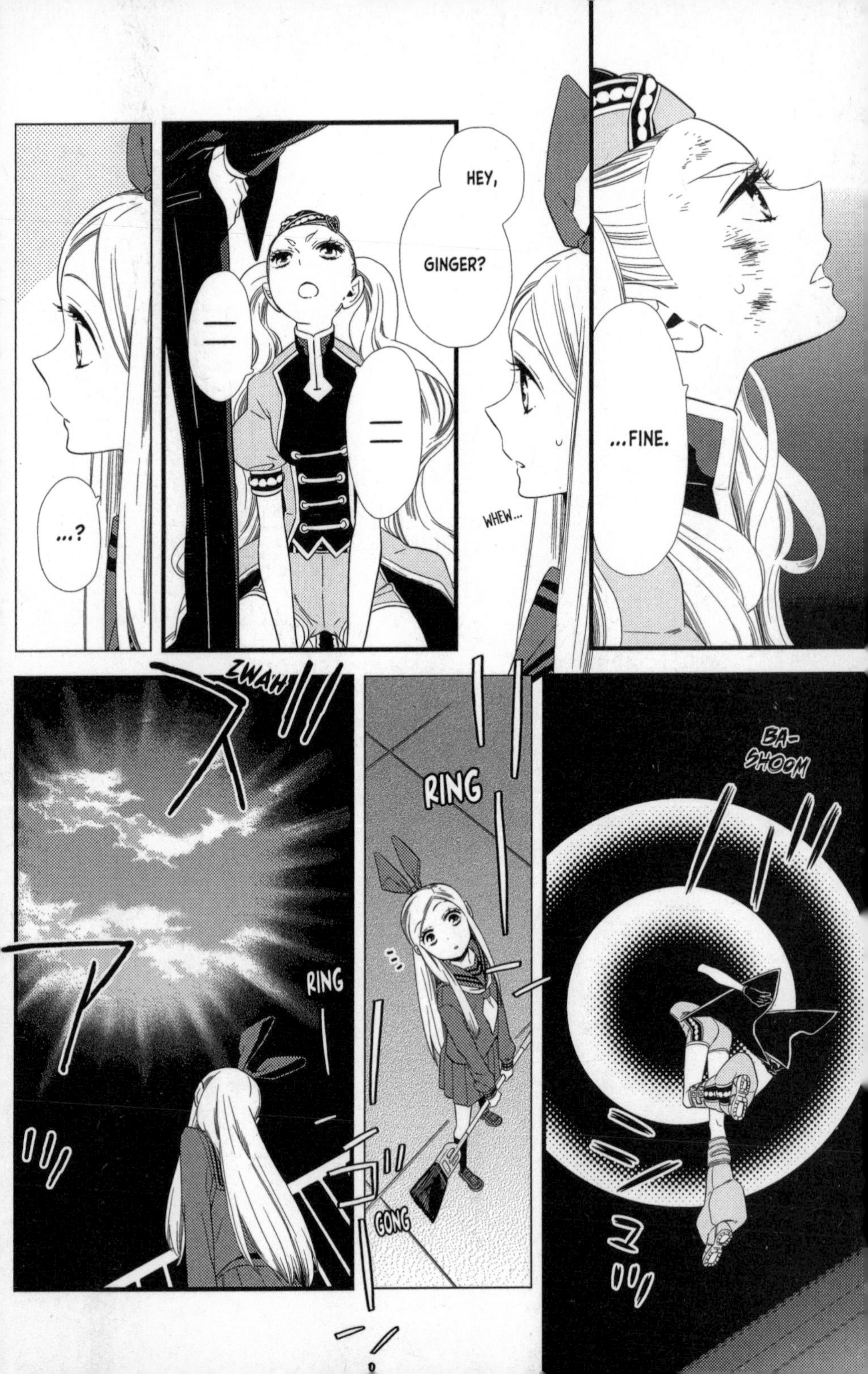
...FINE.
WHEW...
HEY,
GINGER?
...?
BA-SHOOM
RING
GONG
ZWAH
RING

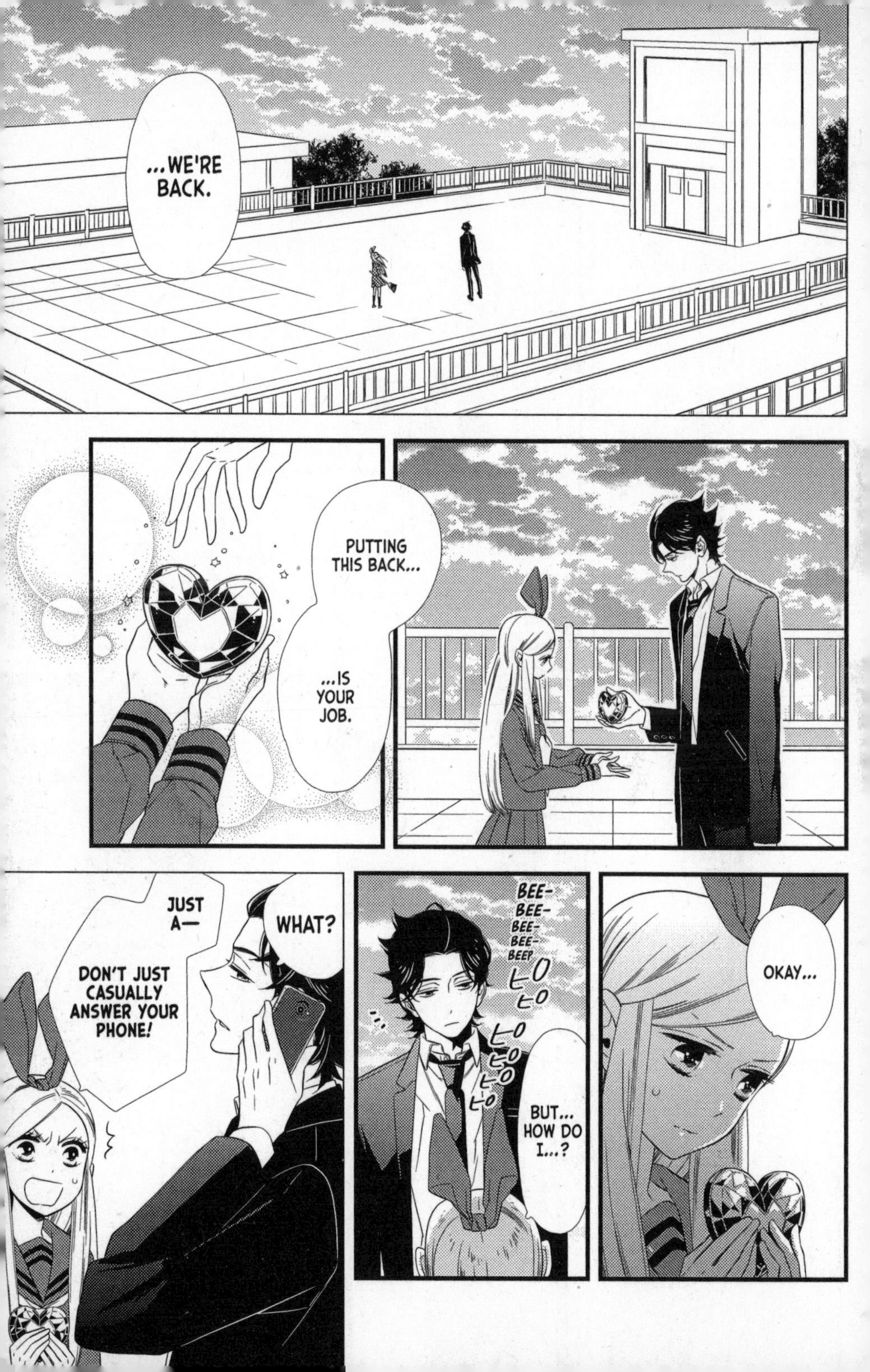
...WE'RE BACK.
PUTTING THIS BACK...
...IS YOUR JOB.
OKAY...
BEE-BEE-BEE-BEE-BEEP
...
BUT... HOW DO I...?
WHAT?
JUST A—
DON'T JUST CASUALLY ANSWER YOUR PHONE!

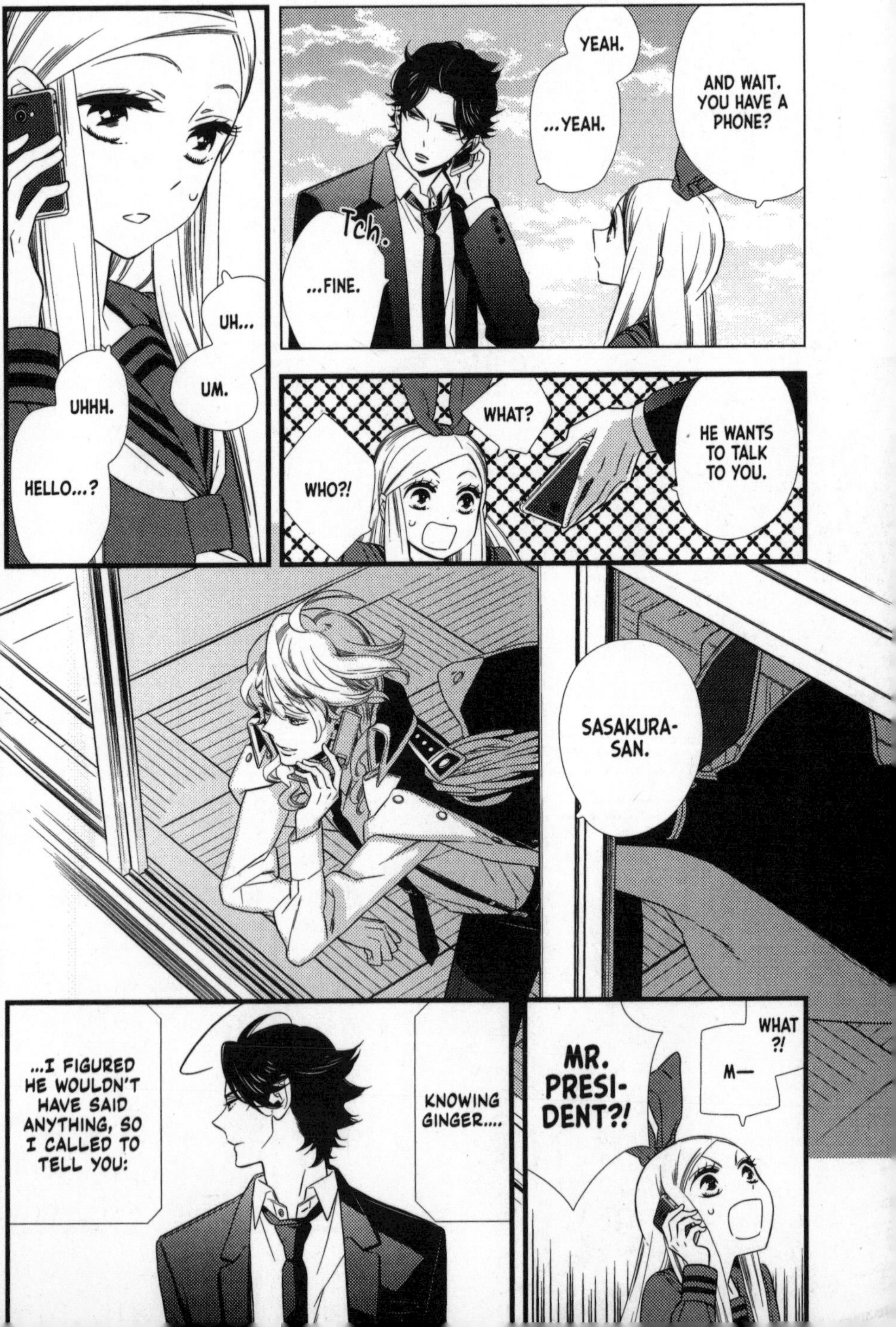
AND WAIT. YOU HAVE A PHONE?
YEAH.
...YEAH.
Tch.
...FINE.
HE WANTS TO TALK TO YOU.
WHAT?
WHO?!
UH...
UM.
UHHH.
HELLO...?
SASAKURA-SAN.
WHAT?!
M—
MR. PRESIDENT?!
KNOWING GINGER....
...I FIGURED HE WOULDN'T HAVE SAID ANYTHING, SO I CALLED TO TELL YOU:

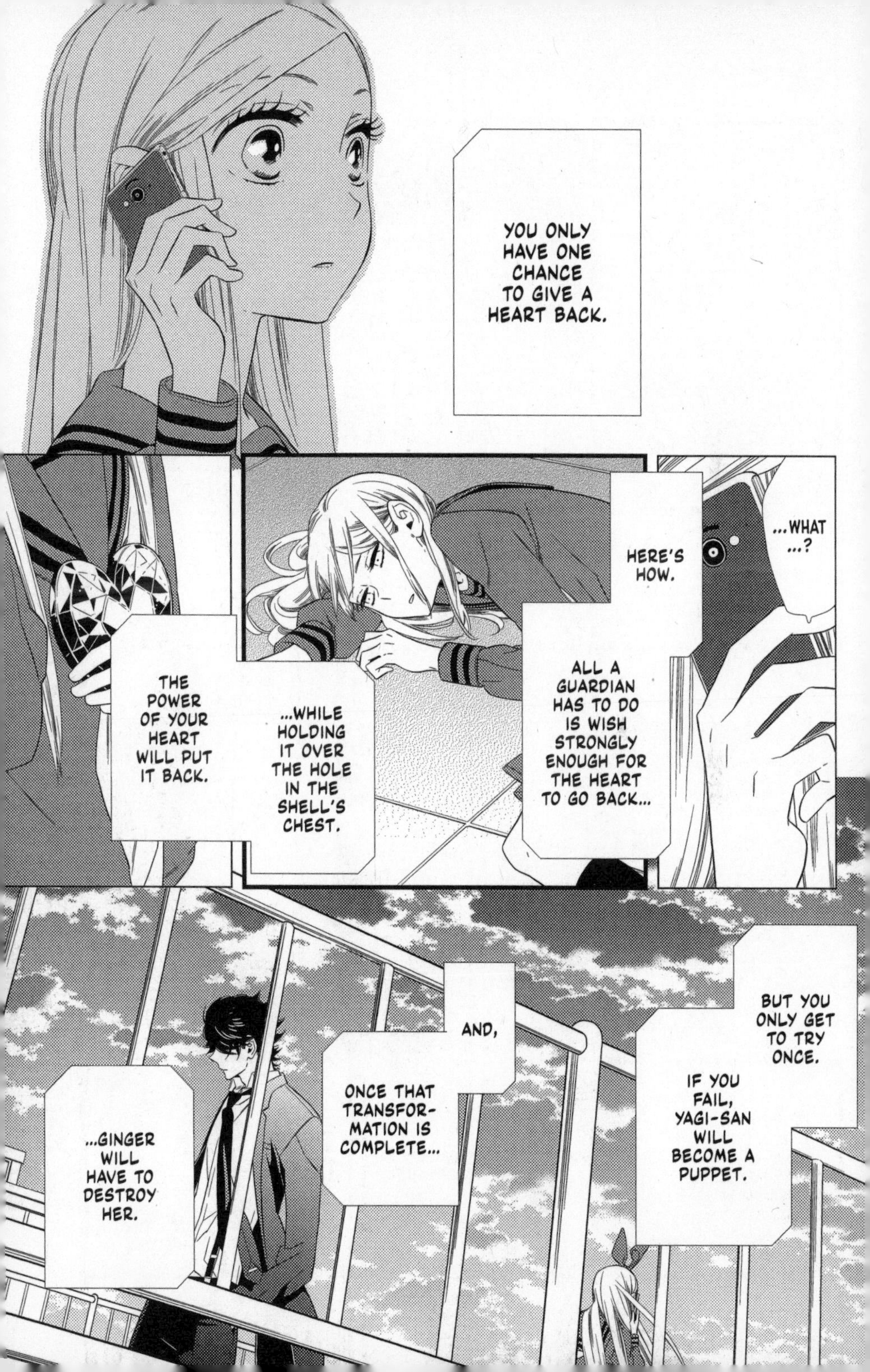
YOU ONLY HAVE ONE CHANCE TO GIVE A HEART BACK.
...WHAT ...?
HERE'S HOW.
ALL A GUARDIAN HAS TO DO IS WISH STRONGLY ENOUGH FOR THE HEART TO GO BACK...
...WHILE HOLDING IT OVER THE HOLE IN THE SHELL'S CHEST.
THE POWER OF YOUR HEART WILL PUT IT BACK.
BUT YOU ONLY GET TO TRY ONCE.
IF YOU FAIL, YAGI-SAN WILL BECOME A PUPPET.
AND,
ONCE THAT TRANSFOR-MATION IS COMPLETE...
...GINGER WILL HAVE TO DESTROY HER.

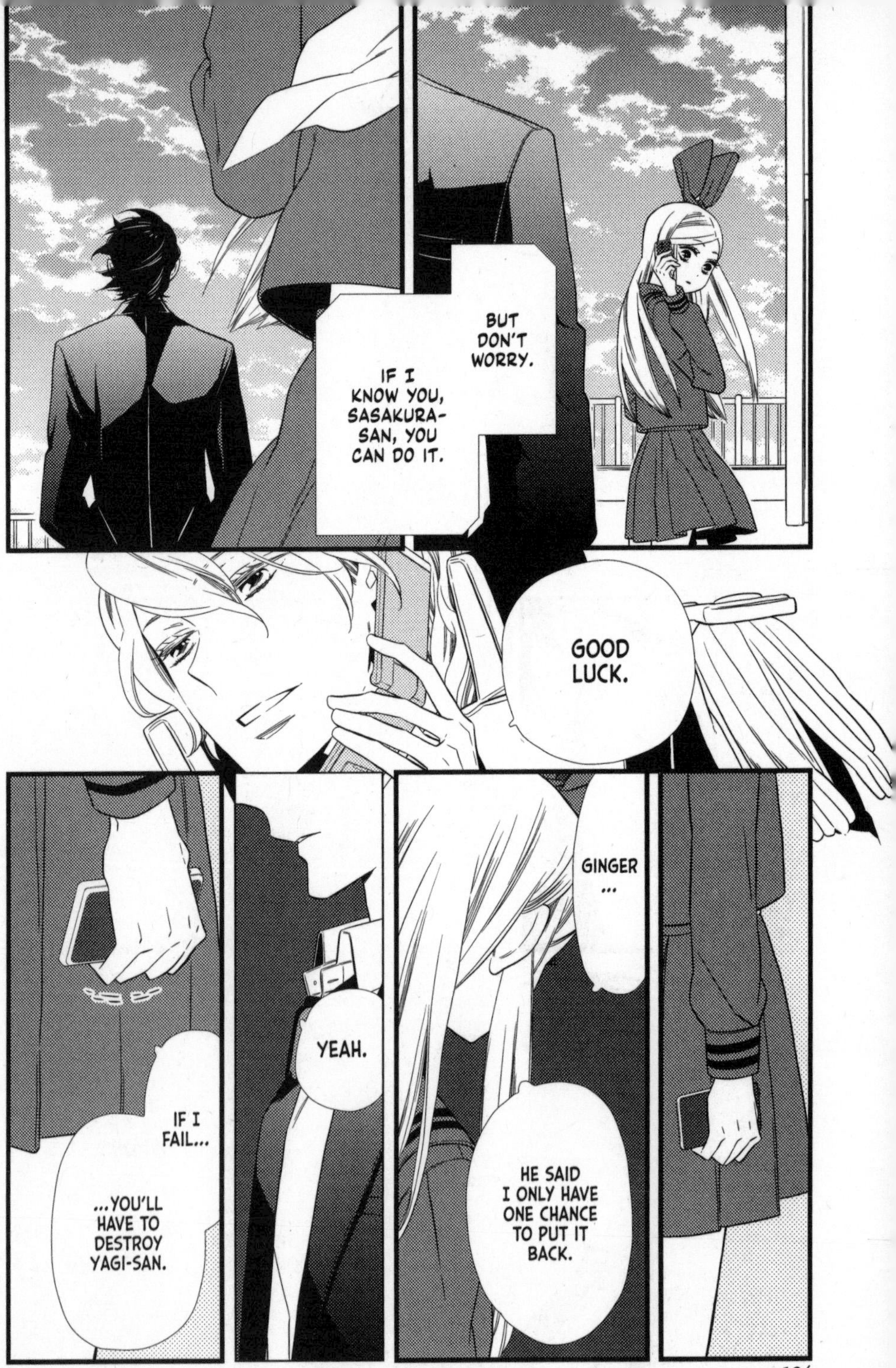
BUT DON'T WORRY.
IF I KNOW YOU, SASAKURA-SAN, YOU CAN DO IT.
GOOD LUCK.
GINGER...
HE SAID I ONLY HAVE ONE CHANCE TO PUT IT BACK.
YEAH.
IF I FAIL...
...YOU'LL HAVE TO DESTROY YAGI-SAN.

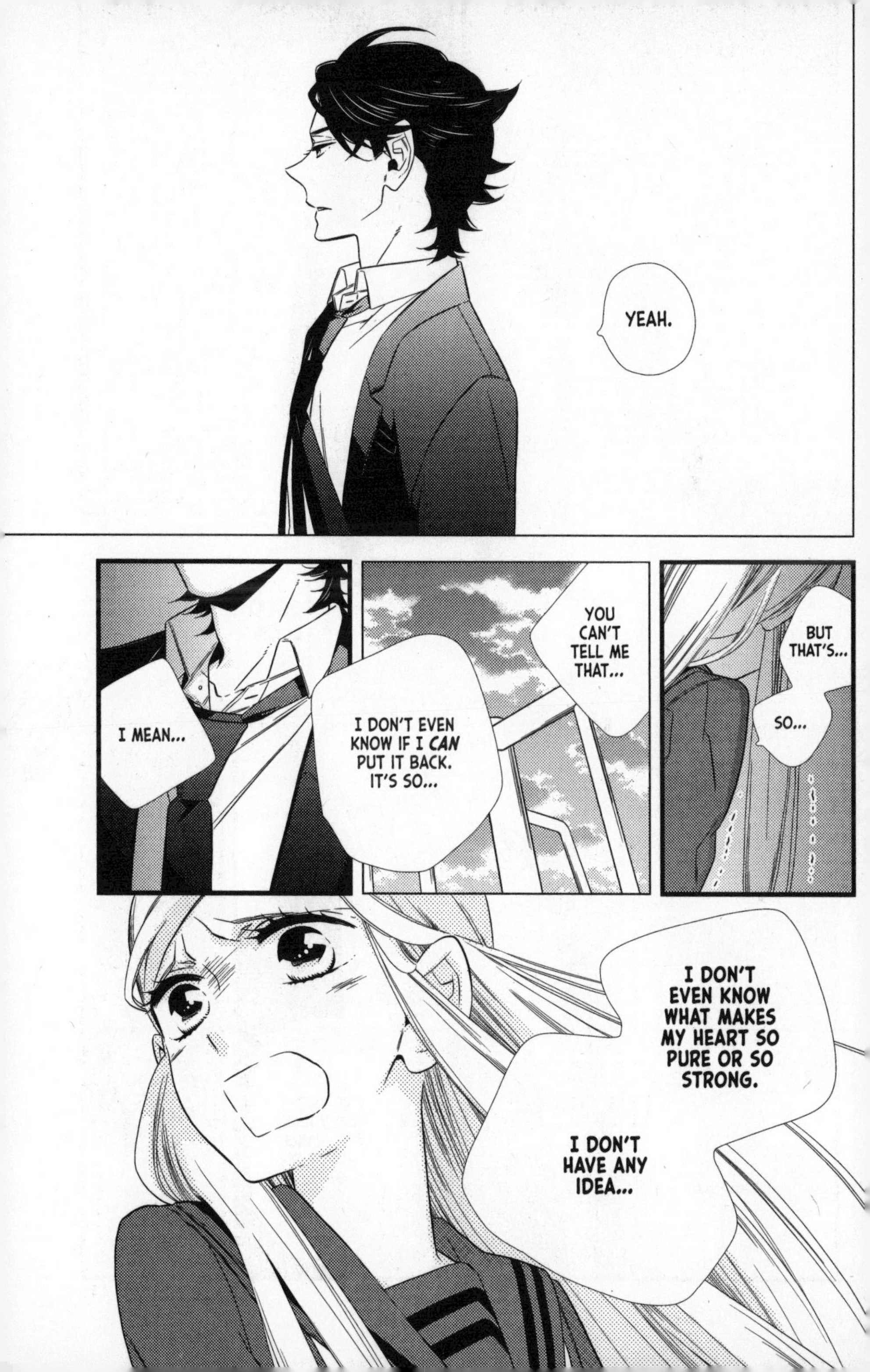
YEAH.
BUT THAT'S...
SO...
YOU CAN'T TELL ME THAT...
I DON'T EVEN KNOW IF I *CAN* PUT IT BACK. IT'S SO...
I MEAN...
I DON'T EVEN KNOW WHAT MAKES MY HEART SO PURE OR SO STRONG.
I DON'T HAVE ANY IDEA...

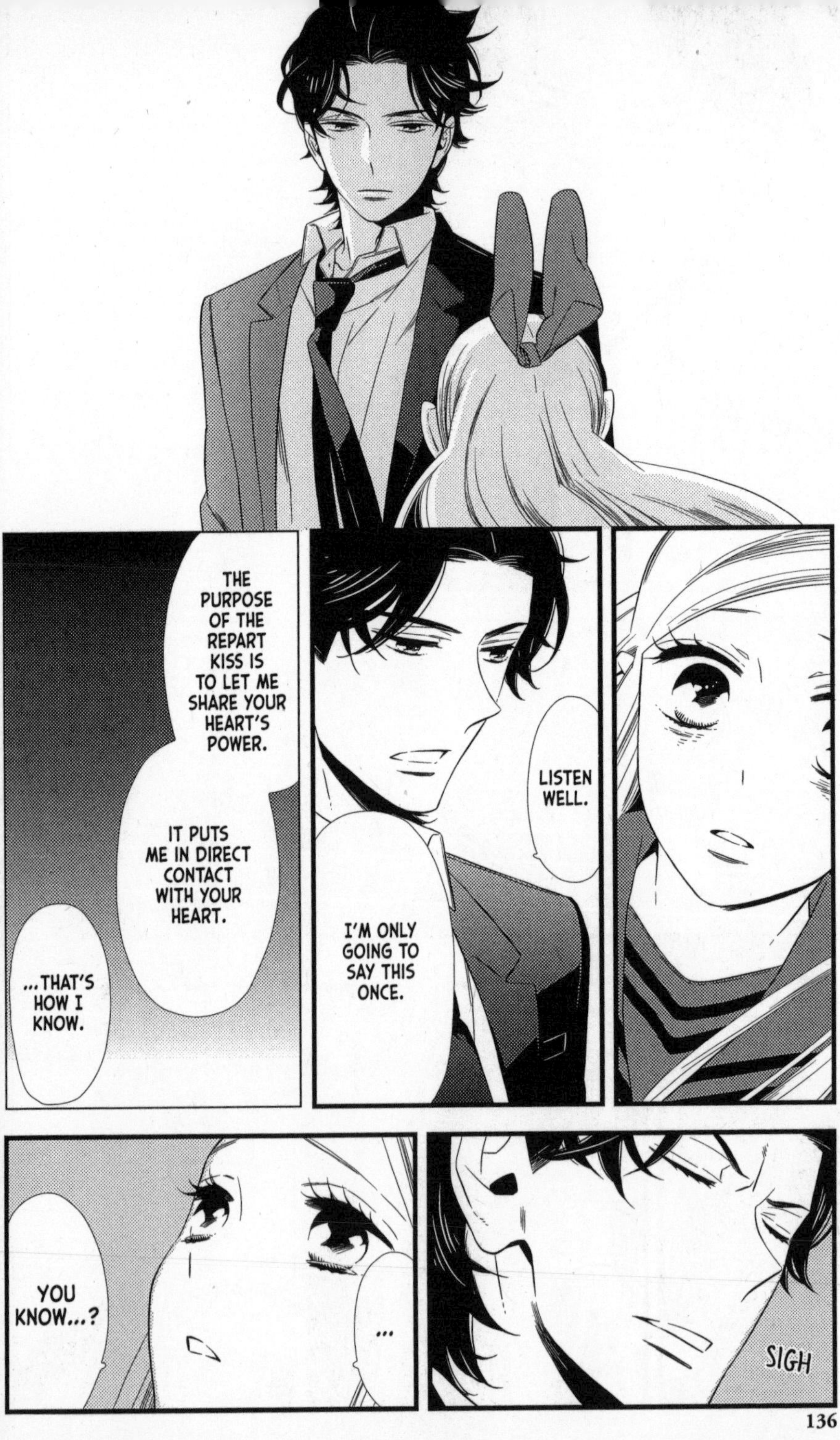
LISTEN WELL.
I'M ONLY GOING TO SAY THIS ONCE.
THE PURPOSE OF THE REPART KISS IS TO LET ME SHARE YOUR HEART'S POWER.
IT PUTS ME IN DIRECT CONTACT WITH YOUR HEART.
...THAT'S HOW I KNOW.
SIGH
YOU KNOW...?
...

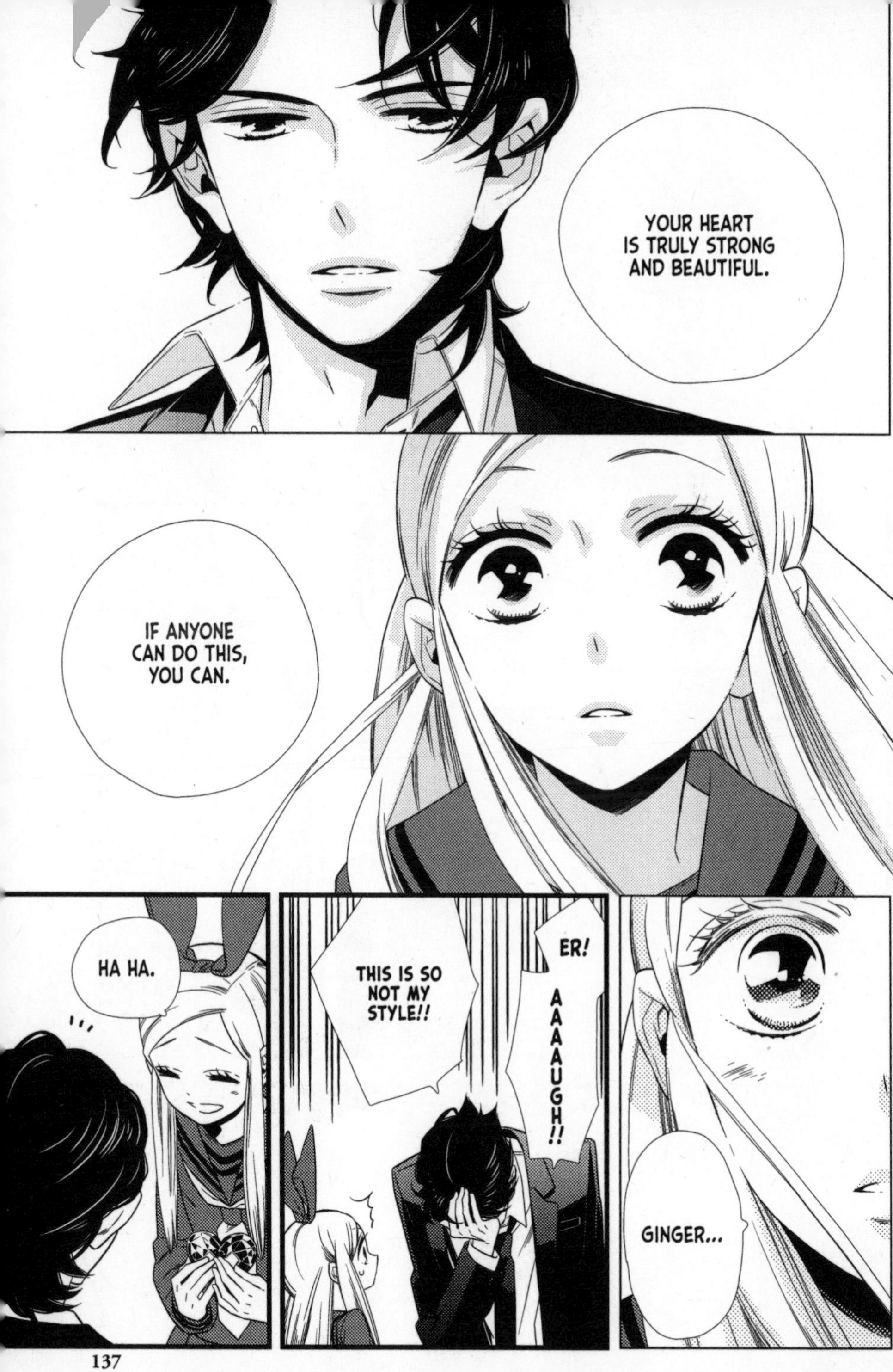
YOUR HEART IS TRULY STRONG AND BEAUTIFUL.
IF ANYONE CAN DO THIS, YOU CAN.
GINGER...
ER!
AAAAAUGH!!
THIS IS SO NOT MY STYLE!!
HA HA.

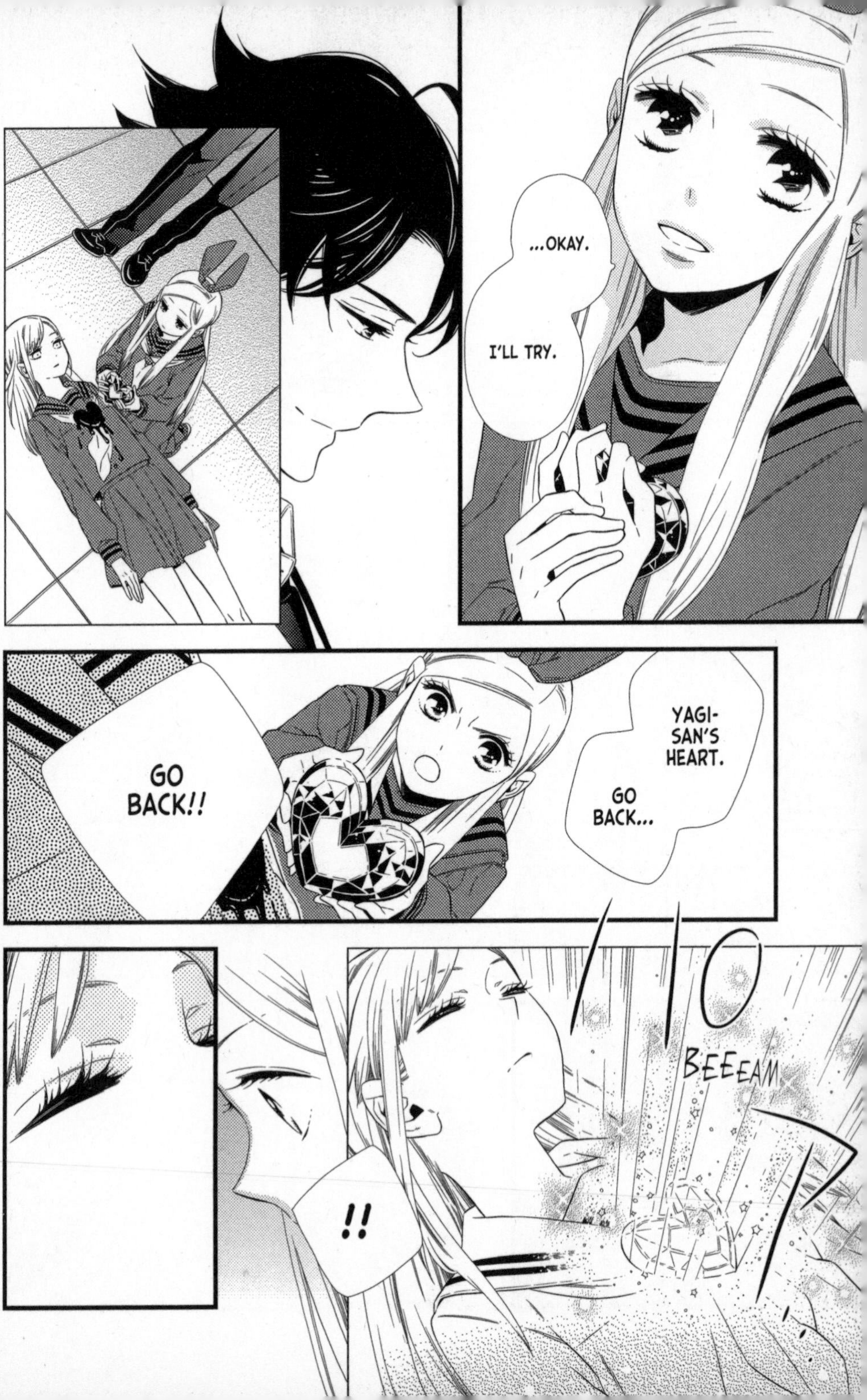
...OKAY.
I'LL TRY.
YAGI-SAN'S HEART.
GO BACK...
GO BACK!!
BEEEAM
!!

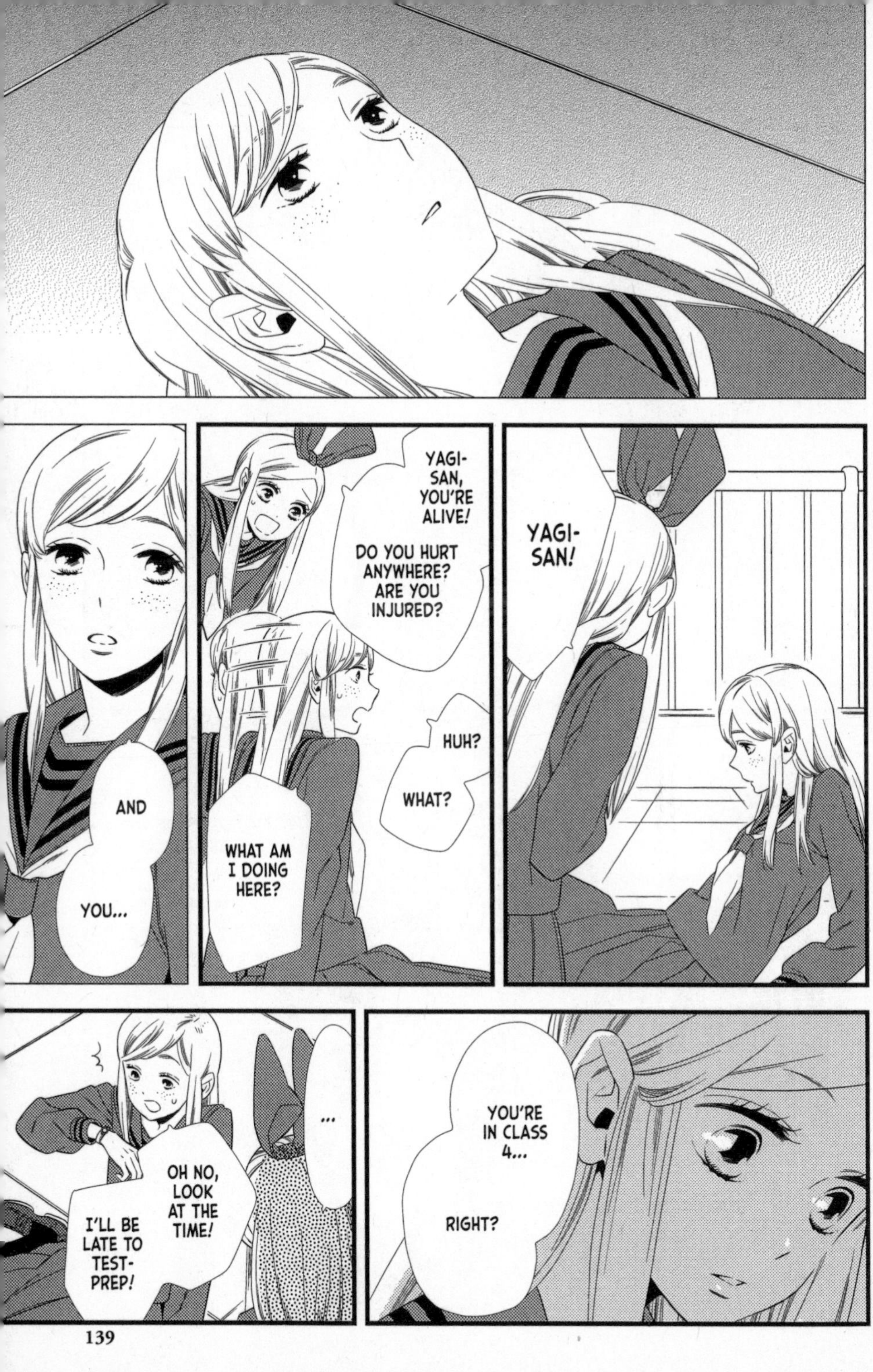
YAGI-SAN!
YAGI-SAN, YOU'RE ALIVE!
DO YOU HURT ANYWHERE? ARE YOU INJURED?
HUH?
WHAT?
WHAT AM I DOING HERE?
AND
YOU...
YOU'RE IN CLASS 4...
RIGHT?
...
OH NO, LOOK AT THE TIME!
I'LL BE LATE TO TEST-PREP!

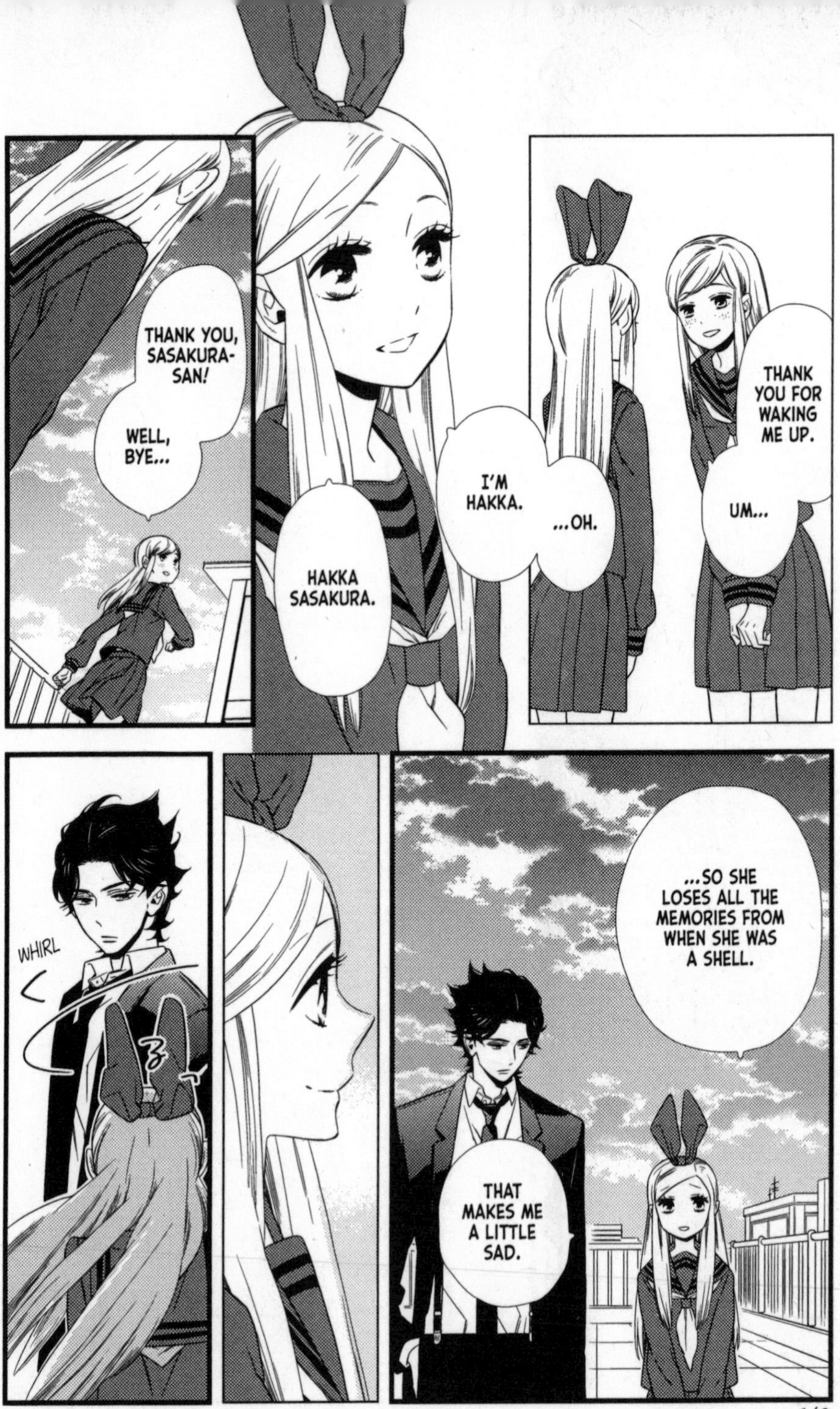
THANK YOU FOR WAKING ME UP.
UM...
...OH.
I'M HAKKA.
HAKKA SASAKURA.
THANK YOU, SASAKURA-SAN!
WELL, BYE...
...SO SHE LOSES ALL THE MEMORIES FROM WHEN SHE WAS A SHELL.
THAT MAKES ME A LITTLE SAD.
WHIRL

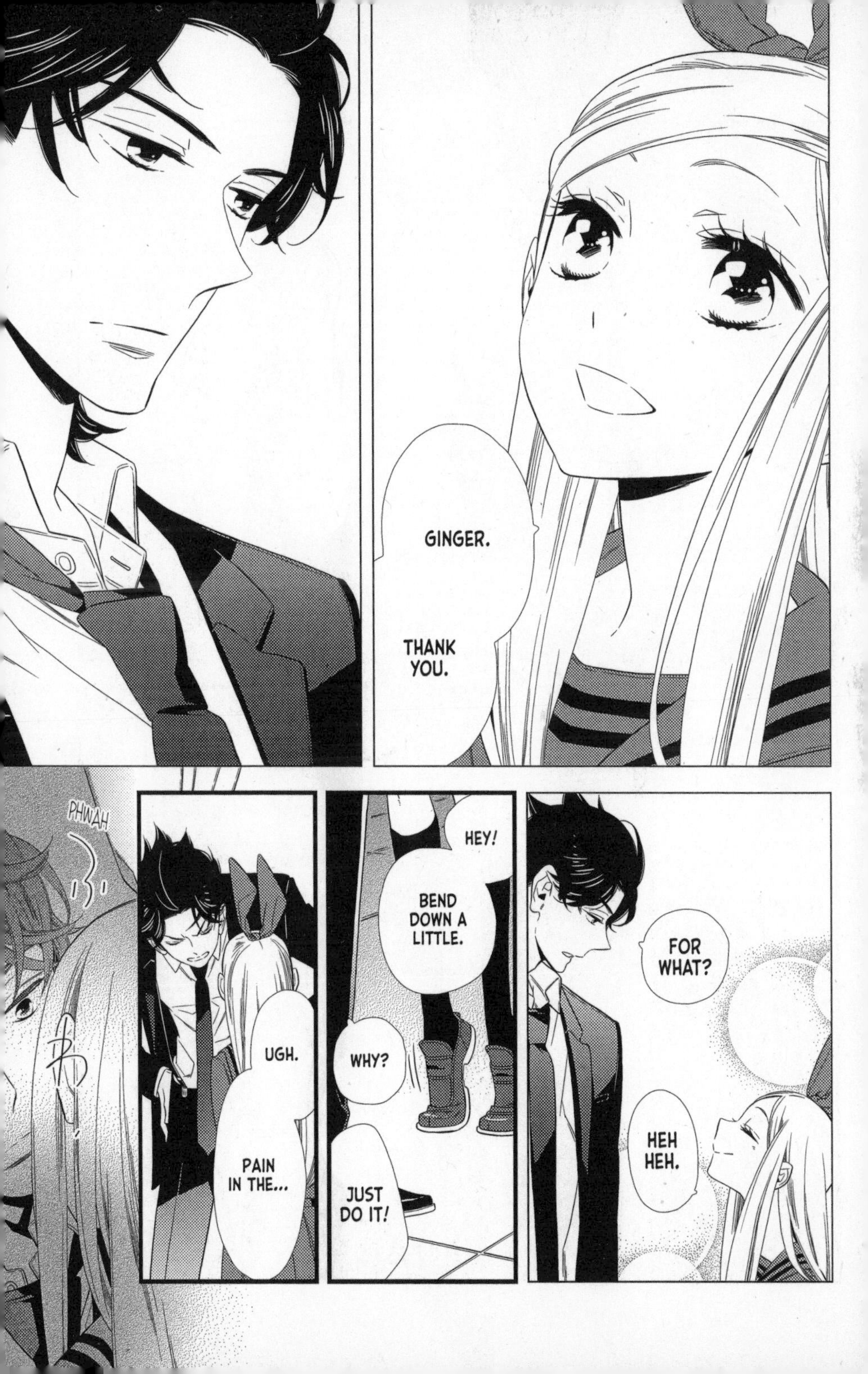
GINGER.
THANK YOU.
FOR WHAT?
HEH HEH.
HEY!
BEND DOWN A LITTLE.
WHY?
JUST DO IT!
UGH.
PAIN IN THE...
PHWAH

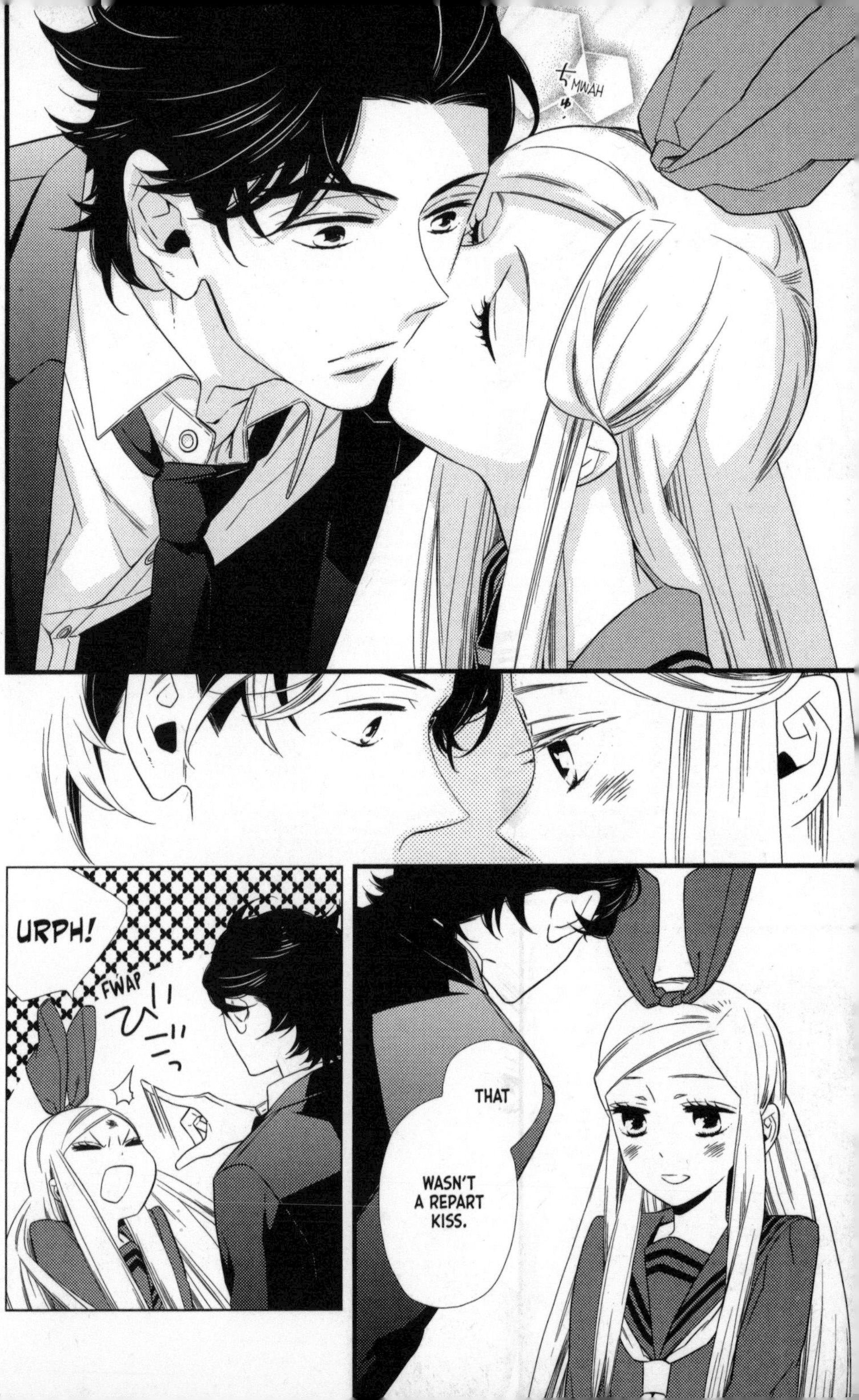
MWAH
THAT
WASN'T A REPART KISS.
URPH!
FWAP

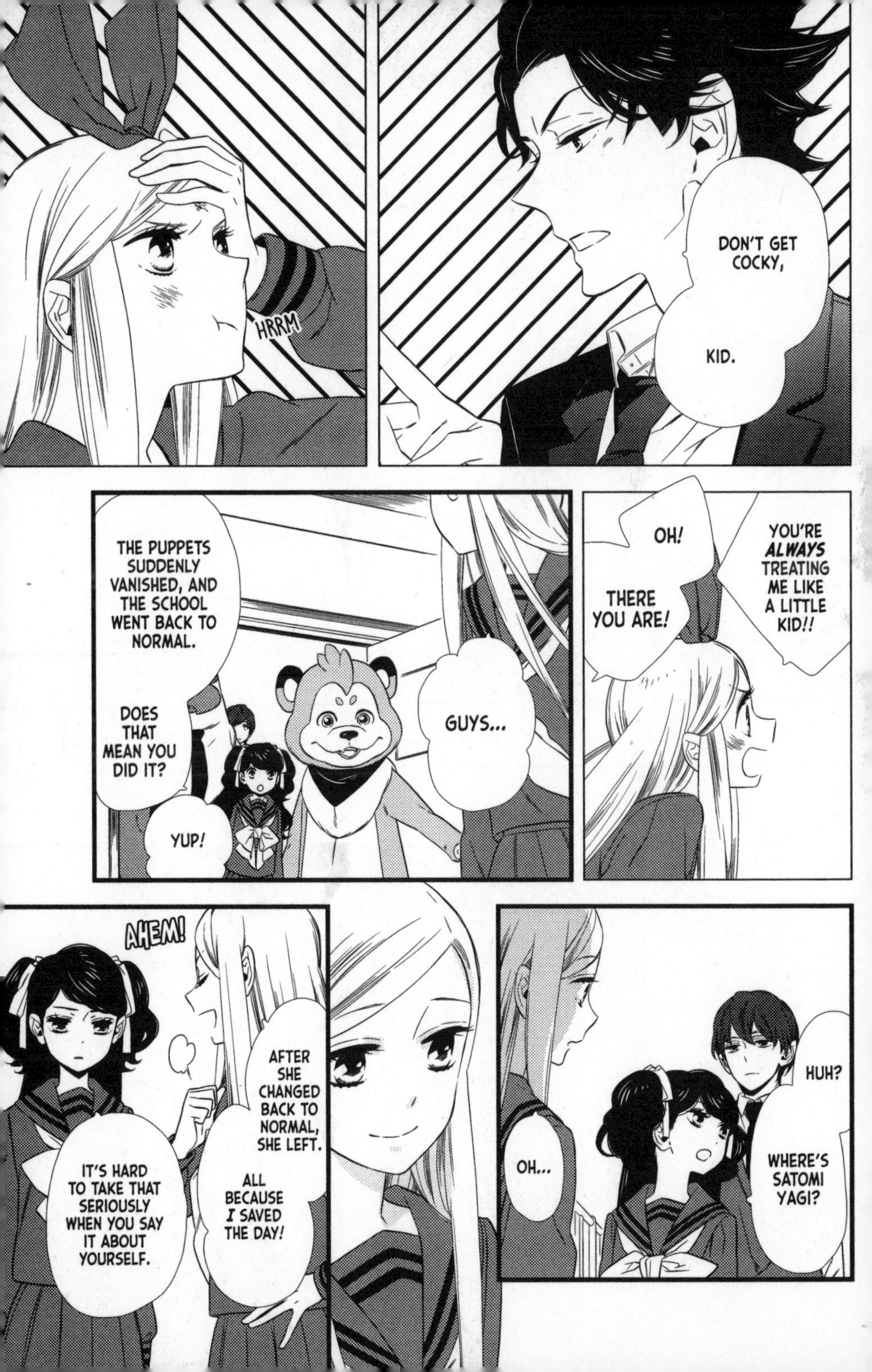
DON'T GET COCKY,
KID.
HRRM
YOU'RE *ALWAYS* TREATING ME LIKE A LITTLE KID!!
OH!
THERE YOU ARE!
GUYS...
THE PUPPETS SUDDENLY VANISHED, AND THE SCHOOL WENT BACK TO NORMAL.
DOES THAT MEAN YOU DID IT?
YUP!
HUH?
WHERE'S SATOMI YAGI?
OH...
AFTER SHE CHANGED BACK TO NORMAL, SHE LEFT.
ALL BECAUSE *I* SAVED THE DAY!
AHEM!
IT'S HARD TO TAKE THAT SERIOUSLY WHEN YOU SAY IT ABOUT YOURSELF.

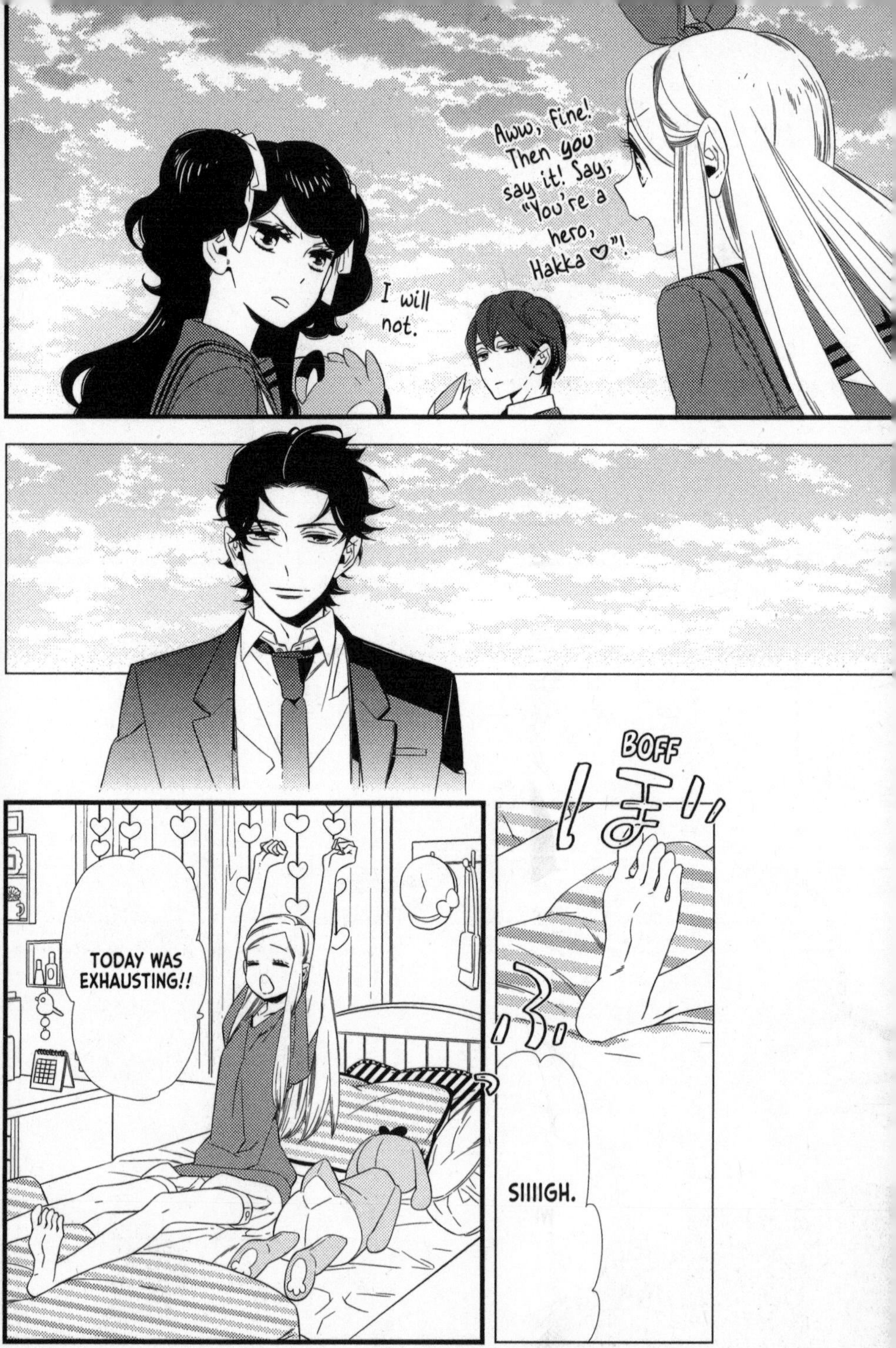
Aww, fine! Then you say it! Say, "You're a hero, Hakka ♡"!
I will not.
BOFF
SIIIGH.
TODAY WAS EXHAUSTING!!

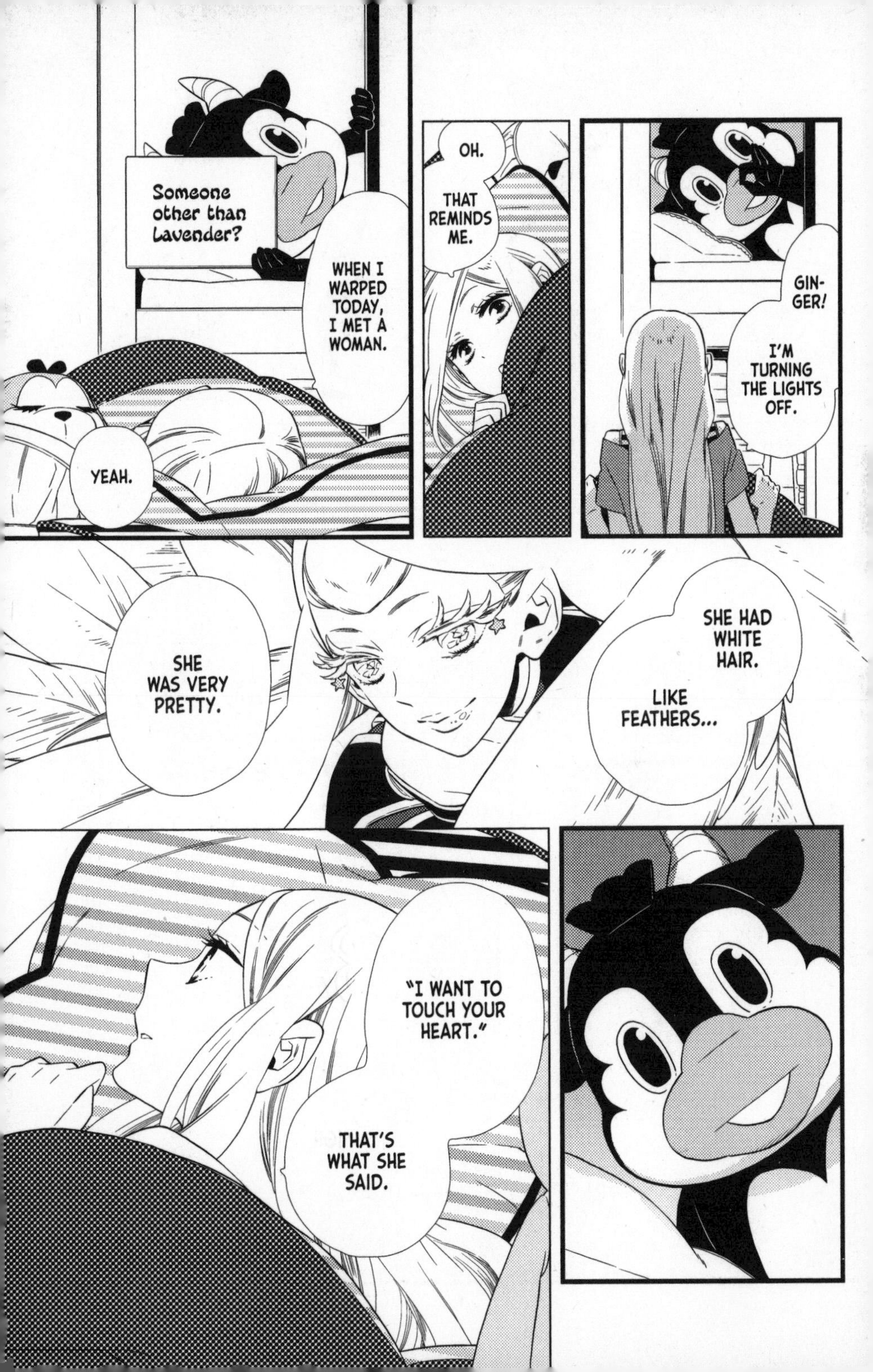
GIN-GER!
I'M TURNING THE LIGHTS OFF.
OH.
THAT REMINDS ME.
WHEN I WARPED TODAY, I MET A WOMAN.
Someone other than Lavender?
YEAH.
SHE HAD WHITE HAIR.
LIKE FEATHERS...
SHE WAS VERY PRETTY.
"I WANT TO TOUCH YOUR HEART."
THAT'S WHAT SHE SAID.

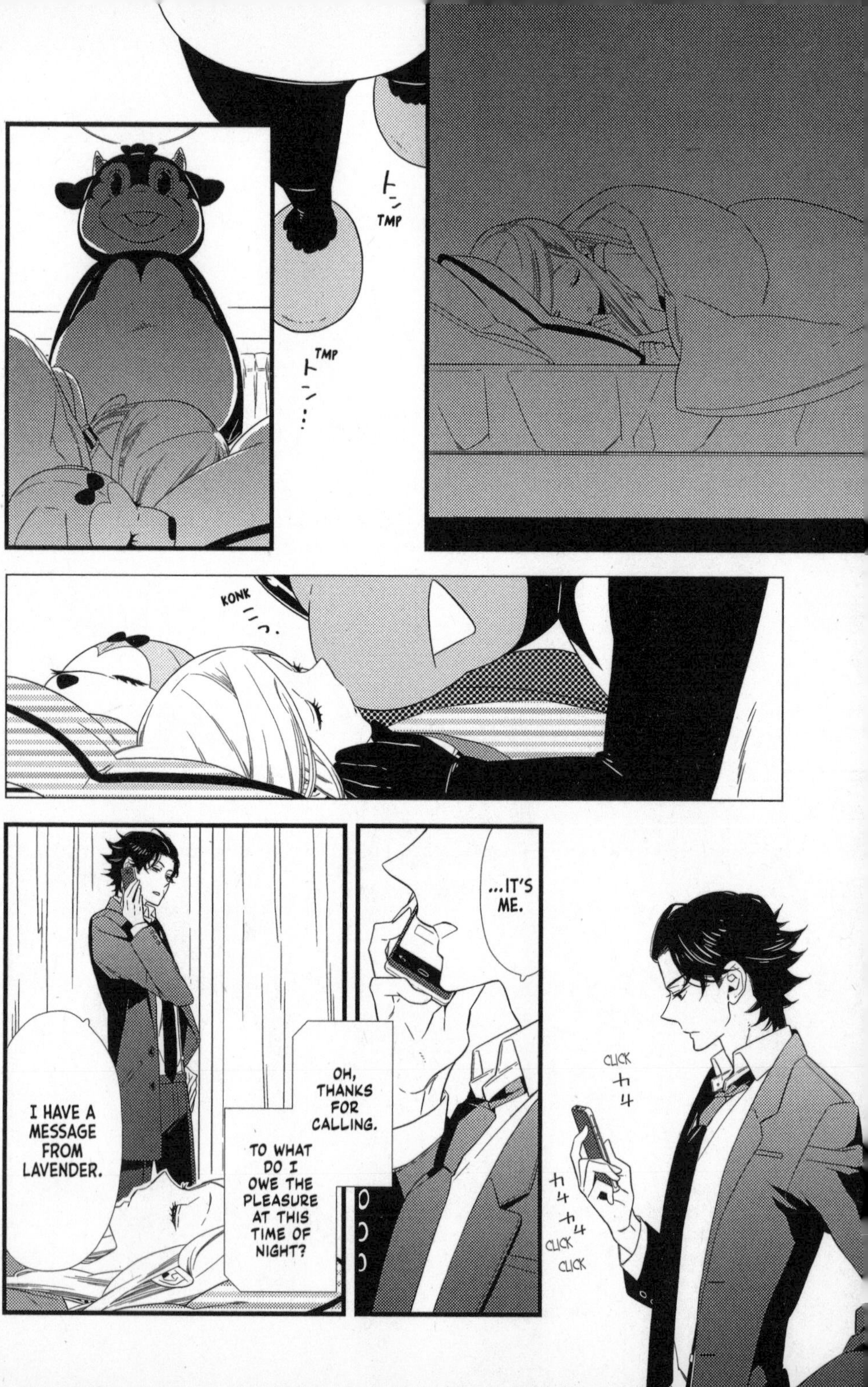
トン
TMP
トン…
TMP
コン
KONK
カチ
CLICK
カチカチ
CLICK
CLICK
...IT'S ME.
OH, THANKS FOR CALLING.
TO WHAT DO I OWE THE PLEASURE AT THIS TIME OF NIGHT?
I HAVE A MESSAGE FROM LAVENDER.

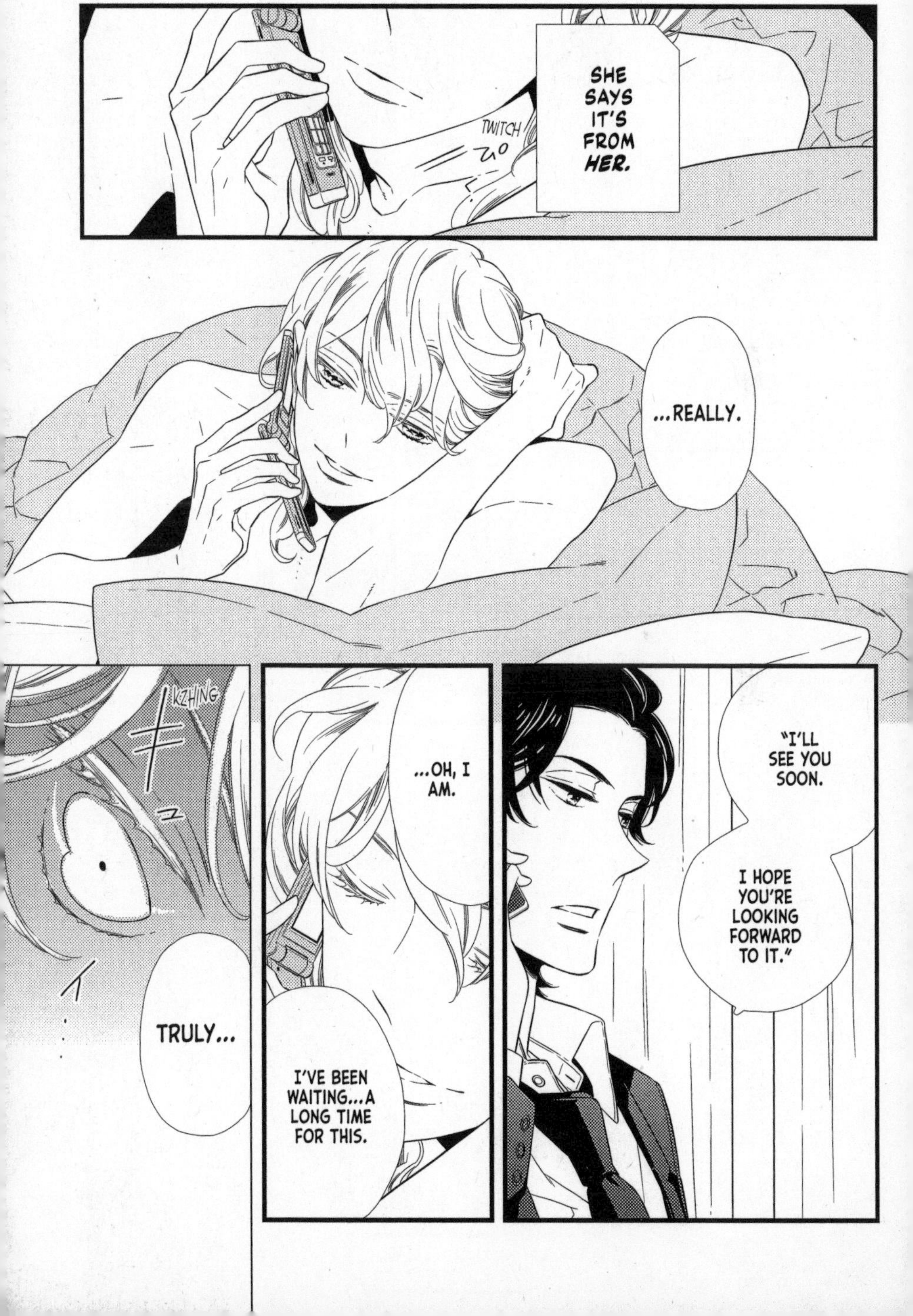

TWITCH
SHE SAYS IT'S FROM HER.
...REALLY.
"I'LL SEE YOU SOON.
I HOPE YOU'RE LOOKING FORWARD TO IT."
...OH, I AM.
I'VE BEEN WAITING...A LONG TIME FOR THIS.
KZHING
TRULY...

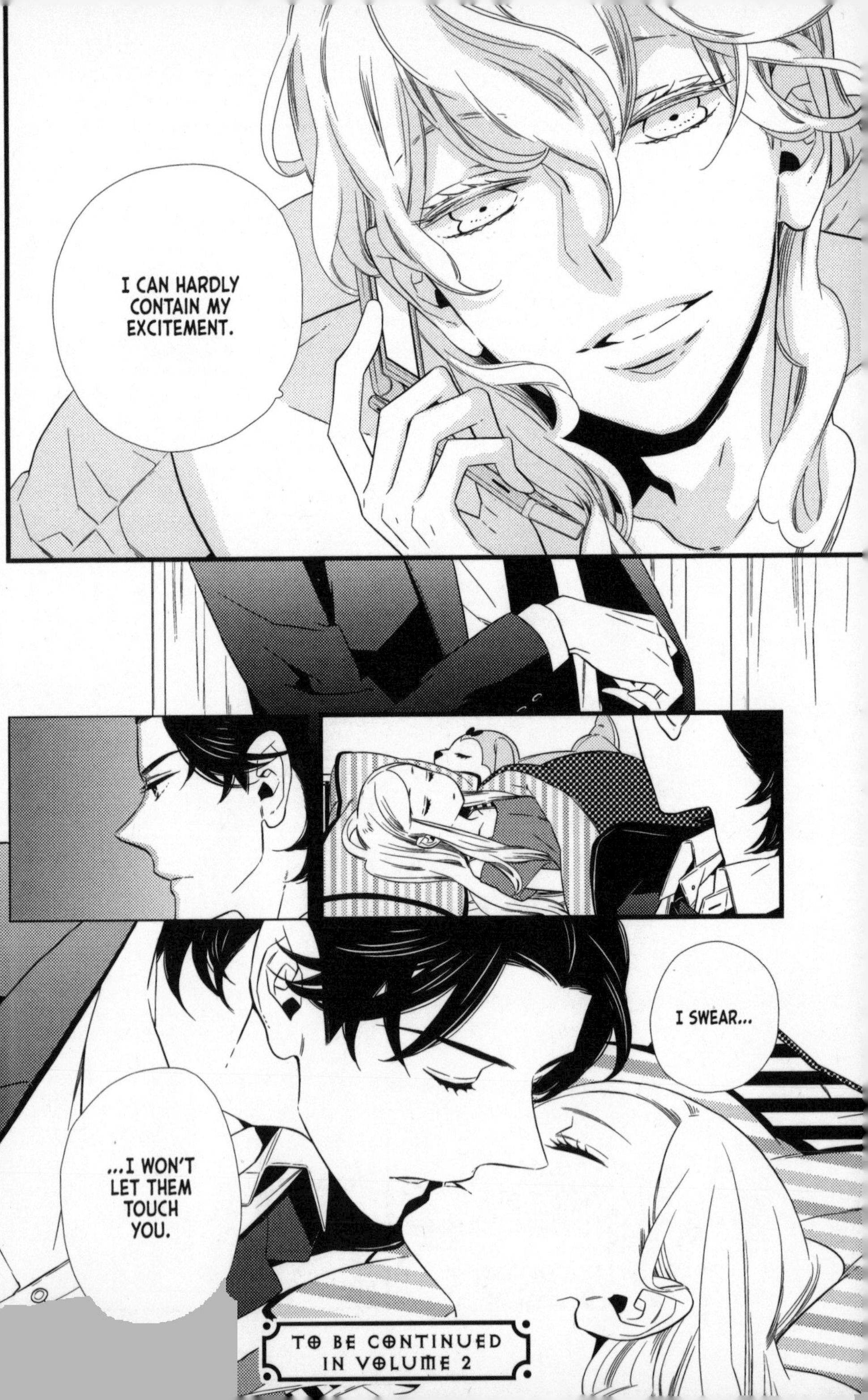
I CAN HARDLY CONTAIN MY EXCITEMENT.
I SWEAR...
...I WON'T LET THEM TOUCH YOU.
TO BE CONTINUED IN VOLUME 2

Kigurumi
GUARDIANS

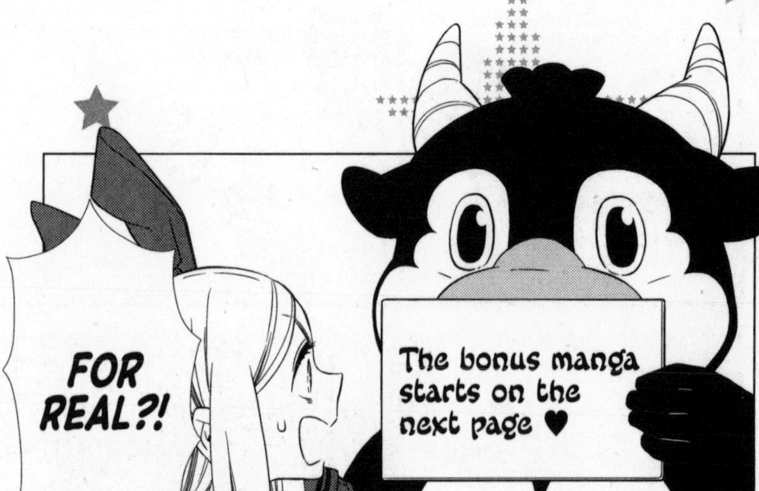
The bonus manga starts on the next page ♥
FOR REAL?!

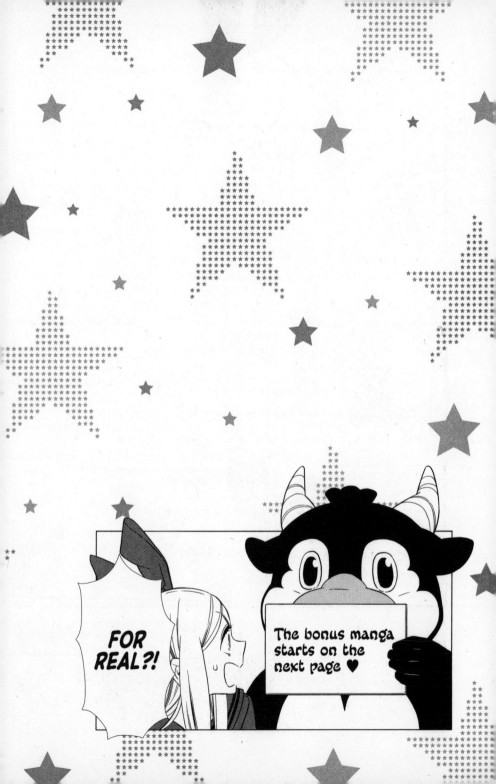

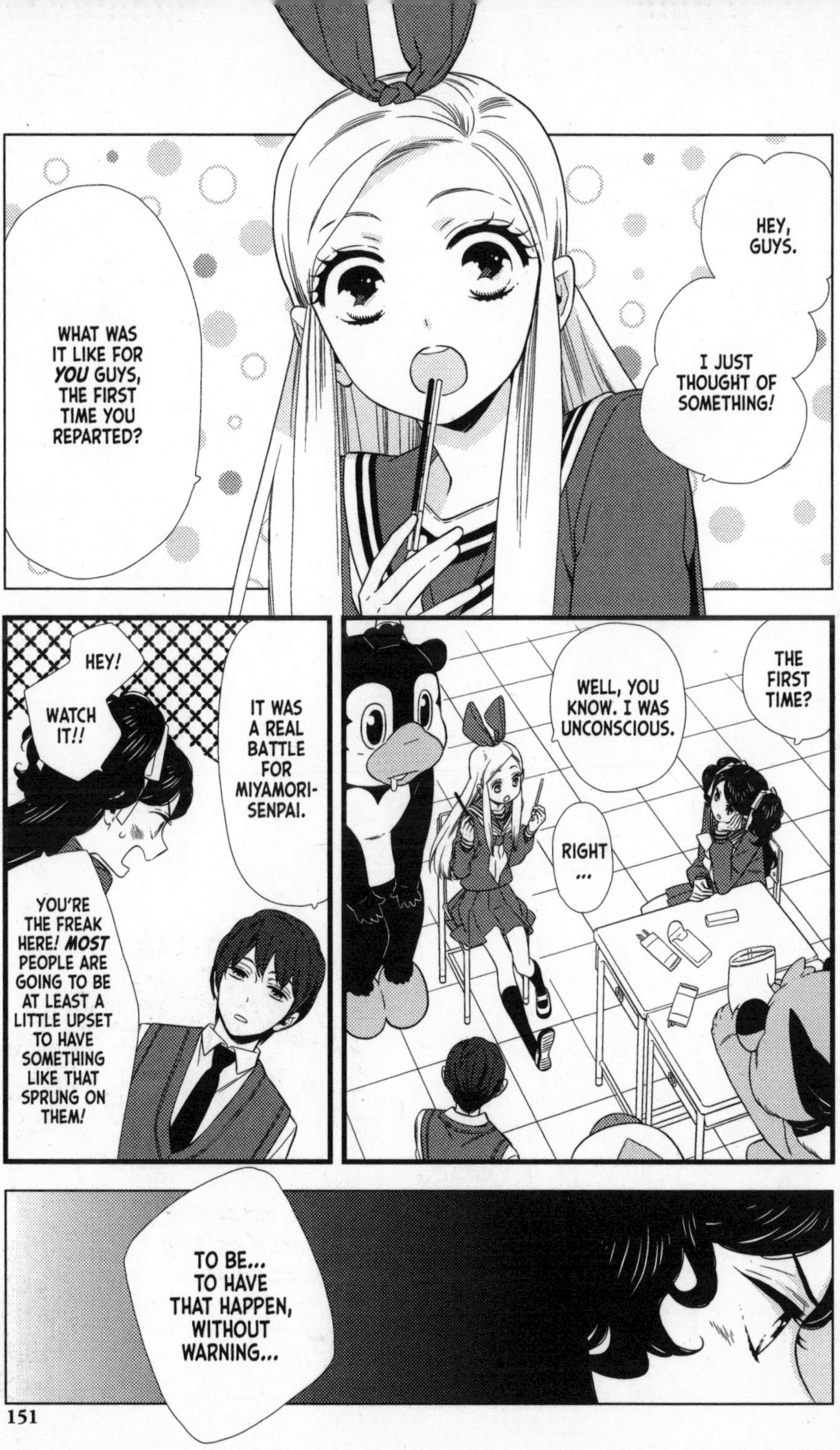

HEY, GUYS.
I JUST THOUGHT OF SOMETHING!
WHAT WAS IT LIKE FOR *YOU* GUYS, THE FIRST TIME YOU REPARTED?
THE FIRST TIME?
WELL, YOU KNOW. I WAS UNCONSCIOUS.
RIGHT...
IT WAS A REAL BATTLE FOR MIYAMORI-SENPAI.
HEY!
WATCH IT!!
YOU'RE THE FREAK HERE! *MOST* PEOPLE ARE GOING TO BE AT LEAST A LITTLE UPSET TO HAVE SOMETHING LIKE THAT SPRUNG ON THEM!
TO BE... TO HAVE THAT HAPPEN, WITHOUT WARNING...

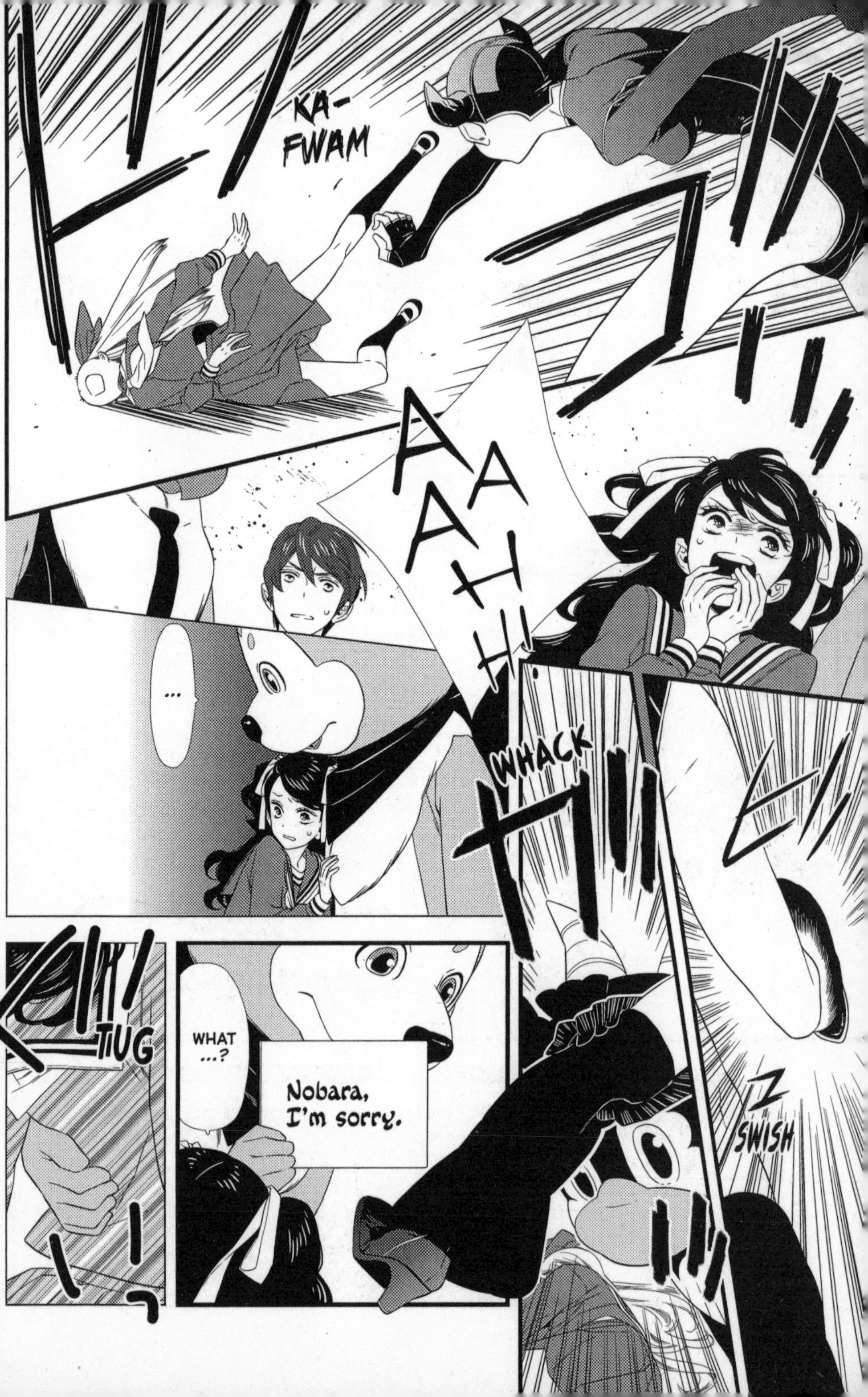
KA-
FWAM
AAAHH!
...
WHACK
SWISH
WHAT ...?
Nobara, I'm sorry.
TUG

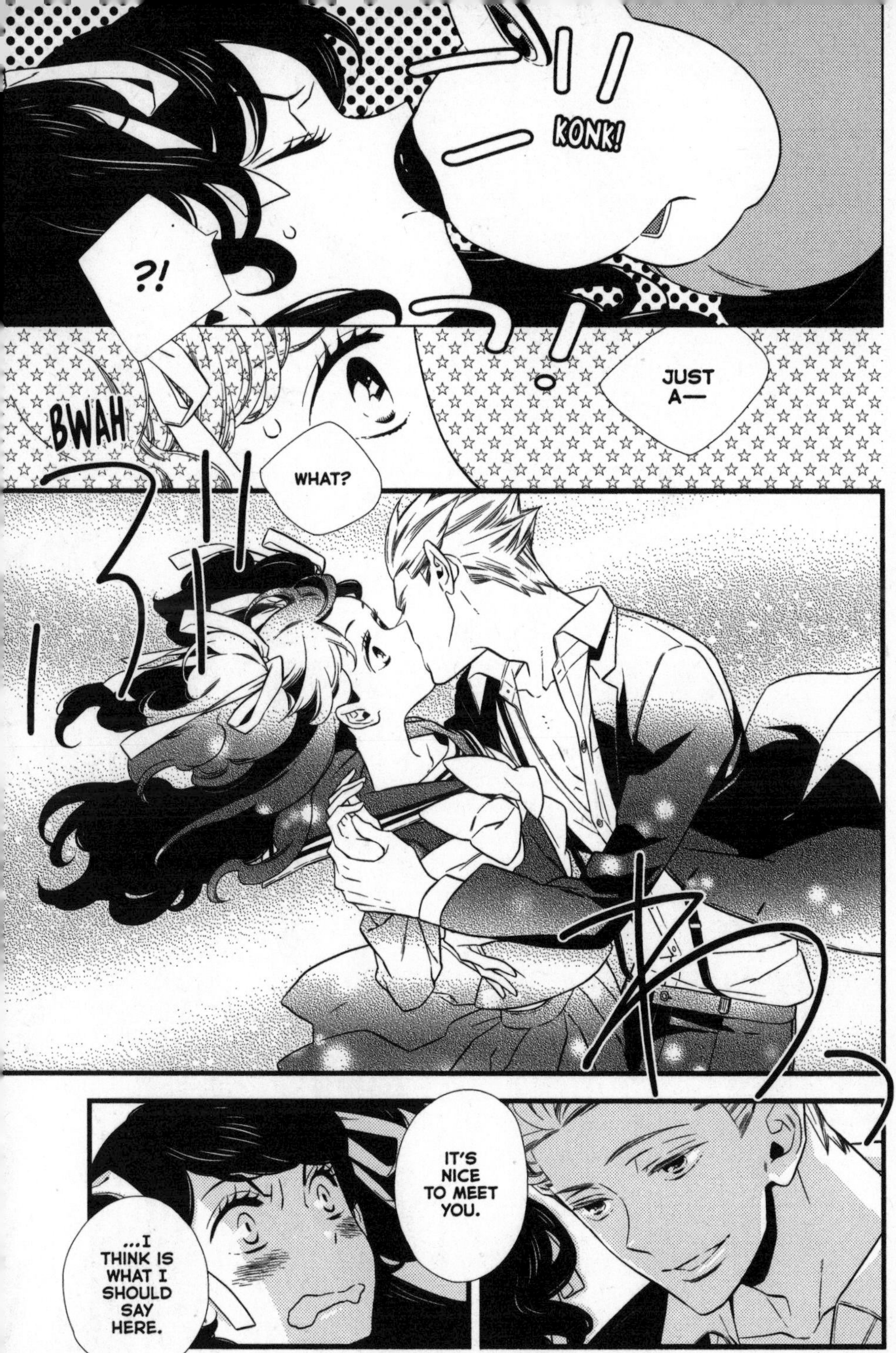
KONK!
?!
JUST A—
WHAT?
BWAH
IT'S NICE TO MEET YOU.
...I THINK IS WHAT I SHOULD SAY HERE.

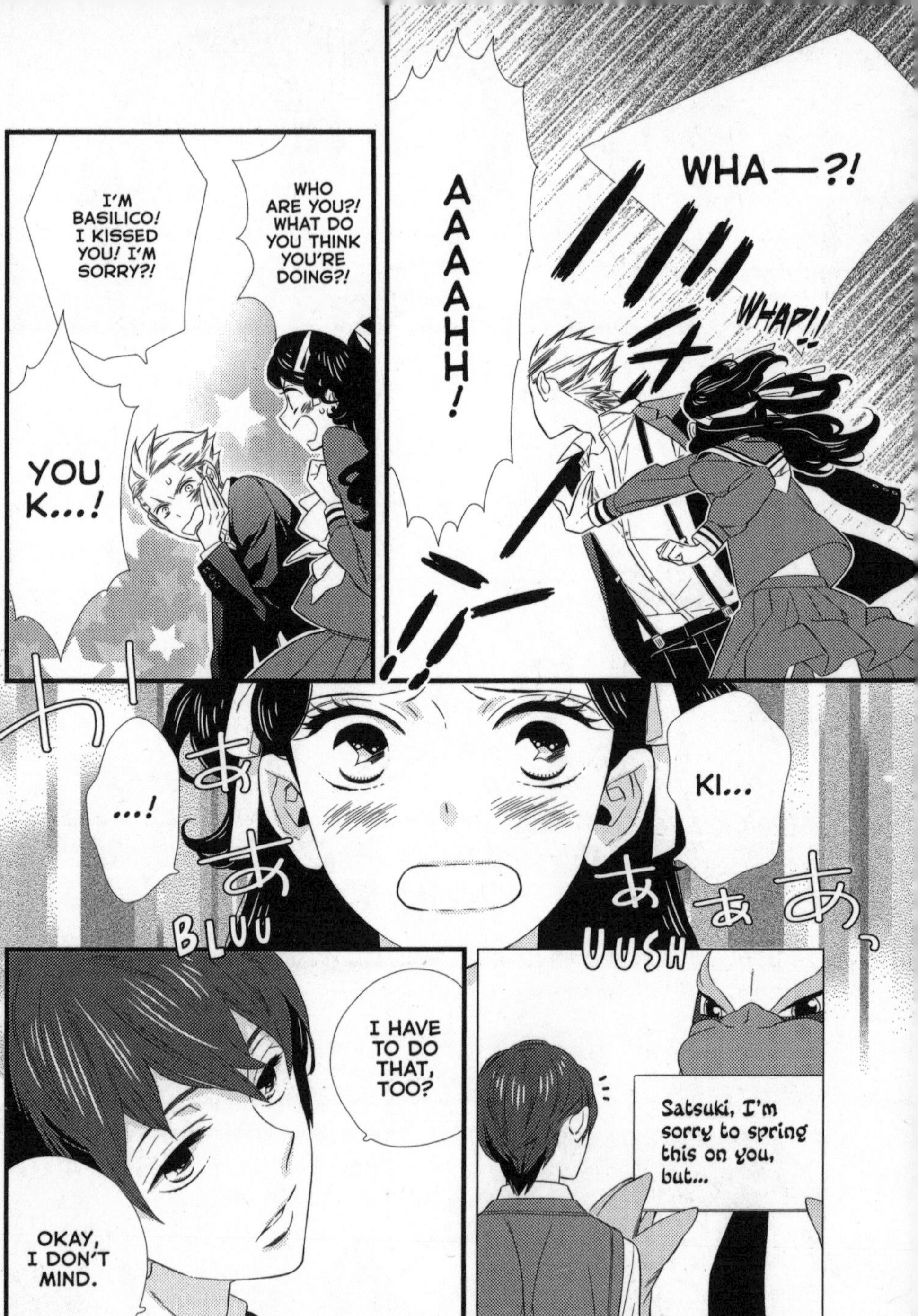
WHA—?!
AAAAAHH!
WHAP!!
WHO ARE YOU?! WHAT DO YOU THINK YOU'RE DOING?!
I'M BASILICO! I KISSED YOU! I'M SORRY?!
YOU K...!
KI...
...!
BLUU
UUSH
Satsuki, I'm sorry to spring this on you, but...
I HAVE TO DO THAT, TOO?
OKAY, I DON'T MIND.

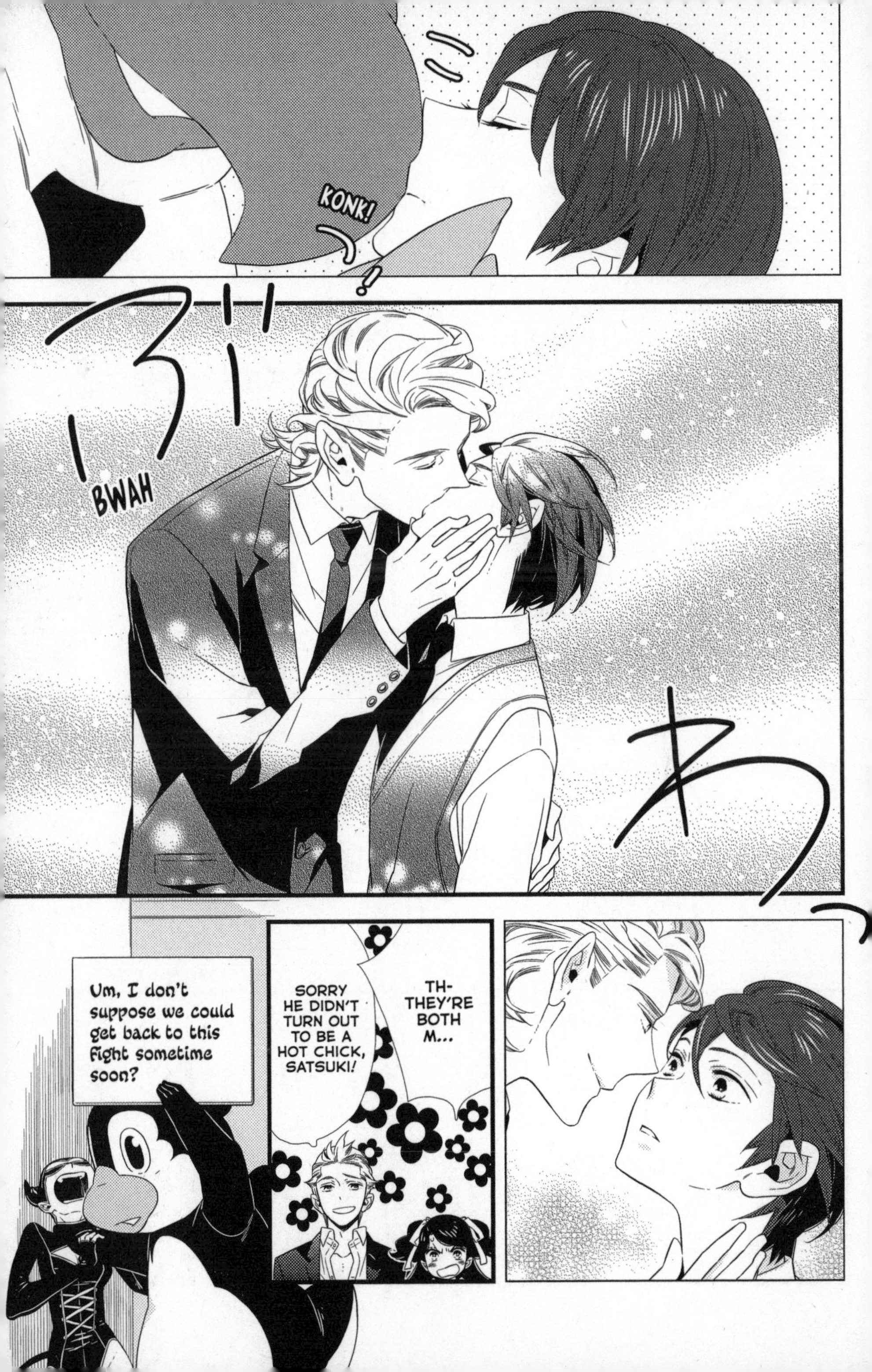
KONK!
BWAH
TH- THEY'RE BOTH M...
SORRY HE DIDN'T TURN OUT TO BE A HOT CHICK, SATSUKI!
Um, I don't suppose we could get back to this fight sometime soon?

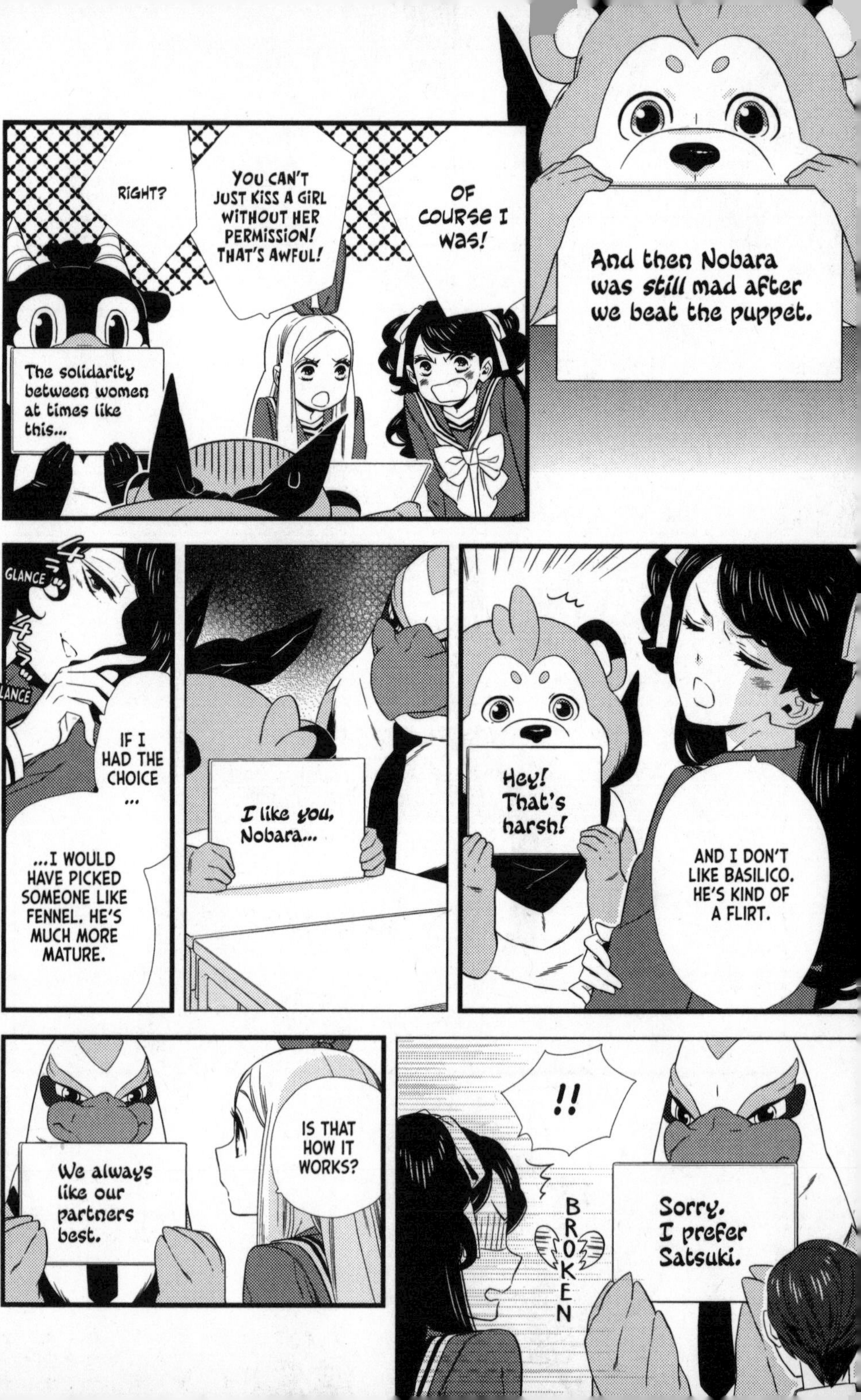
RIGHT?
YOU CAN'T JUST KISS A GIRL WITHOUT HER PERMISSION! THAT'S AWFUL!
OF COURSE I WAS!
The solidarity between women at times like this...
And then Nobara was *still* mad after we beat the puppet.
GLANCE
GLANCE
IF I HAD THE CHOICE ...
...I WOULD HAVE PICKED SOMEONE LIKE FENNEL. HE'S MUCH MORE MATURE.
I like you, Nobara...
Hey! That's harsh!
AND I DON'T LIKE BASILICO. HE'S KIND OF A FLIRT.
We always like our partners best.
IS THAT HOW IT WORKS?
!!
BROKEN
Sorry. I prefer Satsuki.

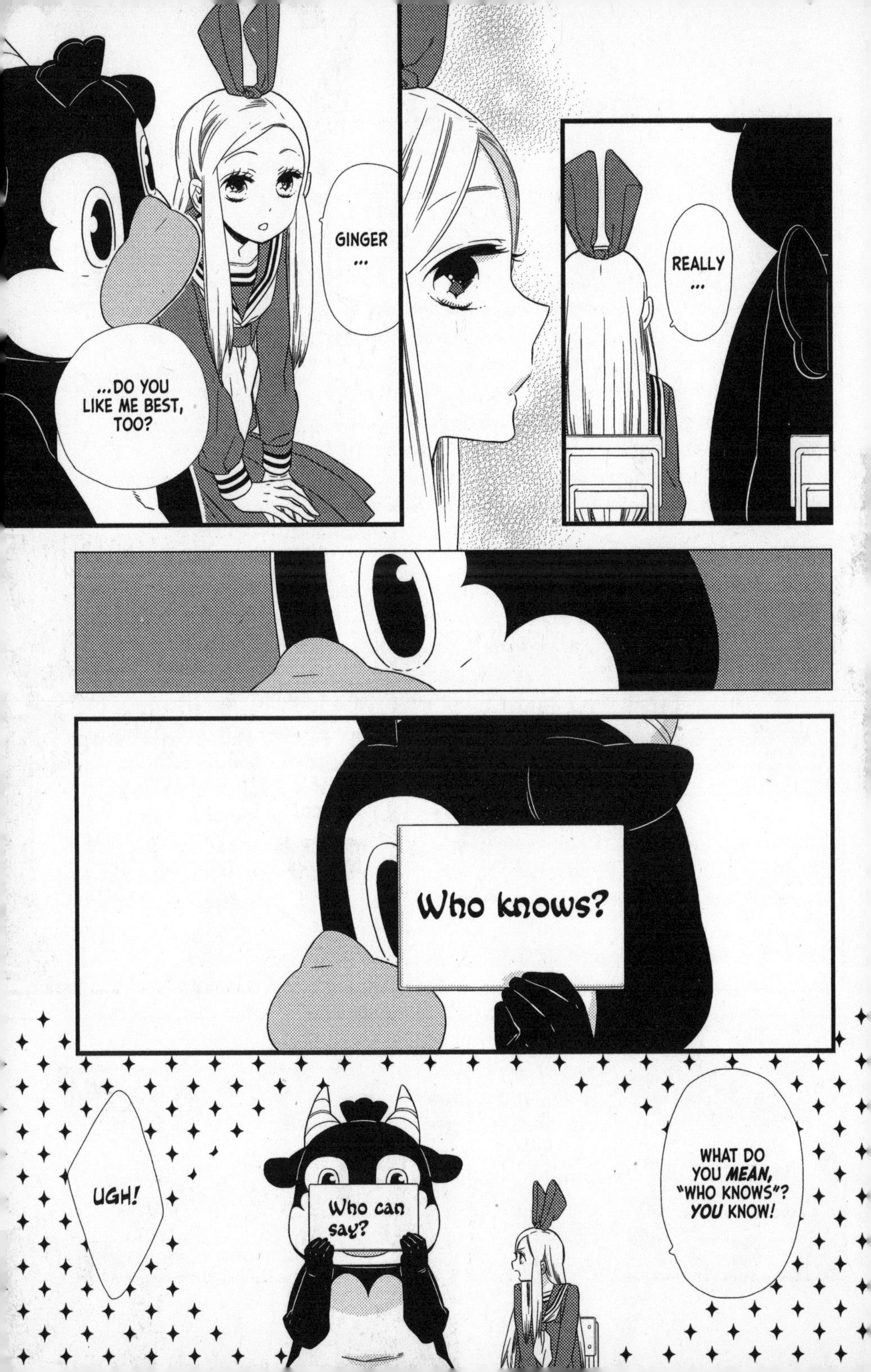
REALLY ...
GINGER ...
...DO YOU LIKE ME BEST, TOO?
Who knows?
WHAT DO YOU *MEAN*, "WHO KNOWS"? *YOU* KNOW!
Who can say?
UGH!

TRANSLATION NOTES

Kigurumi, page 13

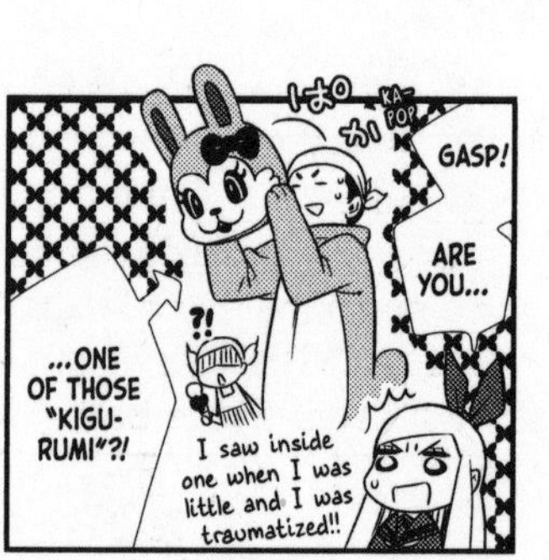
KA-POP
GASP!
ARE YOU...
...ONE OF THOSE "KIGU-RUMI"?!
I saw inside one when I was little and I was traumatized!!

The word *kigurumi* has gained popularity in English in recent years, mostly in reference to full-body animal pajamas. Many readers may already know that the word also refers to more elaborate animal costumes of the variety used for sports mascots and popular characters at theme parks. The word *kigurumi* is an abbreviation for *jintai chakuyô nuigurumi,* which means "life-sized wearable doll." (The *ki* is an alternate pronunciation of *chaku,* or "to wear.") In Japanese, a noun can be both plural and singular, so the use of *kigurumi* in this manga may refer to one or the group, depending on context.

Use honorifics, page 19

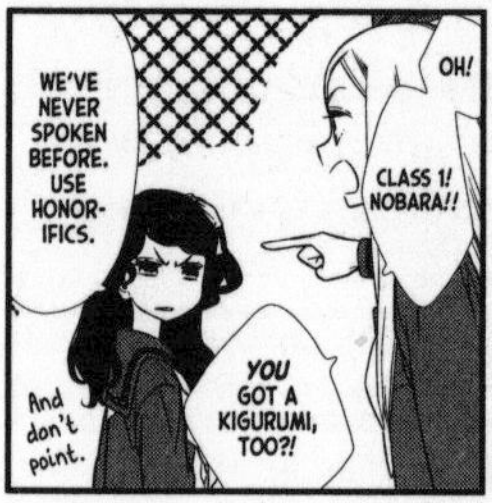
OH!
CLASS 1! NOBARA!!
WE'VE NEVER SPOKEN BEFORE. USE HONOR-IFICS.
YOU GOT A KIGURUMI, TOO?!
And don't point.

In Japan, it can be very rude to address someone you don't know well by their given name. Sometimes it's appropriate to ask someone how they prefer to be addressed, but when that's not feasible, the safest bet in most circumstances is to call them by their surname and add the honorific -san (similar to the English "Mr." or "Miss"). Because they have never spoken before, Nobara would not be out of line in expecting Hakka to address her as Miyamori-san. Other honorifics in this volume includ "-chan" (which denotes friendship or closeness, and is usually reserved for children and younger women), and "-senpai," which is for one's direct seniors in school or other organizations.

Look that way now, page 33-34

Here, Ginger and Hakka are playing a game that is often considered a

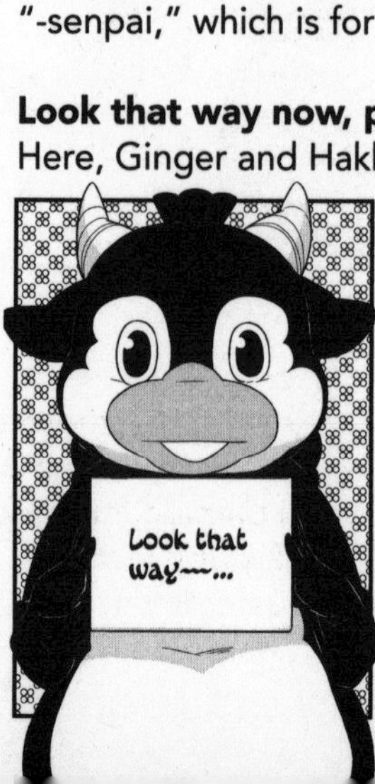
Look that way~~...

"sequel" to rock-paper-scissors. After the players have thrown out their rock, paper, or scissors, the winner says, "Look that way ***now!***" and points up, down, left, or right. The loser of the rock-paper-scissors turns his or her head in a direction as well, and if the finger and the face are pointed in the same direction, the rock-paper-

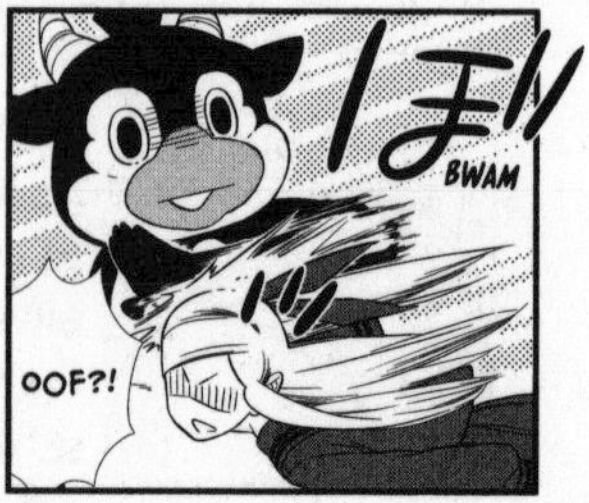
BWAM
OOF?!

scissors winner wins again. If they point in different directions, they start another round of rock-paper-scissors.

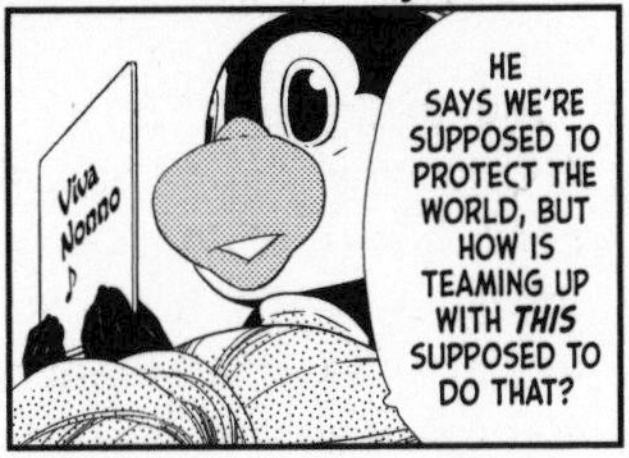
HE SAYS WE'RE SUPPOSED TO PROTECT THE WORLD, BUT HOW IS TEAMING UP WITH *THIS* SUPPOSED TO DO THAT?
Viva Nonno ♪

Viva Nonno, page 46

Technically, this phrase is Italian for "long live grandfather!" but it is a variation of "viva non non," a nonsensical shout from the Drifters' cover of the Duke Aces' 1960s single "*Ii Yu Da Na.*" The title of this song means, roughly, "Ah, what a nice bath," which is probably also what Ginger means when he says, "Viva Nonno."

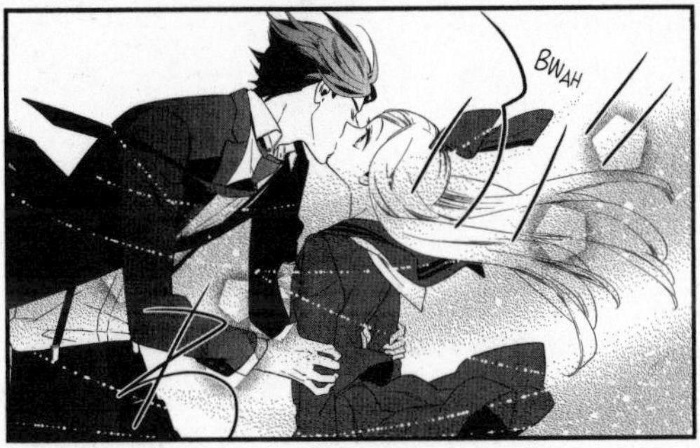
BWAH

Repart, page 53

Pronounced "ree-part," the exact etymology of this term is unclear—the translators would not be surprised if Chigaya made it up himself. A reasonable theory is that is comes from the French word *repartir*, which means "to restart." It may also come from the Italian *ripartire*, with the same meaning, but it doesn't really match the imperative (command) forms of either.

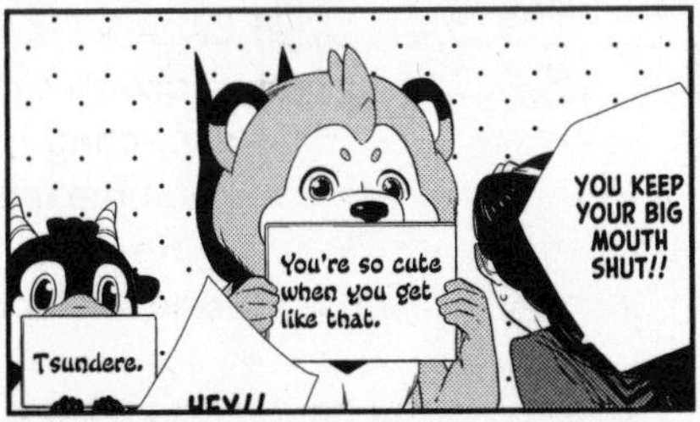
YOU KEEP YOUR BIG MOUTH SHUT!!
You're so cute when you get like that.
Tsundere.

Tsundere, page 83

Readers may be familiar with the *tsundere* trope, describing characters who are often sarcastic and mean but will occasionally reveal hints that they actually do care about another character. For the uninitiated, *tsundere* is a combination of *tsun-tsun*, meaning "bad-tempered," and *dere-dere*, meaning roughly "lovestruck." The word usually refers to one person who shows both traits, but in this case, it would seem that Nobara is *tsun-tsun* while Basilico is *dere-dere*.

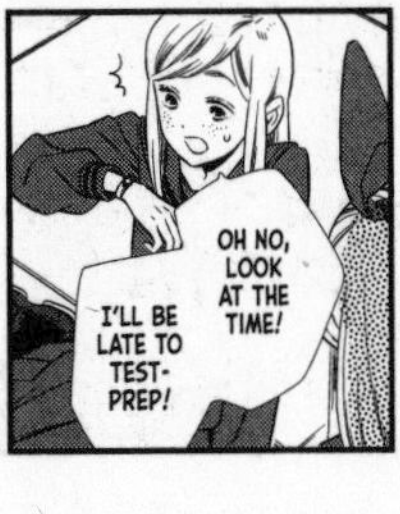
OH NO, LOOK AT THE TIME!
I'LL BE LATE TO TEST-PREP!

Test-prep, page 139

In Japan, many high schools require their potential students to pass an entrance exam before they can enroll. The more elite the school, the harder the exam. To prepare for these tests, students can attend *juku*, a type of supplementary school specifically geared to help them get into the high school, and eventually college, of their choice.

Kigurumi
GUARDIANS

A Kodansha Comics Trade Paperback Original.

Kigurumi Guardians volume 1 copyright © 2013 Lily Hoshino
English translation copyright © 2017 Lily Hoshino

Published in the United States by Kodansha Comics, an imprint of Kodansha USA Publishing, LLC, New York.

Publication rights for this English edition arranged through Kodansha Ltd., Tokyo.

First published in Japan in 2013 by Kodansha Ltd., Tokyo.

ISBN 978-1-63236-490-6

Printed in the United States of America.

www.kodanshacomics.com

9 8 7 6 5 4 3 2 1

Translation: Alethea Nibley & Athena Nibley
Lettering: Lys Blakeslee
Editing: Lauren Scanlan
Kodansha Comics edition cover design: Fawn Lau

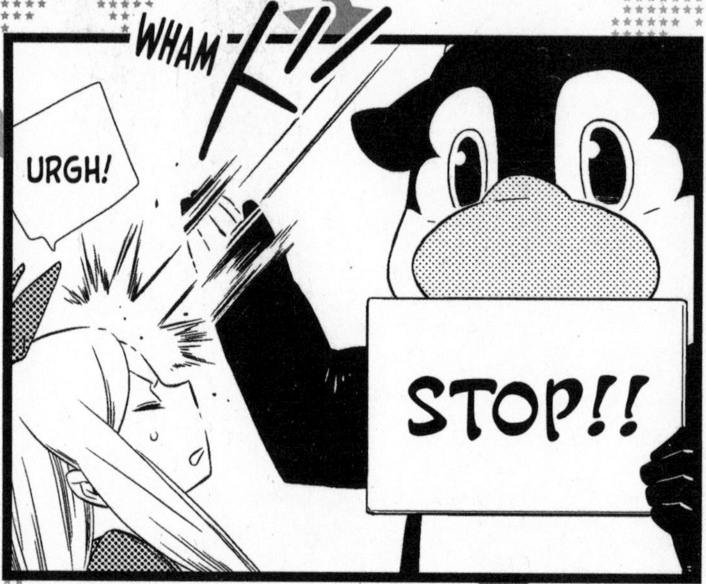
WHAM
URGH!
STOP!!

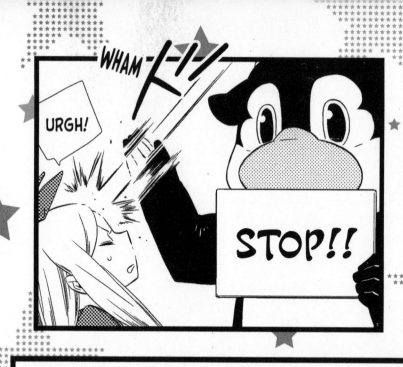

You're going the wrong way, kid!

Manga is a completely different type of reading experience. To start at the beginning, go to the end! Authentic manga is read the traditional Japanese way—from right to left, exactly the opposite of how American books are read. It's easy to follow: just go to the other end of the book, and read each page—and each panel—from the right side to the left side, starting at the top right. Now you're experiencing manga as it was meant to be!